HANOI
RELEASE JOHN NASMYTH

A FAMILY LOVE STORY

Hanoi Release John Nasmyth is about two simultaneous struggles: the struggle of Nasmyth and his fellow POWs to keep hope alive in the face of the brutality of their North Vietnamese captors, and his sister Virginia Nasmyth Loy's struggle to keep his memory alive among her fellow Americans. In this moving account, brother and sister together remind us of what true heroism is all about — the heroism of those who served in Vietnam and especially those who endured years of hardship in the Hanoi Hilton, and the less conspicuous but equally impressive heroism of the loved ones who supported them and waited at home for their return.

Richard Nixon

For John —

Glad you made
it here. Thanks

Virginia Nardozzi
'97

HANOI
RELEASE JOHN NASMYTH

A FAMILY LOVE STORY
BY
VIRGINIA NASMYTH
AND
SPIKE NASMYTH

V. PARR PUBLISHING
Santa Paula, California 93060

Limited Edition

Printed in the United States of America
ISBN 0-9613991-0-4

Some names of former prisoners of war
have been changed to protect their privacy.

FOR MOTHER: I LOVE YOU

**FOR YOUR FIERCE DETERMINATION
AND CONTAGIOUS ENTHUSIASM**

Author's Note

This book, this labor of love, was begun one afternoon in 1969. I wanted to write a chronicle of what it must be like to be a prisoner of war in North Vietnam, and what it was like to have someone you love suddenly fall under the dubious title of 'missing in action.'

All we knew then was that Spike had been shot down. By publicizing our family's story, I hoped to stir up public support for our POWs. Our strenuous campaign at home, with trips and speeches and demonstrations, kept adding chapters to my book.

Then, when Spike was released in 1973, when he had been stateside only a few days, I asked him to tell me his story so I could complete my book. His own struggle to cope and survive was such an integral part of the overall story.

That night, the second or third of March, 1973, I picked him up at the March Air Force Base Hospital. We drove to my father's apartment, drank loads of coffee, I held his hand and he began. We talked for twelve hours—it must have been all night. Sometimes Spike's eyes would glaze over or he'd look past me, far off as if I weren't there. His voice would come from deep, deep inside him. I just held his hand as his story unfolded. (Thank you, big brother, for going through all that again for me.)

He didn't at all seem mentally stunted from his isolation as a POW. In fact, I was struck by how vivid his memory was. He'd been studying foreign languages, writing dictionaries—it was amazing how sharp and alive his mind was.

When I think about the minute details and conversations he recalled (I taped his talk that night) I realize how he could have remembered the early days of his capture so clearly. He had been in solitary for many months at first; that's a long time to dwell on what's happening to you. There's no outer world at all—just your own world.

As I was putting Spike's story and our family's story together, my daughter Jenny came along, then Mary. I got my work started again when Mary was around two years old. I must have been working on the fourth re-write when 'little Spike' was born; then Dad died, which was so sad for us.

Now that my fourth child, baby Bodie, is two, I have been able to piece together enough time to complete this project.

This is a project which, for me, simply had to be done. This is a story which needs to be told. It occurs to me that there is an entire generation of young people who know so little about Vietnam, about what happened to the men who went there and their families behind at home. It has taken this country a decade to recover from the floundering times we were all experiencing then.

I want young people to read this story, to know what happened to Spike and our family. I want mothers and politicians to remember the valiant struggle of our wonderful POWs, as well as their dedicated families who educated the world about the value of our individual men.

We must never, never, allow an American to wait so long in a prison camp again.

Acknowledgements

Ann Farmer
> It all started with Ann. She enthusiastically edited the original manuscript when it was only 250 pages long. She liked it and urged me to persevere. I can never thank Ann enough for her warmth and devotion.

Vivian Reifers
> Vivian allowed our family to erect the original 'Hanoi Release John Nasmyth' billboard on her property. She was happy to leave it there until Spike got home, which is part of my story.

Clorice Baber
> She typed my original manuscript and wanted to see it in print.

Tulia Hydinger
> Tulia, beautiful Tulia taught me enough French in a hurry to converse with the North Vietnamese around the world.

Carr Flournoy
> He read the original manuscript and urged me to complete it.

Laura Miller
> She worked after hours retyping the completed manuscript.

Bob Dornan
> His enthusiasm never ebbed.

George Putnam
> I cannot say enough. George lent me his entire file on the Nasmyth

campaign years, over one hundred pages. George helped us bring our campaign to the world, and he allowed me to use some of his writings.

Patty Fry
For believing in my project and introducing me to my editor.

Michele Holmes
Michele, weeping over the phone while reading my book, singing its praises, was relentless in urging that I finish this story, one that, in Michele's words, "simply had to be told."

Sarge Budy
A man my father's age who read the completed manuscript for me. It was partly his masculine reaction to my story which caused me to carry on with the job of publication.

Richard Nixon
The former President brought the POWs home. He saved their lives. And, he has supported me in my life's project with his touching contribution.

John H. Nasmyth, Sr.
Difficult as it was for Spike's Dad, our Dad, to relive the campaign, he did it for me.

Pete Nasmyth
Our brother Pete took time out from his hectic days to share his stories with me.

Gebo Berger
Our sister Gebo worked so hard on the campaign for Spike.

Virginia Nasmyth
Our Mother. Thank you, Mother, for everything.

Spike Nasmyth
Thank you, Spike, for telling me your story. I shall never forget watching you and listening to you tell about those six and a half years of your life.

Carmen Nasmyth
She gave me her moral support those first difficult years.

June Laurie Behar
My editor. She took the manuscript and with enormous energies guided me. Together we produced this beautiful book.

Rick Loy
My husband. Rick was unfailing in his devotion during the 'campaign.' He was wonderful. I appreciate all his support.

Jenny, Mary, Spike, and Bodie
All four children have watched mama go to the office, or sit down at the kitchen table to work. Somehow they all seemed to realize how important this book is to me. I can never thank my sensitive, generous children enough.

HANOI
RELEASE JOHN NASMYTH

A FAMILY LOVE STORY

You've never met my brother, Spike.

AUGUST 5, 1964

Everett Alvarez, Jr., twenty-six, shot down in his A-4 Skyhawk, became Hanoi's first American POW.

Telegram

September, 1966

SPIKE, with his dusty blond hair and pale green eyes, is a sexy, hell-raising, jet jock. I've always had a crush on Steve McQueen's character, Josh Randall, the bounty hunter in *Wanted Dead or Alive*—he reminds me so much of Spike. Spike is a great listener. He's tough as nails, handsome and lovable, above all lovable. You know the type, he makes money and friends wherever he goes. Children and women are crazy about him. He can be like a magnet attracting 'tight situations,' and makes it through them effortlessly. Spike's motto in life is 'don't sweat it.'

Mine is a wonderful big brother, showering me with praise and gifts whenever he's home. I always wear the sapphire ring he picked up for me on his last trip to the Orient. I guess Spike is the most generous person I've ever known. He really knows how to treat his little sister.

Before Spike left for Vietnam with the Triple Nickel Squadron, he took me to a going-away party for his best friend, George Volk. George was about to leave for Vietnam as an army pilot. The party lasted all night and I came to know and love the Volk clan.

Spike took me to the drag races and the next week we visited our sister in Phoenix. He and I sat around and talked a lot at night back at home. Just 'B.S.-ing' one night, we got into a 'what if' discussion. Little sister happily giving him one of the back rubs he relished, I asked, "Well, Spike, what if you get shot down?" Spike shrugged it off. I was still concerned. He assured me, "Baby sister, don't worry, I'm an officer. If they get me, I'll be okay."

On the morning he was to leave for Vietnam, I drove my fearless, healthy, tough, wonderful, twenty-five-year-old big brother to the airport. Going up the escalator I felt so proud with Spike holding my hand. Here I was, a seventeen-year-old girl holding this handsome jet jock's hand. I looked over at Spike, standing there in his dress blues. He smiled back at me, squeezed my hand. He held my hand all the way through the air terminal. I watched his plane take off, thinking, I'm sure gonna miss my big brother, Spike.

The summer of 1966 while Spike was in 'Nam, I worked on a farm in Israel and traveled in the Middle East and Europe, a tremendous spiritual experience. Baptized in the Jordan, the Holy River, I came away filled with an overwhelming love toward man. I sent Spike a postcard almost every day and came home virtually glowing.

A couple of days after arriving home, I finished up the summer by going up to Bass Lake with my girlfriend's family. We planned to spend a week or so waterskiing, dancing at the Falls, and hiking trails.

On September first, we were cruising up the lake near some campgrounds when we saw a young guy swimming toward us, thumb up. That was a pretty original way to get a lift, so we threw him a ski and gave him a ride. That's how I met Rick Loy. We waterskiied, hiked up the river, and went to the Friday and Saturday night dances together.

It was at the second dance, about midnight, when I felt an overwhelming need to be home. I had never hitchhiked before, but I felt I must go home and that was all there was to it. Rick cut his vacation a week short. We drove the three hundred miles to my house.

That was September third.

Rick dropped me off at my house about seven in the morning. I took a bath, pulled on a blue shift, and then the doorbell rang. It was an Air Force chaplain. He wanted to see Mrs. Nasmyth. She wasn't home, nobody else was either.

"Does this have something to do with Spike?"

The chaplain: "Yes."

I asked, "Is it good?"

He said, "No."

Tears flowing down my face, I whispered, "Spike's not dead?"

The chaplain said, "I can't say."

He had an official-looking piece of paper. He would only give it to my mother. I begged him to give it to me, but he wouldn't. I grabbed at it as he was holding it up over his head. He just held it there. I tried to drive over to the house my mother was painting, but I couldn't control the car. The chaplain drove me. I was screaming, pounding his dashboard with my fist. When we got there, she had already left for home. He turned back toward home and I just kept screaming. When I saw my mother at the end of the driveway, she was thirty yards away, but she knew what had happened. It was the most terrible moment of my life. I watched my mother's face crack into pieces.

The chaplain handed the telegram to mother. We read it together:

Oh God, we were torn apart . . . "A fireball, oh, Jesus."

We had a terrible time holding the piece of paper. It just kept slipping. Crying, furious, "Damn you, God."

I have never before seen Mother cry. She was crying and shaking, struggling to read that piece of paper. Mom let the paper and her hand fall to her side and we held on to each other, sobbing. Finally, Mother sat down at the kitchen table and began to read the telegram again.

"Mother, what shall I do, who's gonna tell Dad?"

Mom mumbled, "I can't do it, call someone."

I got on the phone, tried to dial several times until I got through to our neighbor, Paul Lee. I could hardly talk. "Paul, Spike's been shot down. Please come and help us, somebody's got to tell the family."

Paul said, "Oh, no, of course, we'll be right over."

The chaplain sat quietly watching the whole scene. Finally he said, "Is there anything I can do? Would you like me to stay?"

"No," Mother said. "Please go."

Sola

Umm, good, that's good. Sola, you're so soft. I love your dark brown hair . . . mmmm, hey baby, what a nice way to wake up.

Oh hell. This isn't my place. I've been dreaming. Damn! I'm still in this shit hole.

I don't want to lose that feeling, daylight's sneaking in . . .

Jesus, my tailbone's killing me, ahh, my shoulder blades, knee, my elbow's stiff. Sitting up's making my head throb. Look, the new bites are already starting to itch. Those goddamn mosquitos.

Terrific. I've got my feet on this filthy floor, my eyes are beginning to unstick, one at a time and there's my damn mosquito net, it fell down last night. My face really ate it. I hate it when they're inside my nose.

How could anything taste as bad as this crap on my teeth? This place smells like a cesspool.

There's John. Mouth wide open, snorting every time he inhales. No wonder he didn't hear the gong.

The peephole in the door opens, the idiot guard yells, "Mi, shet up! No schleep!" Three bowls filled with hot sticky rice, with some onion greens slopped on top, slide through. That's breakfast for John Brown, John Blevins, and me.

Since I'm already up, I carry Blevins' bowl over to him. He looks miserable in the morning, says he itches like crazy under his cast, couldn't sleep.

Brown crawls out from under his net, picks up his bowl and staggers back to his bed to eat. Blevins begins his morning ritual of shoveling hot rice into his mouth as fast as he can. He eats faster than any other human on earth with all the accompanying sound effects. Jesus, he's noisy, lips smacking, some of the food going down, most of it falling back into his bowl. God damn, now his fuckin' nose is starting to run again . . . sniff,

sniff, snort, snort. Holy shit! Pigs don't make that much noise.

Brown and I just look at each other, we can't believe it. I always look away while he's eating, but you can't turn off the sound. Sometimes I wish his parachute had failed to open.

How in the hell did I get into this mess?

Up until 1960, the United States supported the Saigon regime only with military equipment, financial aid and 700 advisors for training the military. By the end of 1963, the number of advisors had increased to 27,000, joined by U.S. helicopter pilots. All of this did not halt the advance of the Viet Cong. In February, 1965, President Lyndon Johnson ordered the bombing of North Vietnam, but bombing failed to stop Hanoi. Four weeks after the bombing began, 3,500 U.S. Marines landed at Da Nang. By July, 1965, U.S. combat troops had risen to 75,000. The number of U.S. troops continued to climb until it reached 543,000 by April, 1969.

Thailand

September 3, 1966

Ubon, Thailand, a gentleman's way to fight a war. Unlike the soldiers in South Vietnam who lived in foxholes out in the fields, at Ubon fighter pilots returned to their air-conditioned BOQ's each night, living with a certain amount of luxury.

I had no desire to live in the BOQ on base, so I rented a Thai bungalow downtown among the civilian population. My bungalow, elevated on about twelve-foot stilts, isn't air-conditioned, but screened in. Surrounded by heavy trees, it is always cool inside. The upstairs is divided into two bedrooms. The bathroom on the ground floor has a cold-water shower, American-style toilet and a big mirror. Next to the bathroom is a combination kitchen and parking area for my motorcycle. The kitchen has three little charcoal burners which serve as a stove.

The thing that makes my bungalow extremely attractive is my beautiful Thai girlfriend, Sola. She is a young lady who works in the American Embassy in Bangkok and came to Ubon to visit her cousin. Sola's cousin, a young waitress out at the Air Base, introduced us.

Sola and I have been enjoying a rather fine romance. Fact is, she helped me pick out my bungalow and helped me decorate it.

Last night, beautiful Sola and I went out to a nice little Thai place called the Nit Hoi Club. Sola and I spent the evening eating, drinking Thai beer and enjoying ourselves. We went home pretty late.

She got me up real early. I had to be at the base by 4:30 a.m. I kissed her goodbye, jumped on my motorcycle and headed for the base.

My little Honda 125 has provided me with many exciting moments going to and from the base. If you've ever driven in Tijuana, Mexico, you know exactly what Thai traffic is like—it's every man for himself. More than once, I've had to ditch my bike in a rice paddy to keep from getting run over by a bus.

When I arrived at the base there were half a dozen other pilots there in various states of semi-wakefulness: hung over, under the weather, red-eyed, feeling bad, looking forward to getting into their aircraft and turning on the one hundred percent oxygen to get their functions back to normal.

I ran over to the BOQ where I had a room, changed into my flight suit and drove on down to the command post for the 'general briefing of the day.' It covered weather conditions, the expected anti-aircraft fire, and SAM (Surface-to-Air-Missile*) activity in the area the day before; generally, what to expect on the mission, the type of target we were after, the priority of the target, and the possibility of 'rescaping,' (that is, flying a rescue mission for someone who had been shot down the day before, and maybe taking a route in or out to search for the downed man and listen for his radio beeper).

After the general briefing we had twenty minutes or so to kill before the flight briefing. We had a cup of coffee and sat around and shot the breeze about the previous night's activities.

Then we got it together. Our squadron leader gave the 'specific flight briefing,' that is, the actual tactics we were going to use on the way in, the formation we'd use, the position he wanted the aircraft to maintain, and our altitude going in. On a map the captain laid out our route. We all copied it down so we'd know roughly where we were all the time.

We discussed the particular tactics to use if we encountered SAMs or anti-aircraft fire or a MIG aircraft. We looked over our target and generally laid out the flight so every man knew what he was supposed to do under any circumstance.

Before this flight, as before every flight, we checked out our aircraft to see that they carried the proper armament, the missiles were in good shape and the bombs properly attached.

The last thing I did before getting into my airplane was to grab a thermos of beer and tomato juice. One of the best parts of flying a combat mission is hauling ass out of North Vietnam afterwards at 450 knots, sipping a beer.

After completing pre-flight, we climbed into our aircraft, strapped in, and started engines. Over the radio we checked in with flight lead, then taxied down to the 'hot' arming area.

The armament men crawled under and removed the safety pins from our load of bombs, missiles and anything else we were carrying. When the pins were removed, they gave the 'all clear' and we radioed the tower for take-off clearance. In pairs of two, the tower cleared us onto the run-

*Thirty-seven-foot long, surface-to-air guided missile with a 200-pound warhead.

way. We ran our engines up, checked them out, kicked in full after-burner and blasted off.

I was leading a flight of two into the southern region of North Vietnam, twenty miles north of the DMZ. We were on an armed reconnaissance mission, flying around fully-armed, just looking for some action. We'd been flying for twenty minutes or so, running up and down highways, looking for targets. Hadn't seen a damn thing. Our fuel level was getting low, and we were preparing to head for home when I spotted something. Dead ahead lay a gulch where railroad tracks had been cut through a knoll. The tracks had long since been bombed out of existence, but the roadbed was still there. We could see truck tracks, which told us that at night the Vietnamese were moving their supplies southward through this gulch. I took her down to 200 feet, just above the treetops, going 450 knots or so. As I made a pass I saw a glimmer of light. It looked like a reflection off a windshield. I called to my wing man, "Buzz down there and take a closer look."

Apparently, a bunch of Vietnamese hiding under the natural camouflage of trees in this gulch thought they had been spotted. As my wing man made his pass, he saw perhaps a dozen North Vietnamese abandon their vehicles hidden under the boughs and leaves, and run like hell.

An excited voice came over the radio, "There's a bunch of them down there right in the ditch!" I pushed up the power, lit the burner, got the thing going pretty fast and came around to make another pass. At about 100 feet, 480 knots, I lined up on my target and pickled off four napalm cans. The automatic timer let them fall a fraction of a second apart so they strung out in a long line. The napalm hit in front of the first truck and spread out over most of the vehicles in the gulch. I got a beautiful hit. My wing man was right behind me. He was pretty excited. Things were blowing up all over down there. He dropped his napalm right in the middle of the fire I had already started. We pulled around to take another look. We were getting a lot of secondary explosions, which meant the trucks we hit had been carrying fuel or ammunition. We were coming in low so we got a good look at everything. Things were burning pretty good.

I called the Airborne Command Post, told them what we had found and that we had a bunch of good fires going. The guy in the Command Post was really excited. You don't often find good targets in the southern part of North Vietnam. He told us to give him our exact location and he'd send in four F-105s carrying two three-thousand-pound bombs each. They went in and hit the smoking ruins of what we had already napalmed and scattered trucks and parts all over the countryside. A three-thousand-pound bomb makes a hell of a bang. Later that day, they sent another flight in to put the finishing touches on the thing. If you don't blow the stuff to bits, the North Vietnamese take all the usable parts off the wrecks and use them on other vehicles. I think that day we completely disintegrated the vehicles in the area. It was a satisfying mission, one of the few times I saw a really good target.

Shot Down

September 4, 1966, 4 a.m. Sola woke me up. I was so hung over I barely remember either leaving or driving out to the base. But, I found myself there at the Command Post in my flight suit listening to the general briefing of the day! Our briefing officer, Lieutenant Colonel Ernie Relak, indicated that our mission this morning was pretty important, although from the looks on the faces in the room, you wouldn't have known it. Our primary mission wasn't particularly tricky, but after hitting our target we were to escort some F-105s. They were after a big oil depot near Hanoi. They wanted us to give them the air cover they needed. The 105s, heavily loaded with bombs, would be very unmaneuverable—easy prey for MIGs.

We were a flight of four F-4s. During the pre-flight, one of the aircraft turned up with a mechanical problem. We decided to take off short-handed.

Start, taxi, arming and take-off all went without a hitch. Just after becoming airborne, the third man in the flight had an emergency and returned to base. That left two of us. We don't like to fly up around Hanoi with just two aircraft; it makes us too vulnerable. Four in the flight is better for self-defense. The Command Post in Saigon told us to go anyway, so we went.

As usual, we met a tanker over Laos, got a full load of gas and headed up toward our target deep in North Vietnam.

After crossing into North Vietnam, I noticed that the weather was different than forecast. (God damn, weathermen don't know shit!) It was supposed to be clear but it was cloudy as hell, a real thick undercast. Now, we just don't like to fly over undercasts near Hanoi. If a SAM missile should come up through the clouds, you probably wouldn't see it until it was too late. Then we got a call from a flight of F-105s. They assured us there hadn't been any SAM activity that morning. If 105 pilots have the balls . . . shit, let's go.

Ray Salzarulo, my back-seater, said, "You think this is smart?" I said "No."

In a few minutes, we are across the area of undercasts and into the clear, no SAMs or flack. Whew! Lots of chatter on the radio. A flight of 105s to the east of us is under heavy 37 and 57 millimeter anti-aircraft fire. Another flight thinks they see MIGs. In my earphones I can hear the sound as Ray's rate of breathing increases. I can hear and feel my own heartbeat. Jesus, I see two SAMs at my two o'clock position coming toward our flight. I call on the radio, "Satan flight, SAMs at two o'clock, break down and right!!!" I roll my F-4 over, pull down into a screaming dive and head for the deck pulling as many 'Gs' as I can without stalling the aircraft. As my airspeed increases, I turn harder, about 6 to 7 'Gs' now. I out-turn the SAMs and they hiss by harmlessly to my left. I start to pull out of my dive and join up with my wing man when my back-seater screams, "Hey, Spike, here comes another . . ."

That's as much of the sentence as he got out, because as I looked to the left I saw two feet from my head what looked like a goddam telephone pole. Instinctively, I blinked my eyes, ducked my head and said "Oh, shit, don't go off." It went off a few feet above my plane. My beautiful F-4 Phantom stopped being an airplane and became a mass of falling wreckage, tumbling end over end, twisting, parts flying off in all kinds of wild gyrations. Holy shit, here comes the ground. (Eject or die, Spike.) I pulled the handle.

It only takes a split second from the time you pull the handle until the ejection seat fires, but it seems like an eternity.

"God damn . . . now this fuckin' thing's not going to work, either."

All of a sudden, I'm flying through the air . . . God, it's quiet! Jesus, my parachute isn't open yet, holy balls, the ground is close.

A couple of seconds later, the parachute automatically opens, no more than 75 feet above the ground.

My parachute ride was mighty short. Very quiet all of a sudden, after all the roar and the noise of being inside the cockpit and the radio chatter, all of a sudden it was deadly silent. Then I heard an explosion as my airplane hit the ground. After that, nothing. Not a sound. It was like being in a tomb.

During the few seconds I was hanging from the parachute, my mind was racing: "As soon as I hit the ground, I'll grab my survival kit and head off toward the jungle. If I can get there before they find me, maybe I can hide a couple of days until they stop looking for me. Then, with some luck, I might make it to a place where a rescue chopper can pick me up."

I hit the ground, and fell on my ass. Trying to do everything as fast as possible, I started to reach up and pull the parachute release. My right arm wasn't functioning. There was blood squirting out of my right elbow. I couldn't move my arm, couldn't move my hand, had to take my parachute off with my left hand. While I was slipping out of my chute harness, I noticed that my gloves, a sapphire ring, and my left boot had been ripped off by the blast of wind when I ejected. All I could think of was "get the hell out of here and hide."

I started to pick up my survival kit, but with one hand I couldn't. (The hell with it.) I took off and headed for the jungle. I hadn't gone more than fifty yards when I looked down and noticed that this clever little trail of blood I was leaving could be followed by a Girl Scout. Starting to get very weak and dizzy. I figured the best thing I could do before bleeding to death was stop the bleeding, then head for the jungle. I sat down on the ground and took a piece of rawhide I had holding my survival knife onto my G-suit, twisted it around my arm, took a pencil from my flight suit pocket, wrapped it tight and squeezed my arm with this tourniquet to stop the bleeding. It worked. The blood stopped squirting out. Now there was just an ooze.

I had been on the ground only about a minute when I started hearing voices. It sounded like a hell of a lot of people, shouting, yelling, chattering, beating their way through the bush. If I didn't make it to that jungle pretty quick I was going to be caught. I made about another twenty or thirty yards before I saw a bunch of Vietnamese coming out of the underbrush behind me. I wasn't sure they had seen me. I was in some pretty thick stuff so I headed for a tree with thick undergrowth around it. I got under the tree. (Maybe they won't find me here.) Wrong again. They had seen me, and I was surrounded.

My last thought before being captured is surprisingly calm. (Well, as far as experiences go, this ought to be an interesting one.)

About two minutes after my landing on the ground, a scrawny old Vietnamese man holding an Elliot Ness-Untouchables type machine gun walks up to me. He has a wild look in his eyes. He's shaking like a leaf. I'm hoping he doesn't shake so hard he squeezes off a round. He gives me the 'put up your hands' signal, which I follow as best I can, but my right arm doesn't work, it doesn't go up. This upsets him, but he sees the blood and besides they have me outnumbered a-hundred-to-one. There are several others, barefoot men, women and kids dressed in dull pajama-like outfits, or naked except for filthy rag loincloths like the one the guy holding the machine gun has wrapped around his middle. They've all got machetes, or sticks or guns of one sort or another and they are chanting and yelling and screaming. They are all pretty excited. Me too!

With the old man holding his machine gun on me, two others take my knife and cut off my G-suit, my flight suit, and my one remaining boot. They strip me down to my underwear. When they tear off my flight suit I notice a piece of shrapnel, about one inch long and a half-inch in diameter sticking out of my right thigh. It must have been the piece of metal that had gone through the crook of my right arm.

By now there are at least a hundred Vietnamese standing around looking at me. One old woman whacks me on top of the head with a bamboo stick. The old man grunts at her and she backs off. I sit down, my back up against a tree. Another little old man comes out of the woods with a dirty Red Cross bag on his shoulder. He comes over and gives me a little first aid on my arm. He takes a gauze bandage, ties it around the wound, then he pulls the chunk of shrapnel out of my leg. It's an ugly puncture wound, a hell of a hole, but there's not much blood.

My life in North Vietnam begins.

I thought about Ray. (I wonder if he got out?)

When the old man finished patching me up, they put a blindfold on me. Somebody took me by my good hand and led me off. I couldn't see because of the blindfold, but mud squished up between my toes and I could hear water running. It smelled like shit. I thought I must have been walking on a dike in a rice paddy. I knew I'd lost a lot of blood, I was weak as hell and for the first time I realized the seriousness of my predicament. As shock wears off fear comes on. Shit! I was scared. The walk seemed endless. (Jesus, where are they taking me?) My head was pounding. I could feel blood oozing down my arm; walking had started the bleeding again.

Someone had me by the hand and was leading me along. Everywhere I could hear people talking. The path we were following must have been lined with villagers taking a look, curious to see what kind of thing this 'Yankee Air Pirate' really looked like. We walked for maybe an hour. The guy leading me grunted to make me stop, and took off my blindfold. I was in the midst of a heavily wooded area. An old man rolled out a ragged bamboo mat, and gave me the 'lie-down' signal. It didn't take me long to learn that you can communicate anything by hand signals. Gestures get the point across. I lay down. It was about eight-thirty or nine in the morning. I spent the rest of my first day in North Vietnam, the daylight hours, lying under this tree. I think every Vietnamese within twenty-five miles came to take a look at me. Literally thousands of people paraded by me that day, stood around just looking. They didn't touch me.

I'm pretty sure there was a bounty for captured Americans. Apparently this bounty was considerably more if the man were alive. The ragged old guy with the rusty machine gun who had captured me stayed by my side. He was more interested in protecting me against the Vietnamese than he was in guarding me. The teenage kids wanted a piece of me, I could tell by their jeers and the looks on their faces. But my guard held them off. I lay there all day waiting for the sun to go down. I could hear our guys flying all over the place. It looked like the Vietnamese were waiting for the air to be clear of RESCAP aircraft so they could get a vehicle through and transport me.

My mind was racing. (Holy shit, why a good guy like me? Why not one of the pricks in the squadron?)

The recurring thought running through my head was, "How in the hell did I get myself in this mess?" I relived the last minute or two of my flight a thousand times. (If I had seen that other SAM I wouldn't be here. If the other guy in my flight had seen it I would have been able to dodge it.) I was pissed off that I hadn't cleared the area well enough to see the other SAM. God damn, if I had just looked around a little better, I might have seen it and been able to avoid it.

My arm was swelling and bloody. I had a pretty good idea it was broken. I couldn't move my hand or wrist. I was hoping it didn't get gangrene and rot off. I'd heard about the horrible infections you can get in the Orient. (Of course that piece of shrapnel could have gone through my head instead.)

The temperature was right around ninety-five degrees, excruciatingly hot and humid. Just lying there, the sweat rolled off my forehead, legs and chest all day long. A bead of sweat rolled off every second or so. Felt like bugs crawling across my body. Nobody offered me a drink. Shit, I was too scared to feel thirsty. I kept thinking, "I'm alive, now what?"

The mosquitos weren't bad during the daylight hours, but as the sun went down they came out in droves. I could take a couple of mosquito bites; I had other things on my mind.

I lay there on my back wiping the sweat off my face, looking up at the sky. (God, I wish I were back up there.)

A few hours after sundown, a small van pulled up. The old man gave me the 'get-up' signal and took me over to the van. I crawled in the back door, ready for my ride to Hanoi.

The men in the van were the first military people I'd seen. The old man who had captured me stayed close until I was locked inside. Some sort of transaction took place between the soldiers and the old man; maybe he got his reward. That's the last I ever saw of that old guy.

Three soldiers had picked me up, a driver and two in the back with me. They had guns; I recognized an AK-47 Russian-made machine gun. The other was just a rifle. Once inside the van, they tied a rag over my eyes. The truck had high windows, so even without being blindfolded I couldn't have seen anything anyway. They had me lie on my back on the floor.

The soldiers riding in the truck with me jabbered to each other once in a while. A couple of times they leaned up and spoke with the driver, but I couldn't understand what they were saying.

We were driving along a dirt road full of big chuck holes. I'd bounce off the floor every time we'd hit a bump. Jesus, I started to hurt.

After a while the pain was excruciating, the van was moving fast, the road was rough as hell and I was bouncing around like a ping-pong ball back there.

I kept hoping I'd wake up from this nightmare. I hurt bad. The soldiers looked down but didn't seem to feel very sorry for me. I wasn't feeling very tough.

The Family

Mom and I were hurting pretty bad. Neither of us could handle getting hold of the family on the phone. We were numb. There was a knock on the door. I looked up and there were Paul and Ruth Lee. They walked into the kitchen and took over, Paul got on the phone trying to contact Dad in Canada. I went out to the front porch, sat down alone and cried.

For the past week Dad, big sister Gebo, her husband Bob and their kids had been at Dad's summer place near Victoria, B.C. This morning Dad and his mother, Louise, had been seeing Gebo, Bob and the kids off at the Victoria airport for their return home to Phoenix. As Dad and his mother were returning to their cabin, they nearly ran over Louise's eighty-year-old husband, Norman, running down the dirt road toward the city. Breathless, he told Dad there was an urgent message to call home. Pretty shook, Dad drove back to town, reached a phone and called. Paul Lee read the Air Force chaplain's letter over the phone. Sobbing, defeated, Dad could only manage, "I guess there's not much more to say; I'm coming home."

To reach Pete, Paul phoned some of his friends in Arcata, California. He left the same message: "Pete, urgent, phone home."
An hour later Pete phoned from a neighbor's. Again Paul read the telegram aloud. Pete just listened, the veins swelling up in his neck and head. Mom and I cried hard and clung to each other as Paul, in a controlled monotone, read: "It is with deep regret . . ."
Pete held his hand to his forehead. Tears were streaming down his face. He walked home, glanced at Carmen, his wife, and said: "Spike's been shot down."
Pete walked into their bedroom and lay down on his back on the bed

just holding his head and staring up. Pete stayed like that for the rest of the day.

Pete's idol for years had been his big brother, Spike. He just lay there, tears welling up, thoughts about Spike filtering through his mind. Spike always did things just on the edge of danger. When Pete had had a paper route, Spike would take him out on it in the jeep. He'd drive off the road at forty miles an hour and scare the hell out of his younger brother. Spike always said, "An inch is as good as a mile."

They used to have wars. Pete would be making a sandwich at the kitchen counter and Spike reading the newspaper, then somehow Pete would get in Spike's way and they'd end up slugging it out. They played and fought continuously. They never did hold grudges, though.

Spike always had the fastest hot rod and threw the best speed shifts. When he was sixteen, he dropped the 'trans' in his '40 Ford. He needed money so he went down to the dairy a couple of blocks away and shoveled enough hundred-pound bags of cow manure at twenty-five cents a bag to buy a thirty-dollar transmission. He put it in by himself out in the back yard.

When Pete was eighteen, Mom and Dad loaned him a credit card so he could drive up and visit Spike at college in Moscow, Idaho. When Pete got there, Spike used the card to have every five-gallon can he could find filled with gas, enough to last him a month. Pete said, "Gee, won't they think I used a lot of gas getting up here?"

Spike shook his head, "No, they won't even notice."

You know, they didn't.

Meanwhile, Gebo, her husband, Bob, and their children Larry and Carol were waiting between planes in the Seattle airport when the P.A. system announced a phone call for them. Bob answered it.

Mother and I listened while Paul Lee told him someone would be waiting for Gebo at the Los Angeles Airport. Mother was too upset to move, so I said I would go. I took the chaplain's telegram and blindly drove the forty miles to the airport. I don't even know how I got there, driving like a madman. I could hardly see because of the tears. I hated the cars that were in my way and swerved around them. Poor Gebo, I had to give this awful telegram to Gebo.

At the same time, seated on the plane, Bob was telling Gebo he had just spoken to Paul Lee. Bob said, "Gebo, Spike's been shot down. Someone from the family will meet you in L.A. with the telegram."

Gebo started to cry. She sobbed and cried out loud all the way to Los Angeles. A disaster—she felt he was lost. She thought, "Hell, if he were alive everybody wouldn't be so upset, upset enough to call me in Seattle."

-19-

She felt a chilling sense of impending doom.

All during the plane ride, thoughts of their childhood flew around Gebo's mind like loose pieces of a jigsaw puzzle.

Scenes flashed by. As a child again, Gebo could see his fair, angelic little face looking up with those big green eyes. She felt like his mother; she talked for him. Spike didn't bother to talk until he was three years old. He didn't have to; he had Gebo to interpret for him. She could almost feel Spike as a toddler, standing there holding her hand. It seemed as though he had spent all his time holding her hand.

She recalled when they were older kids, hiking together in the Monterey Park hills. Pete, Spike, Gebo, two neighbor boys and our dog, Captain, exploring the ravines in those hills, lifting Captain over the crevices. Scenes flashed by in her mind faster and faster. They were melting crayons with matches; she made them neat rings; together they rummaged through garbage cans, made magic potions, rode wagons . . .. Gebo didn't want to think about it now. Her eyes swollen, red, she visualized little Spike hiding the vegetables he didn't like in a drawer, then throwing them out the window to Lloyd Talley, a neighborhood kid. Pete and Spike threw cats out the windows by their tails. Once, while jumping on his bed, Spike flew out the second-floor bedroom window. At night they'd spend their time lying around on the grass looking at stars—and one night there was a meteor storm.

Time was passing swiftly in her head—she was a teenager now, babysitting for the two boys. One time they attacked her with a broom. She took it away from them and whacked 'em. Mad, they decided to spend the night in the top of the huge maple tree in our front yard. She wanted them down before Mom and Dad got home. She got out their own BB gun to threaten them, and ended up squirting them down down with the hose.

Then she remembered last summer, before Spike left for Vietnam, when he drove to her house in Phoenix. They had sat around, talked and drunk beer. He just loved her two little kids. He carried them around on his shoulders and took them to the Air Force base to look at jets. The children loved him.

Bob shook her shoulder: "We're in Los Angeles."

Gebo got off the plane alone and walked over to where I was standing. I ran to her, "Gebo, I'm sorry . . ." I started to bawl. She held me, crying. We just stood there hugging each other, crying.

Gebo read the telegram and asked how Mother was doing. Then, she called home and told Paul Lee that she would be back the next day. She very slowly walked back down through the boarding terminal to join her family.

I watched my sister, crushed now, as she stepped back onto the plane.

In a mental fog I went out to my car.

I reached home from the airport feeling very sick. Gebo had seen the telegram. I gave it back to Mother; nothing had to be said. Mom had hold of herself and was sitting at the kitchen table. I went out on the front porch and began to cry all over again.

It was awful and lonely when it got dark that night. Ruth and Paul went home. Mom and I went to bed. I heard her crying into a towel in her bathroom and I fell into a deep sleep.

Dad arrived home at four a.m. He looked around the house. I stayed in bed. Mom couldn't even talk to him. He did the best he could. He kept walking around around the dark house saying to himself, "What is the use of all this, what is the use . . . ?" Tears welled up in his eyes as he stared out the kitchen window.

That same night, while Gebo was packing for her trip back to Los Angeles, she sat alone in her bedroom thinking about the Air Force telegram. Things simply were not very hopeful.

When Gebo arrived we sat together holding hands, waiting for Pete to come home. Gebo hadn't returned home with any expectations at all. She just wanted to see how everybody was doing. She only really worried about Mother, who's the strong one—and if she wasn't strong we would all be in trouble. Mom was strong.

Being home with the family didn't make Spike's fate seem so final for Gebo. Everybody was upset and scared, but she and the rest of us kept talking about the various possibilities, what could have happened: he could still be alive; he might have ejected; just his radio failed; the beeper might have failed too; he could be hiding in the jungle. We weren't going to assume the worst until we knew all the facts and had talked to everybody possible.

The next morning Pete flew home. Pete is a great, big, strong man. God, it was awful to see him so torn up. He walked into the kitchen actually crying.

We all sat at the kitchen table and stared at each other. When one of us started to cry, he'd go outside or into the living room. We waited, stunned, for the first time all experiencing helplessness. Day after day the veins stood out on everybody's faces each time the phone rang, or when somebody came over, or when we looked through the mail. During those first days of terror and bewilderment, I felt like I had the dry heaves. The strain knotted up our stomachs, made us speechless. When we did talk about Spike it would end up sending us off in different directions to cry or to get a grip on ourselves.

We would wait for the phone to ring and run to the mailbox each morning. We would sit around the table together discussing the possibilities. If anybody could make it, Spike could.

We watched Dad sitting in his patio chair, quietly smoking, not flicking the ashes, just staring off with the tears running down his cheeks. We had never seen our father cry.

Pete told us something eerie that he couldn't get off his mind. On September third, the same night I had spent hurrying home from Bass Lake, Pete had a dream about Spike. In the middle of the night, about 4 a.m., Pete woke up in a cold sweat. His wife, Carmen, was awakened by his tossing. Pete told her about his strange nightmare.

Pete had seen Spike's plane blow up. He saw Spike eject through the flames and land on the ground. Pete explicitly described Spike standing in a rice paddy in a small valley. Clearly he could see Spike wearing only his shorts and there was a stream of blood running down his right shoulder. Pete saw Spike's hands tied behind his back as a number of people marched Spike up a hill and out of sight.

Pete was absolutely convinced that this is what had happened. He had seen it. That first week Spike was missing was especially traumatic for Pete because he felt Spike had been captured; he could see Spike walking around with a bowed head, subjected to mental and physical abuse. Pete saw Spike transformed from a flier to a prisoner of war.

Again and again, sitting across from Pete at the kitchen table, I'd ask, "Well, what do you think, Pete? Does he have a chance? Is he . . .?"

"Nah," was Pete's reply. "He made it, Virginia. I know he made it. I can see it. Hell, I can feel it."

Pete was so positive, so sure of himself. He gave me something to hold on to.

We had all come together at the home where we grew up to help each other and to be together when more news of Spike arrived. Hourly we expected more information.

The telegram, that impersonal, pessimistic, official letter of condolence was all we had to live with. We followed the instructions in the text explicitly. We did not discuss Spike outside the immediate family. Spike had always been the center of the family's conversation and the talk of the neighborhood, but this telegram struck such fright into us that we couldn't talk about what might be happening to him.

Torture

The truck arrived in Hanoi about two o'clock in the morning. I was dragged out of the truck and taken into what I later found out was the Hanoi Hilton complex. The Hanoi Hilton has several different sections, all of which we gave pet names to: New Guy Village, Little Vegas and Heartbreak Hotel.

The Hilton originally was a jail built by the French. All the buildings were brick, plastered, then whitewashed, with red tile roofs. Before being occupied by Americans it was used by the North Vietnamese to confine their own people.

I was taken into a little room about twelve feet by twelve feet in New Guy Village, the Nobby room. It had a primitive plaster job on the walls and ceiling. I was told to go sit in the corner on the floor. There was no furniture in my end of the room. Only a table and chair stood in the opposite corner.

A few minutes after arriving, I met my first English-speaking interrogator. I never saw this guy again after my first week in Hanoi. I had a pet name for him, 'Shakey.' His hands shook like a leaf as he chain-smoked cigarettes. He smoked them down till they blistered his lips. Very intense. Shakey asked me who I was, asked my rank and serial number. Then he started asking for more information.

I told Shakey, "I can't answer anything other than name, rank, and serial number."

He replied, "You are a very foolish young man. In some days you will be begging to answer these questions. Other Americans have learned to think clearly here and so will you." Shakey asked me several more questions which I refused to answer. He left the room.

I sat there alone wondering what was going to happen next when a guard walked in. He had some ropes in one hand. He rather professionally came over to me. He gazed at my injured right arm, studied the problem for a minute. He probably hadn't encountered this problem in the last few days. He was going to have to use a new technique.

It didn't take him long to come up with a new plan of attack. Intuitively I sensed one thing you didn't do when a guard was doing something to you, you didn't resist.

He tied my ankles together with a fancy slip knot. (Not too tight, not bad.) Next he tied a rope around my left wrist, yanked my left hand across my back toward my right shoulder and down around the rope between my ankles. As he started cinching it up I felt a burning sensation on my shoulder. The rope was taking the hide off there. He kept pulling. It drew my feet up toward my butt and drew my left hand up the right side of my back. I couldn't believe I could stretch any further, when with one more cinch my left hand appeared up over my right shoulder.

The guard propped me up in the corner on my tail bone and disappeared out the door. It wasn't too bad, but it hurt. The most uncomfortable thing was the point of my tail bone resting on the cement.

It seemed like hours before Shakey came back and asked me, "Are you ready to talk?"

I told him, "No."

He left.

Propped up in the corner there on my tail bone, I was convinced that there was no way they could make me say anything other than name, rank, and serial number.

Shakey came back in perhaps an hour. He sat down in the chair behind the table at the other end of the cell. He sat there and smoked a couple of cigarettes, didn't say a word, just looked at me. He drank a couple of cups of tea and then asked me if I would like some water.

I nodded my head. I hadn't had anything to drink. I'd been sweating all day and had developed a terrific thirst. I said, "Yeah, I'd like some water."

"When you're ready to talk we'll give you some water," he said as he set a big cup of water on the table in front of me. "I won't talk to you," I replied. He looked a little disgusted, shook his head: "What a fool, you're wasting time." Then he grunted something in Vietnamese and walked out. Back came the guard. He walked over to me and untied the knot at my feet.

I thought, "Well, he's untying me. I showed 'em I was tough. It's all over, they couldn't put up with me." (Stupid Gooks!) Then I discovered why he untied the knot. Now he really cinched up the rope, pulling me into a tight ball. (Jesus Christ, does he think I'm made of rubber?)

I began to notice I was becoming a contortionist. My left hand was beginning to creep further over my right shoulder. I could see my entire hand. There's just no way your hand gets over your opposite shoulder without quite a bit of help.

They left me for an eternity. My circulation was cut off both in my ankles and my hand. I couldn't get my old Boy Scout Handbook out of my mind: "If you have a tourniquet on, you've got to release it every hour or you'll get gangrene and your limb will fall off." (Damn, I wonder if these stupid bastards know that? This guy better come in pretty quick and untie me or I'm going to lose two feet and a hand.)

I thought of something I'd heard at Air Force Survival School. An instructor had said, "Orientals always use the 'good guy'—'bad guy' technique. First, the 'bad guy' will torture the hell out of you, he'll take you to the breaking point. Then the 'good guy' will come on the scene and come to your rescue:

'I see my friend has mistreated you. This is not how we treat our prisoners, I will take care of you, please, you must not think badly of our people because of one man's actions.'

"The 'good guy' will try to win your confidence and get you to answer his questions. If you don't talk, he will leave and the 'bad guy' will return. This will be repeated until you are so glad to see Mr. Good Guy that you'll talk to him."

(God damn, where is Mr. Good Guy?)

I don't know where that survival school instructor got his info, but the 'good guy' never showed up. Waiting for him was the main thing that kept me going, and damn near got me killed.

Again the rope man left me propped up against the wall, incapable of moving. The only thing I had free was my broken right arm, which was a useless, bloody mess.

Cinched up in the pretzel position, it was kind of an insidious pain. Not really a horrible pain, it just built and grew, spread till pretty soon it seemed like my hand and everything was on fire. God, I was starting to hurt.

I couldn't stand it any longer when the guard came in and untied me. He didn't say a word, just looked at me. He gave me a couple of grunts which I figured meant to stay there, and disappeared.

As soon as he left I started to pick myself up from the floor, tried to straighten out my legs. Right away I noticed I had no feeling in the ends of my fingers, they were numb. (Oh hell, they've ruined me, my fingers are dead.)

There was no way to tell time, no windows, one door I couldn't see out of, and a bare light bulb, glowing day and night.

I sat there on the floor, leaning my head back against the wall, sweat running down my face. A guard looked in every few minutes. In sign language he got across: "If I catch you sleeping, I belt you." I was so incredibly tired by then that despite the wake-up guard I'd dose off for a minute or two every time I was left alone.

That morning another Gook came in. He looked like a Gook medic. I could tell because he wore a filthy-looking smock. He unraveled the filthy blood-soaked bandage which was still wrapped around my arm. He took a look at the wound, wrapped it back up with the wet, caked bandage and disappeared.

Shakey came back in: "Ah, the doctor just looked at your arm. You're getting infection, you need medical attention very badly."

I said, "Yeah, that's a good idea, let's go get some medical attention."

Shakey answered, "Ah, when you are ready to talk to us I shall send you to the hospital; until then you will get no medical attention."

I got the message. (Dirty bastard. I hope when my plane hit the ground, it hit your village.)

I told Shakey I wasn't going to make any deals. According to international law, prisoners of war must be given medical treatment.

He laughed. "You are not a prisoner of war. You are a criminal. You will be treated as a criminal until you repent of your crimes against the heroic people of the Democratic Republic of Vietnam.'

With that I told Shakey I had to piss.

He said, "No."

"Then I'm going to piss on the floor."

"Okay. Go outside."

I had a horrible urge but the only thing that came out was thick and dark orange, just a few drops. My penis was bright red and swollen. (Jesus, my arm is broken, turning black; I can't piss; I'm a prisoner of savages, dying of thirst; infection is setting in; and now my cock is falling off. Dirty yellow bastards!)

Back inside, Shakey told me to sit in the corner. He began to give me a lecture: "Many of your friends have talked to me. It is certainly foolish of you to resist. It is a silly thing for you not to cooperate. Why should you go through this? The medic tells me that your arm needs medical attention. I feel bad not letting you go to the doctor. Why don't you think clearly? (A favorite Gook phrase.) Now you must think clearly."

I just sat there and shook my head. Shakey shrugged, went outside and hollered in Gook.

A moment later the rope man walked in, a whole coil of ropes slung over his shoulder. He grabbed me and put me back in the ropes, not even trying to be gentle. My left arm was so stiff it would barely bend, but he bent it.

Instantly, I was in agonizing pain. The muscles must have been torn. He didn't get my hand nearly as far over my shoulder this time as he had the night before. Christ, it hurt. He cinched the slip knot tighter and tighter. This time I ended up with my back bent damn-near double and my feet drawn up really tight. The bastard walked out the door.

God, I had the most awful backache and my hand felt like it was on fire, felt like it was being cut off.

Shakey had taught me one Vietnamese phrase, 'bao cao.' "When you're ready to talk, say, 'bao cao' to the guard and he will come and get me."

Later I learned that 'bao cao' means something close to 'report.' That's what you were supposed to say to a guard when you wanted to talk to an English-speaking Vietnamese officer.

I didn't bother remembering 'bao cao.' (What the hell do I need that for? I ain't gonna talk to this guy.)

The guard didn't leave for very long this time. About fifteen minutes later he came back in and cinched me up even tighter, right back to where I was the first night. I was still expecting a Charlie-Chan-looking cat with big thick glasses to come in and say, "Ah so, my friend, you have been mistreated. I will report the bad officer . . . " But he never showed. I was like that for another long time when the rope man came back in and put still another cinch in the ropes.

(God damn, another quarter of an inch tighter and my arm, or my neck or my back or something is gonna break.)

God, how long have I been like this, I'll count to a minute, one to sixty. One, two, three, four . . . One, two . . . I never got past thirty. Seemed like thirty minutes, not thirty seconds.

Shakey came back. He was a little agitated this time. "I am very busy now. I do not have much time to put up with you." He asked, "Would you like a cup of water?"

I said, "Yeah." This cup of water had been sitting on the table all night. He picked it up and threw it in my face. I got a mouthful.

"Now that I have given you water, you are ready to talk."

Somehow Shakey had the idea that if I took his water I would talk to him.

"Now answer my questions."

"I don't have anything to say to you."

"Oh, you promised if I give you water . . . " He took the metal cup and started banging on my forehead, face and eyebrows. He was really getting mad.

As he worked himself into a rage he began trembling like a leaf: his head, hands, whole body shaking. His lips were quivering when he talked, foam at his mouth . . . .

(Jesus Christ, he's crazy!)

I didn't talk. After he had banged on my head with the cup for a while, he stomped out of the room in his rage.

My right arm still had the original bandage on it, so I couldn't get a good look at the wound throbbing under the wrapping, tight and swollen. The bandage was oozing red and dark blue over the caked, dried blood. I was thinking about that and thinking about my hand falling off; the pain was really getting miserable.

I began to think. (Hey Spike, I don't know how long they can keep this up, but I don't think you can keep it up indefinitely.) One thought occurred to me: I must be a weak slob, I'm sure other guys have gone through this and never talked to them.

Later, when I couldn't take it any longer, the rope man came back in. He grabbed at the ropes. I didn't look up. He untied me. I had been thinking of nothing else, waiting for some relief. But when the ropes came off, it hurt even worse. Fresh pain shot into my hands and feet, with every heartbeat.

I was leaning back in the corner on the cement slab, beat, head throbbing, feeling sorry for myself when for the first time I heard something from outside the room. From some room not too far off, a man let out a blood-curdling scream. It sounded like they were pulling out fingernails or sticking him. A death scream. Then he hollered, "You sons of bitches, get me out of these fuckin' ropes. I'll talk to ya rotten bastards." Followed by another American voice, "Don't sweat it, buddy, we're all behind you."

Then I heard the guards shouting and yelling, running around. I could hear somebody just getting the hell beat out of him—bang, bam, grunts and groans. It was then I realized there were other Americans close by and that someone else was hurting and about to say something beyond name, rank and serial number.

Shakey came in a little later. "You see some of your friends are here also, they are also criminals. Your friend is ready to talk, you heard him."

"You aren't following the Geneva Convention with this guy. You're torturing him."

"You are not prisoners of war. You are criminals. Tonight I am very busy and have something else to do. I allow you to stay here in the cell and to think about your crimes. Think seriously, and tomorrow I will come back to speak with you. The doctor told me you are badly wounded. Think clearly and seriously of your crimes tonight. After we talk tomorrow you will go to the hospital."

(Fucking Gooks and their screwed up logic. This dumb bastard's telling me that it's my fault. It's my fault he's withholding medical treatment. Where the hell is the 'good guy'?)

I was so damn tired I was asleep the instant my head hit the floor.
"No schleep! No schleep!"
(What the fuck's going on?)
"No schleep! No schleep!"
(Whaddya mean no sleep?)
A guard kicked me in the stomach, then hit me on the side of the head, still screaming, "No schleep! No schleep!" Whenever I dozed off he'd remind me with a blast from his foot.

"No schleep!" The longest night of my life finally passed. It was sunup when Shakey returned.
"Now we talk. Where did you fly from? Who was your commander? What was your target?"
"I cannot answer your questions."
Shakey got pissed. He virtually screamed something in Vietnamese and in came the rope man. Shakey pointed to me muttering in Gook to the guard.

"Now my guard will remove your bandage so you can see your wounds. Then you will think more clearly."
The guard unraveled the gauze.
(Oh, my God, I've got gangrene!) My arm was the size of a football, a bluish purple mass, seeping yellow pus. The smell was horrendous. Several small wounds were scattered around a big one on my forearm. I could see a hole in the top of my forearm and a hole in the bottom and a big gash where there ought to be a bone.

"Now my guard will leave the bandage off so you can see your arm as it gets worse. Soon you will know that it is time to cooperate."
The 'no schleep' guard repeated last night's routine.
(Oh, Jesus) Bugs began crawling all over my arm. (Fly away you bastards.) They got stuck in the pus. (What the hell smells so bad? Jesus Christ, it's me!)
The morning of the fourth day, Shakey came to my cell.
"Now will you allow my doctors to take you to the hospital?"
"Sure, I'm ready right now."
"Ah, you are ready to answer my questions. Now you are thinking more clearly."
"No, I didn't say that, I said I wanted to go to the hospital."
This time the rope man wasn't even half-way nice about it.
(My God, he's gonna tear me apart.)

He just went berserk, kicking, hitting, slapping and screaming like a wild man, while the sweat and blood went flying.

Shakey stood there watching. "You see, my guard is angry. You have caused him to stay up late. He is a very busy man. He has other things to do, you are causing him to stay with you. He is angry."

Shakey walked out. The guard sat at the table glaring at me. Every few minutes he'd come at me, kicking and screaming.

I felt like puking but I couldn't. Then in my ears I started hearing a loud roar and suddenly the room started to spin; I became violently dizzy.

Lying there on my back, tied up, I tried to tell the guard that I had to vomit. He wouldn't even look at me. He just spat in my direction. He kept saying "Bao cao?" I didn't even remember the words then, I didn't know what the hell he was talking about. I started vomiting but nothing came out—the dry heaves.

Later the rope man jerked the sticky, smelly ropes off and threw my 'good' arm to the side; it was just like a noodle. He stomped off. For a long time, lying there, I couldn't feel anything below my wrist. The damn thing had been tied up so long, I wondered if it would ever work again.

The fifth day, a guard whom I had never seen before came in. He was holding two bananas, a bowl of rice, and a bowl of green soup. He set them down in front of me. There was a spoon in the soup. He grunted something like 'eat.' I wanted to but I couldn't pick up the spoon, so I put my hand in the rice. Just plain, tasteless rice, but when I put it into my mouth it made me sick. I couldn't take food. I looked at that bowl of green soup and Jesus, just the smell of it, it stank. I didn't touch it. I did manage to pick up the two bananas and devour them.

That afternoon the medic came in. He looked at my wounds, grunted and left. Pretty soon the medic and another man returned.

"The medic says you need to go to the hospital."

"Let's go."

"No, first you must confess your crimes against the heroic Vietnamese people."

More: "No schleep, no schleep."

The sixth night, I was propped up against the wall again, when Shakey came in and gave me a long lecture. "Look at your arm, it's in very bad condition, very swollen. The medic has given me a report. If you do not go to the hospital very soon we will have to cut it off. You force us to treat you severely. We want to show you the lenient and humane treatment we give to criminals who repent of their crimes."

Listening to this, barely able to hold my eyes open, I started to conjure up stories in my mind. I knew there couldn't be many more days of this before I was going to start talking. I started making up lies, anticipating the questions he'd ask me.

That night when the rope man came in, instead of putting me in the ropes, he banged me around for a while. I was so dizzy, every time he knocked me down I'd just lie there. The roar in my ears kept getting louder. Some of the scabs broke loose, not blood but green-yellow pus oozed out. The smell was pungent.

I spent most of the following day studying mosquitos. There were hundreds of bites all over my body; my eyes, ears and lips were swollen to double their normal size. I watched a big one, a real pig. He sucked so much blood out of my arm he couldn't fly. I was too tired to reach over and squash him.

(God I'm a mess. Look at me, pus and blood, filthy. I wonder why I'm so dizzy? Wonder what causes this noise in my head? Shit, I don't think I can get up.)

That night when Shakey came back in, he found me lying on the floor. This really made him mad.

"Do not lie on floor!"

I couldn't get up.

"You have broken the camp regulations. Now you must be punished. The Vietnamese people are tired of dealing with you. If you don't cooperate we will be forced to kill you."

The rope man came in and kicked me around for awhile. It didn't seem to hurt much and he soon lost interest.

(Jesus, the room is spinning. Wonder if I can pick up my head? Maybe I'm getting better, it doesn't seem to hurt much anymore. My arm sure is a funny color; look at all those bugs.)

Shakey was back. "If you answer these questions I will send you to the hospital."

"How old are you?"

"Twenty-five."

"What airplane did you fly?"

"F-105."

"Who is your commander?"

"Colonel Smith."

"What was your target."

"Oil tanks."

"What was the name of your commander?"

"Colonel Jones."

"What is the speed of the F-105?"

"Two thousand miles per hour."

-31-

"Who is your commander?"

"Colonel —a—a—Miller."

"You lie! You lie! Now you will be punished. You will learn what happens to black-hearted criminals."

The room was spinning as the rope man tightened the knot. (I've got to remember what I said. Oh shit! I think my left arm's broken too.)

He's cinching me up tigher. (I've got to make him stop, say something . . . What were those damn words?)

It's getting dark—or—maybe it's getting light. I'm not sure.

Shakey looked down at me. I started to say something but nothing came out. (Jesus Christ, now I can't talk. I can't do anything.) I tried to take my left hand and give him a signal. I did it, but then I looked down and the damn thing didn't work. (Well shit, they've gone so far I'm gonna die. What the hell!)

I felt kind of calm actually, almost relieved. I just laid my head back and looked up. I could see this guy clear as a bell, but he was spinning like hell. I could hear noise, this roar, but he wasn't saying anything.

After a while Shakey got up, walked over in slow motion, put his hands on his hips, stood over me and looked down at me. I looked up at him, tried to move my mouth. (There ain't no way.)

He just looked at me and walked out.

Later four guards came in carrying a narrow wooden door. They laid it down beside me. The English speaker said, "Get on."

(Shit! Are you kidding? I can't get on that damn board, I can't walk, I can't even wiggle.)

Jabbering, one guard holding his nose, the officer said something to them. They weren't gonna touch me. They rolled me up onto the board with their feet, picked it up and carried me out to a jeep.

Pine Box

We were all incapable of facing the fact that Spike had just disappeared. All we had left of him were memories.

Gebo's and Pete's responsibilities were calling. Eventually they had to return to their own families, in Phoenix and Arcata.

Then, a few weeks later, a large pine box carrying all of Spike's personal possessions arrived from overseas. Mother and I put the box in his bedroom, sealed and untampered with.

Hospital

The jeep left the camp and went down to what must have been their hospital. They actually had an X-ray machine. After a few pictures were taken, the guards picked up the door I was lying on, carried me to another room and laid me on a hospital bed.

I heard water running. I could move my head and eyes. I saw the backs of several men in white smocks, washing their hands.

(Boy, this is really neat, just like Ben Casey. They're washing their hands, cleaning up. Great! It's gonna be sterile. Things are going to be okay now.)

Then I looked at the ground. The floor of this room was an inch deep with dirt, dead cockroaches and bugs by the thousands, and to top it off these so-called medics were all barefoot.

They came over and took some kind of gadget, grabbed hold of the scabs on my arm and pulled them off. I couldn't see. I was remarkably calm, at least for a little while, until I felt a sawing action on my arm.

(God, they're cutting my arm off!)

There was a guard standing there with a gun. He had a sneer on his face, he gave me a 'cut off your arm' signal. I still couldn't see; they had a white cloth between my eyes and my arm. I couldn't move. (Oh shit, it's got gangrene, they're sawing it off.) It felt like they were sawing it off right where the wound was, shuu shuu shuu. (Oh, this is it, man. They are doing it. They are cutting the damn thing off.)

When they finished and moved the cloth, I still had an arm. They must have been filing the rough edges where the shrapnel had gone through the bone. It sure felt like a saw. When they removed all the pus and blood and stuff, it wasn't nearly as bad as I expected. Half of the swelling turned out to be this caked mass of crap on it. They didn't clean up my arm, just wrapped it and put on a rough Gook cast.

My 'hospital' visit was over. They they took me for a ten-minute drive which ended up in a place we called the Zoo. They drove the jeep into the camp, pulled me out of the back, took me into a room, laid the door I was lying on down on the floor and left me there.

That morning a guard came in, threw a mosquito net at me, a blanket, a pair of short pants and short-sleeved shirt and a pair of long pants and a long-sleeved shirt. All of the clothes were red and grey striped.

Later in the morning a guard came in, kind of a friendly guy. He was called Happy.* He was going to be my 'turnkey' for the next three or four months. Happy gave me three cigarettes, stuck one between my lips and lit it for me.

Around noon another guard opened up the door and brought in some food, my second meal since I arrived in Hanoi, nine days ago. A bowl of rice, a big bowl of green soup and a side dish. (Ugh!) I didn't even try to eat it, but I emptied the little teapot of water.

At night I covered up with my blanket and pulled my mosquito net over me. I couldn't hang it up.

I had no water to clean myself with. That old saying that you get used to your own smell is bullshit. I smelled so bad it made me want to puke.

After two days in this cell, Happy came in, told me to get up and roll up my stuff. I stuck the mosquito net, blanket, and clothes under my arm. He led me to another cell. The second cell was big enough for six to ten people. There was no one there except me.

Happy didn't speak English. He pointed, indicating, "You live there in that bed, hang your mosquito net up there." He showed me a place to tie it. I said, "Okay." He gave me my day's ration of cigarettes, then he left.

I put everything in the corner wadded up, and laid down on the board bed. I was so tired, instantly I went to sleep.

About the fourth day at the Zoo, a guard called Magoo came in. Magoo turned out to be one of the super bad-asses. Magoo had a piece of paper in his hand, 'The Camp Regulations.' The English was atrocious but understandable.

Magoo didn't say anything, he just pointed.
1. It is forbidden to communicate with other criminals in other cells by any means, by coughing, making loud noises, or tapping on the wall. Any criminal caught violating this regulation will be severely punished.
2. When you want something say in low voice, 'bao cao.' The guard will report it to an officer.

*All the guards had names: Happy, Clyde, Frog, Magoo, A.B. (After-Birth).

3.   All the criminals must keep cells neat.

4.   Get up and go to bed according to the gong.

The gong is an empty cannon shell; when they banged it with another piece of metal, that meant get up. They would bang it at eleven a.m. or so, that meant nap time; bang it at two p.m., that meant get up; they'd bang it at night, it meant go to bed.

One of the regulations said, "When you are met by the Vietnamese officers or guards, you must greet them in the proper way." I didn't have any idea what it meant at the time.

There was a bucket in the corner of the room. Magoo pointed and said, "Bo," that was their word for bucket, my toilet.

I was shaking my head like yeah, I understand the camp regulations. I didn't know what a lot of them meant. I was going to learn pretty fast.

In sign language Magoo stood me up, walked me over to the door, shut the door like he was leaving. Then he opened the door. He said "Bao." I though it was some Vietnamese word, I just stood there looking at him. He came over and hit me hard alongside the head with his fist. He said again, "Bao." I shrugged like, "I don't know what the hell you are talking about." "Blam!" We played the game again, like he was just coming in the door. He opened the door and said, "Bao." I still didn't know what the hell he meant, sounded like "bow."

It was. He blasted me in the head. Again he opened the door, but this time he grabbed me by the hair and pulled my head down, "Bow." I got the picture. You're supposed to bow when he opens the door.

(That's a bunch of bullshit!)

Magoo left and came back with an officer called Spot. Spot explained to me very carefully that any time he met me or a guard met me or any other Vietnamese met me, opened my door, or window, I must stop and bow.

I couldn't believe this guy. (You bow every time you meet some Vietnamese? That's the most humiliating thing I've ever heard of in my life. I bet nobody else is doing this bowing shit.)

"You are criminals, you must greet the guards in the proper manner." As Spot left and I was sitting there on the bed, Magoo slapped my face, screaming, "Bow, bow!" (Now I find out that you're supposed to bow when they come and when they go.) I didn't bow. Magoo came over, grabbed my head and 'bowed' me. They left.

The cell had one window but it was covered with a bamboo mat. I went over to it. It was woven pretty tight; you weren't supposed to see out. I peeked around and sure enough I found a little hole where I could see out. All I could see was a short piece of sidewalk in front of the building across the way. I was peeking out this little hole when all of sudden I saw two Americans walk by. I had no idea where they where going when all of a sudden they stopped. They each gave a deep bow. (What the fuck's going on?) Then I saw a Vietnamese guard walk by.

(Jesus Christ, they're serious about this bowing shit.)

That afternoon Magoo came back with some rope in his hands. When he opened the door, I just sat there on my bed. He gave me the stand-up signal and said real low, "Bow." I didn't get up.

He walked over to me and, God damn it, in a few minutes I was right back in the ropes. (You're shittin' me, this is where I started!)

Magoo said, "Bow, bao cao," meaning, when you're ready to bow say, "Bao cao." I lay there for a long time. I thought about those other guys bowing out there and said, "Screw it. I'll bow for 'em." I was just hurting so bad. Magoo came back a little while later, untied me and demonstrated to me the art of bowing.

We decided later that bowing was probably the most degrading thing they ever did to us. They had full colonels on down to ensigns bowing every time they saw an officer, a guard, or a Vietnamese woman. But it was bow or suffer.

A couple of years later when I was communicating, I heard about one POW who lived in the same cell block. He was walking out toward the bath area and this little Vietnamese dog walked by. He bowed to the dog. (Oh God.) The guard got the right implication; he was insinuating the Vietnamese are dogs. Boy, they just beat the piss out of that guy.

Another funny thing happened to two of the POWs. We were never supposed to see other Americans. But every once in a while the guards would screw up. In this case, two POWs coming from opposite directions walked around a corner, practically bumping into each other. They stopped, bowed majestically, then walked on while the guards went berserk. They both received their 'just punishment.'

My first two weeks at the Zoo were a blur. The infection in my arm kept me flat on my back. I had constant headaches, those throbbing miserable things behind your eyes. It felt like my head was going to explode with every heartbeat. The damn things lasted twenty-four hours at a time. I thought they would never stop.

One day Happy opened my cell door, handed me a small towel and a chunk of lye soap. He signaled for me to follow him. My right arm was in a huge cast and I had a patch on my right leg and a piece of gauze around my neck for a sling.

Happy led me to the wash area and signaled that I had five minutes. There was a small cement trough with a hose trickling water into it. The trough was green with moss, and little bugs were buzzing around on top of the water. I dipped water with my tin cup and washed with one hand. My first bath in two weeks sure felt good.

I slid right into the prison routine.

A guard would ring the gong about 5:30 a.m. That was the signal to get up. I'd take my mosquito net down and roll up my blanket. An hour or so after the gong, a guard would appear at the peephole in my door; I'd stand up, bow, and he'd give me three cigarettes and a light.

The next event of the day could happen any time in the morning. The cell door opened, the guard would say, "Bo"—time to empty my bucket and wash. The number of times you got to wash each week depended on the mood of the guards—sometimes every day, sometimes once a week.

Chow arrived around 11 a.m. The guard opened the door, I'd bow and walk outside to an old door lying across two sawhorses. On the door were several rations of food. It would take three trips for me to get my food into the cell. Using one hand I'd pick up a bowl of rice, a bowl of green soup and maybe a side dish of pumpkin, melon, cabbage, or something I didn't recognize.

Ten, fifteen, or twenty minutes later the guard would open my peephole and I'd pass my dishes out. Then he'd light my second cigarette of the day.

Later I would hear some Americans come by, pick up the dishes and go to the bath area and wash them. I'd hear them bitching and moaning a little in low voices.

At noon the gong would ring again: the beginning of nap time. For the next two hours there wouldn't be a sound in the camp. Every day during nap time, the roving guards would sneak up on my door and pop open the peephole as fast as they could. Trying to catch me doing something, damned if I knew what. I didn't have the strength to do anything but lie on my bed. (Maybe they think I'm digging a tunnel!)

The gong sounded again at two, signaling the end of nap time. Most of the time nothing happened in the afternoon until the food arrived. The food routine was repeated, followed by the third and last cigarette of the day. Just after dark the gong sounded for the final time, and it was under the net till morning.

(Am I ever going to see another American? Those guys I saw through the hole in my mat, how did they happen to be together? Why am I by myself?)

It was kind of funny, they had issued me a woven bamboo mat about two and a half feet wide by six feet long. When Happy brought it in, I didn't know what it was. I laid it down beside my bed for a place to put my feet. Happy came in a few days later, shook his head, "No, no." He picked the mat up, shook it off and laid it on my bed.

Two weeks after Happy showed me how to use my sleeping mat, he came into my room in the Stable and gave me the roll-up-your-stuff signal. I rolled my gear up in my mat, stuck it under my arm and followed Happy out the door. This was the first chance I had to look at the prison. Every building had several windows. Each window was covered with bamboo mats, hiding all but the top few inches of the opening. The open space was too high for anyone to see out. There were bars on all the windows. The buildings were separated by walls. Mats were hanging everywhere, the mats and walls an attempt to keep everybody in complete isolation.

Happy lead me over to a square building, then inside into a very small dungeon, about five feet wide and eight feet long.

A bare light bulb hung from a cord. There was one window covered with a mat and a cement bed which took up most of the room. Happy pointed to the bed. I laid my belongings down and just stared. He pointed to the camp regulations which were glued on the wall and to a bucket in the corner. This was my new home, cell four, the Office. Compared to the cell I had just left, this was a real hole—dark, damp and tiny.

A few days later an English-speaking officer came into my cell and explained the camp regulations to me for the tenth time: "You must keep your room neat and clean at all times."

There were thousands of mosquitos smashed on the wall. The officer accused me of doing it.

"If you kill any more mosquitos on the wall, you will be punished."

I don't know how he would have known if I had squashed any new ones. There were already millions of corpses. He also warned me about communicating: "If you are caught knocking on the wall or trying to communicate with the other criminals you will be severely punished."

I knew there were other prisoners in the same building. At chow time I'd see many bowls of rice and that awful green soup. I could hear guards yelling at people, men shuffling to and from their cells, but so far in my POW life I had not communicated with another American.

I was lying on my bed one afternoon when on the wall right next to my head, I heard, tap-tap ta-tap tap. A minute or so passed, tap-tap ta-tap tap. A few minutes later, tap-tap ta-tap tap. I answered: tap tap. Whoever was on the other side of the wall started tapping like mad. It didn't make any sense, nor did I consider the possibility of a code.

(Poor devil's been here too long, lost his mind.)

I couldn't get enough sleep. Every minute that there wasn't a guard at my door, I spent on my bed. I was sleeping more than twenty hours every day and I was still exhausted.

Being in solitary didn't bother me much. I didn't worry about being alone in this little box of a cell at all. All I thought about was sleep.

I was trying to keep track of the days, I guess, but I just wasn't able to do it. I don't really know exactly what was going on. I had a fever a lot of the time, it seemed to accompany those headaches. Just a daze. It didn't quite seem real. I just wanted to be left alone, so I could sleep.

Another month went by. I was getting used to my little dungeon, felt secure there. Then they moved me to cell four of the Pig Sty. I could think of no reason for the move. I spent a couple of weeks there. I don't know why they moved me. There were three beds in this cell but I was alone. The walls were brick, covered with grey plaster. The room was fourteen feet square, had two windows covered with mats and barred. I didn't do much peeking out while I stayed in the Pig Sty. I was still constantly sleeping from one day to the next.

A few weeks later Happy told me to roll up and follow him—right back to the little dungeon. (These Gooks are weird.) I was glad to be back though; it was darker there and easier to sleep.

My cell door opened. A guard signaled to me to put on my long-sleeved shirt and long pants even though the temperature must have been in the eighties. I followed this guard to a part of the camp I'd never seen before. The guard stopped at a door, spoke to someone inside, then motioned for me to go in.

Sitting behind a desk was a Vietnamese officer, an interrogator, the dread of the camp, Dumb-Dumb.

"What is your name?"

"Nasmyth."

"Nahshit, shit down!"

(Jesus, where'd they get this guy?)

"Now you have seen the lenient and humane policy of the Democratic Republic of Vietnam towards captured American air pirates. We allow you to confess your crimes."

(What the hell is he jabbering about?)

"Do you agree?"

"I don't understand."

"You are a criminal. You must confess. Do you agree?"

"No." (This one is a real nut.)

"Do you refuse?"

"Refuse what?"

"You must confess or you will be punished."

"I don't know what you are talking about."

"Nahshit, I will have you killed and that could be very dangerous for you."

(Holy shit, is he for real?)

"Why you laugh? You must be punished. Kneel down!"

"I don't understand."

"Kneel down!!!"

The guard kicked me off my stool! I kneeled on the cement floor.

"Hands up!! Hands up!! High over head!!"

"How can I put my hand over my head? I have a broken arm."

"The other one. Queek!! Queek!! Keep hands up or I will allow guard to beat you, you have broken the camp regulations. You must be punished so you can think clearly."

(What the hell is he so bent so out of shape over? I don't have the foggiest idea what this is all about.)

As my left arm started to sag I felt a terrific blow to the side of my head.

"Get up!! Get up!! Kneel!! Kneel!! Hands up!! When I return you must be ready to think clearly. Now think of your crimes."

For the next couple of hours I stayed there on my knees trying to hold my left arm up in the air. Every time it drooped the guard would flatten me. My knees were killing me, my arm felt like it weighed a ton, sweat was pouring off me. The worst headache of my life was pounding in my head, and I was so dizzy I could barely keep my balance.

Dumb-Dumb returned.

"Shit down! Now I give you paper and pen and ink to write story of your life."

"I can't write, I have a broken right arm."

"Use other."

"Now return to cell and write."

"It's pitch black in my cell."

"You have light."

"It's so dim I can barely see."

"Do not be obdurate. Go!"

(Wonder what that was supposed to mean?)

I was born in the United States   I never know who my father was my mother worked hard as a servant to buy my clothes and send me to school I had no brothers or sisters but one cousin whose name I forgot. My mother name is the ~~same~~ same as mine except for the first and that's different. I went to college in the same place I was born and studied to be a business man but I was drafted and sent to ~~———~~ became a pilot. When I was a pilot they sent me to Vietnam. I flew an unarmed photo plane. I was shot down on my first mission. My navigator whose first name is all I remember got killed. I was only a lieutenant so they didn't tell me anything. After the war I want to be a doctor   John Nesmyth

Facsimile confession written with partially paralyzed left hand. Spike is right-handed.

First Christmas

None of us had ever seen Mother cry. In fact, I don't think she ever had. September 4, 1966, the day Spike was shot down, Mother cried all day. She had always been the one to take control in rough situations, like when our horse died or when the neighbor's dog killed our duck, Donald. Now for the first time she was a basket case, completely helpless.

The night of September 4, when the neighbors left, Mom and I were home alone. I didn't know what to do. I couldn't stop crying, couldn't talk and when I looked at Mom or touched her, she would burst into sobs.

Mom says she never cried after that first day. But I remember lying in bed listening to her cry her heart out, a towel held up to her face. I heard her that first night and every night for the next four months.

Mom did some other things which seemed out of character. She began sleeping twelve to fourteen hours a day. I guess this was her escape from reality. And she stopped gardening. Gardening had been Mother's joy, but now she hardly went out into the yard. I think it was because Spike and Pete had always helped her mow the lawn, prune the fruit trees, plant roses, etc. It was just too sad working in the yard with Spike gone.

Most distressing of all was that Mother could not be moved from the house. She was glued to the telephone and the mailbox. Of course, it was a comfort for the rest of us going to school or going to work to know that Mother was there waiting for word. But the strain and anxiety every morning at 10 a.m. when the mailman came, turned into a very long, sad vigil.

Dad spent a lot of time at home, very quiet at first. He was no help to Mother in her emotional distress and she was unable to buck him up. Mom and Dad were totally unable to come to grips with Spike's situation together. They didn't talk about Spike nor the various possibilities of what could have happened. Dad began to spend more and more time alone. After work every night he would walk the family dog, Slasher, up and down

Drayer Lane. They would go up and down ten times. Dad talked to himself and the dog, "Dear God, take care of my son, wherever he is." From the first dispatch we got, Dad thought it was all over for Spike, but he couldn't admit it. This made it impossible for us to comfort him or talk about the situation in his presence, because we were all trying to convince ourselves that Spike had somehow made it.

Feeling it was all over took its toll on Dad. He developed an ulcer. Dad had known the family doctor for over twenty years. Feeling very depressed and with stomach pain, he went to see Dr. Halley and told him about Spike. Right then and there, the Doctor pulled out Spike's records and wrote across the front 'deceased.' It was horrible.

Gebo was home now with her husband and two children in Phoenix. She and Bob could not begin to discuss what might be happening to Spike. The afternoon of September 4, in flight between Seattle and Los Angeles when Bob quietly told Gebo that her brother had been shot down and that he was sorry, was the last time they discussed Spike.

So Gebo was trying to come to grips with Spike's missing-in-action status alone. At home, carrying out the duties of housewife and mother, she was preoccupied with what could have happened and thought about the possibilities all the time. She thought he could be down in the jungle somewhere wandering around uncaptured, or hauled around from jungle camp to jungle camp or in a prison someplace.

At night when it was quiet, she tried to intuit whether or not he was alive, but she never could do it.

Sometime after she returned to Phoenix, a nightmare recurred to her several times in a week. Spike was in it. He was in danger. She couldn't reach him. She'd wake up scared and afraid and feeling very much alone because she couldn't turn to anyone for help.

Gebo had this constant dull feeling which ruined everything for her. As the months dragged by with Gebo waiting for news, a dreamlike vision of never hearing, which had permeated all her thoughts, slowly became a reality.

Pete was so sure that Spike was alive. We must have discussed a thousand possibilities that week while Pete was with us waiting for news. Pete became the strong big brother; he really braced us up before he left for his wife and two babies in Arcata, California.

At home in Arcata, Pete and Carmen also were not able to discuss what might have happened to Spike. Pete found himself physically exhausted, sleeping long hours through those first few weeks.

Spike was always foremost in his thoughts. After the initial period of exhaustion wore off, Pete took out his anxiety by doing things Spike used to, drinking or shooting pool.

Pete never doubted that Spike was alive—not for a minute. He constantly found himself thinking, "God, I wonder what they're doing to him?"

In his dreams he vividly pictured Spike looking just like he used to after a football game, head bent, hot and sweaty, harassed by those bastards. He knew Spike had been afraid at first, but he also knew he could keep his cool.

Pete needed someone to talk to. He and Carmen just couldn't communicate on this sensitive level. So he turned to his close friend, Warren Hitchcock. They spent countless hours sitting in bars talking about Spike. Warren constantly assured Pete, "Spike is alive, I know he is. He's a tough son-of-a-gun, believe me, he'll make it!"

Warren's enthusiasm would start snowballing and pretty soon Pete, the bartender, and anyone else around would be slamming their fists down on the bar. "Hell, yes, he'll make it, the tough son-of-a-bitch." They'd have one for Spike.

Those first couple of weeks passed in a pathetic blur. Everybody was hurting so much. We didn't cook; the neighbors brought food over. We didn't eat much, just waited. My boyfriends called for dates. I told them I didn't think I'd be dating for a while. A few days after Spike had been shot down, Rick Loy called. I told Rick what had happened and that I wanted him to come over. Rick came to my parents' house one evening that first week when the whole family was there. He was so sensitive. He assured me that Spike had made it! We sat on the front porch that night and I cried and talked about Spike and all my fears. Rick listened and made me feel that things would turn out okay. Rick came over once or twice a week for the next several months. We talked about Spike and I cried. I was so able to confide in Rick that when I would get upset at school or at night, I'd call Rick and we would talk about it.

High school resumed two weeks after Spike was shot down. Nobody bugged me, so I came and went as I pleased. Mother had phoned my high school counselor and teachers and told them that I had had a horrible emotional shock, and that they would have to be patient and understanding with me for a while.

The first play my English class read was *Antigone. Antigone* is terribly emotional—a young Greek girl is forbidden to bury her dead brother whose body lies outside the city. I had known the story for years. That first day when my teacher announced our reading list, I broke down in class and fled the room. I didn't go to English for two weeks. I spent that time crying on the steps outside the class, staring off through the chain link fence. It was so impressed upon me not to talk about Spike's missing status that I couldn't even tell Mr. Hinkle, my teacher, what had happened.

I went to the beach alone a lot. It felt good to look out in the direction of Spike and watch the sunset. I really felt close to Spike when I could look out over the ocean we shared.

I spent a great deal of time over the following months crying in the nurse's office. I don't remember doing anything or even going to school at all. But I remember the nightmares I had.

I've seen him burn up in that damn plane, watched a Vietnamese walking through the jungle wearing Spike's star sapphire ring. Sometimes I envision the ring just lying on the jungle floor. In the worst dream, which I've had several times, he is trapped by an octopus who's stuck to a great cement wall, and waves crash up on them, and I can't get Spike loose. He's drowning when I wake up crying.

Those first months not another damn thing mattered to me—especially the pettiness of high school.

Then Mom suggested I keep myself busy, get my mind off Spike. So I took three jobs as well as going to school. I worked in a warehouse weekends, ushered in a theater week nights and clerked in a department store afternoons. Three new responsibilities kept my mind occupied.

I worked frantically up until the twenty-fourth of December trying not to face Christmas without Spike. On Christmas Eve I threw up on the floor of the department store where I was employed. I came home and spent the next few days with the family.

That first year Spike was gone I started falling apart, plagued with a barrage of ailments. They all turned out to be emotionally related. Spike was always on my mind.

For the past several months I've spent a lot of time imagining what Spike is doing. I've been talking about it with Rick. We go over and over it. I'm terribly worried that Spike does not realize that we're sure he is alive. I think that must worry him. And I don't want him to worry.

Roommates

Every day at least one quiz (our POW word for interrogation). Sometimes two or three. I never knew who was going to be there. One time it's the Rabbit; he wants to talk about psychology. The next day I'd go up and there's Spot. He tells me about American war crimes in South Vietnam.

My favorite quizzes were with the Elf. If he walked into the room right now there would be no doubt in anyone's mind why we nicknamed him Elf. Ninety pounds soaking wet with a face exactly like a fairy-tale imp.

Elf was a master of the hyperbole. "Do you know how many piratical U.S. aircraft the heroic people of Vietnam have shot down?"

"No."

"Ten thousand at least."

"Really." (Christ, that's more than we have.)

"Most have been brought down with a single rifle bullet. We cannot waste ammunition."

"You don't say, you Vietnamese must be good shots."

"Yes, four thousand years of gallant struggle have caused us to be the best fighters in the world. Even today I can defeat twenty GIs with my bare hands, maybe more."

(Ho ho, my seventeen-year-old sister could wring this little twerp's neck.)

Next morning, a guard opened up my cell. Quiz time again.

(Wonder who it is today, why don't they leave me alone? Oh shit . . .)

Behind the table, dwarfed by his big chair, it's Dumb-Dumb. I give my little bow.

"Nahshit, shit down. What do you wish?"

"Nothing."

"How is your health?"

"Okay."

"You must say sir."

"Okay."

He studies me for a minute. "Nahshit, today the camp commander allows you to live with another criminal."

I stood there looking disinterested. (I'll be damned if I'll show my surprise.)

In walks another American; he bows. We exchange looks.

Dumb-Dumb instructs us, "In the room you can talk only in low tones. Do not try to signal the other criminals or you will be severely punished."

"Now return to the cell."

The guard led us back to cell four of the Pig Sty where I'd been a few weeks earlier. As he unlocked the door I saw another American lying on the bed, one leg in a cast from his toes to his ass.

The guard locked the door, we broke into smiles and started talking a mile a minute.

"Not so loud, that low tone B.S. means a whisper. They catch us making noise and we'll be on our knees holding up the sky."

John Blevins has the broken leg, John Brown is the one who met me at Dumb-Dumb's office. Brown was shot down on Black Sunday,* twenty-eight days before I was. Blevins was captured September 9, a week after me. He broke his leg when his parachute hit the ground. They were both flying F-105s. Brown is three years older than me and Blevins is one year older.

"Man, it feels good to talk," I said.

"Hey! Are there any other Americans around here?"

"Hell, yes! Are you kiddin? This camp has over sixty-five, we know all their names!"

"No shit! How?"

"You don't know the Code?"

"What Code?"

"The Tap Code."

"Jesus, somebody's been tapping on my wall every day for months, you think it was the Code?"

"Sure."

"I thought some poor bastard had gone crazy and was just tapping on the wall. Boy, do I feel like a dummy! I bet he thought I was stupid. Holy Christ, a Code!"

---

*Black Sunday, August 7th, 1966, the U.S. lost 12 planes and 9 crewmembers over North Vietnam.

Brown explained the Code and how the whole communications setup worked.

"Simple, huh?"

"Yeah, but how did you know the Code? Did you learn it in Survival School? I don't remember hearing about it."

"No, just like you, somebody tapped on the wall every day for a couple of days. I guess it became obvious I didn't know what was up. Then one Sunday afternoon when it was quiet he started pounding on the wall up near the window. Then I heard this voice, pretty loud:

'Hey new guy, you hear me?'

'I said yeah.'

'Listen, I'm Major Fred Cherry. This is the Tap Code:

'The alphabet has twenty-five letters, no K. Five lines of five letters. The first tap is for the line. The second tap is the letter in the line. Remember no K, use C for K.'

"Then the Gooks heard him and came running. They raised hell with Fred. He didn't give a shit; he's tougher'n hell."

"I don't think I get the Code."

"Look, it's simple, first tap is the line, second tap is the letter in that line, for example: tap tap tap—tap tap.

"That's the third line, second letter in that line, get it?"

"Let me see, A,B,C,D,E, F,G,H,I,J, K—,"

"No, remember, no K."

"Oh shit!"

"I'll try again, A,B,C,D,E, F,G,H,I,J, L,M, it's 'M'."

"You got it."

"In a couple of days it's no sweat, you'll be sending this stuff like a pro."

"What's this word?"

"Tap tap—tap tap tap.

"Tap tap—tap tap tap tap."

"Let's see—second line third letter—H.

"Second line—fourth letter—I, that's 'Hi'!"

"See, it's a piece of cake."

That day during nap time I sent Tap Code for the first time in my life. Very slowly I told the men in the next cell who I was, when I was captured and that I'd been flying an F-4.

Fred Cherry, John Pitchford and Art Cormier all said, "Welcome aboard, C.U.L."

"What's C.U.L. mean?"

"See you later."

Poor ole John Blevins had the crudest, heaviest cast I've ever seen. It must have weighed forty pounds; he could barely move. When a Gook opened the door, he had to bow sitting down.

Sometimes the Gook at the peephole or at the door didn't like the way one of us bowed.

"Bow!" "Bow!" "Bow!" "Bow!"

He wanted us to bow again but we acted dumb.

Brown looked at me and shrugged, I shrugged—

"Bow!" "Bow!" "Bow!"

Brown looked at me again.

"Bow Wow." "Bow Wow." "Bow Wow."

He barked like a dog and looked at the guard to see if he did right.

I could barely keep a straight face; Blevins had to hold his net over his mouth.

The guard slammed the peephole.

Now that I knew how to communicate, I started learning about the other men in the building. Pop Kerns has been here 16 months; all three guys next door have been POWs more than a year. I heard something that bothered me: Neil Jones has a broken arm that won't mend, and he's not the only one.

Every man in our building has been tortured to one degree or another. Fred Cherry had a dislocated shoulder when he was captured, that's all. Now his body is badly mutilated, all from torture.

The Gooks would tell Fred:

"In the U.S. they call you nigger, so why do you defend your country when they treat you like a slave? Help us; we will treat you correct."

"I may be black, but I'm an American."

The things the Vietnamese did to Fred were obscene.

Communicating was against the camp regulations, and to be caught meant certain punishment, so we were careful. Any time one of us was sending or receiving Code, the other was at the window peeking out a tiny hole watching for guards. When one would sneak up on the peephole we would give the danger signal and sit down. The peephole would fly open, and all the guard saw was three angelic faces.

John Brown turned out to be a hypochondriac with all the classic symptoms. Annoying as it was, he provided me with hours and hours of entertainment, observing as he developed every malady known to man, and a few as yet undiscovered.

Personal Effects

A few months after Spike had been shot down, a van pulled up to the house and unloaded the furniture Spike had kept in storage in Florida. We carefully stored all of Spike's worldly possessions in the pool hall adjacent to our home. This was the same pool hall Spike constructed as a teenager, where he and his friends spent countless hours shooting pool and 'bullshitting.' His high school football shoes and college fraternity paddles hung on the walls. It was very difficult to enter this room now.

Spike is one of the four men who built our family home. Everyone takes great pride in our beautiful redwood living room. Spike's portrait hangs in the living room along with his brother's and sisters' portraits. Upon entering this room, one sees the four Nasmyth children. It seems odd that Spike isn't really here.

> Life is a big up
> Until a great down
> My heart is dead
> I am dying.

All the family waited at our separate homes. We waited for a long, long time. The days passed by slowly, weeks followed weeks, then somehow we found we had been waiting for months. Still no word.

Until Spike was shot down, Gebo had been living a fairy-tale kind of life with her husband, Bob. A marvelous student, she graduated from college in three years so they could be married. Then she held down a fulltime job as an insurance adjuster so they could establish themselves and save for a family. Gebo was in heaven with the arrival of their son, Larry. Two years later the birth of their daughter, Carol, rounded out their family perfectly. Perfectly for Bob, that is, but not enough for my big sister.

Bob was a very content individual. He spent his evenings puttering around the back yard with their two children, hammering, playing ball, working on the yard. He was the perfect house husband, yet he worried. He worried unusually about the little things.

I think they began to drift apart emotionally. They struggled over various family decisions, especially whether or not to have more children.

Anxious to please, to make things right, Gebo threw herself into becoming a gourmet cook. She spent hours planning, shopping for and cooking marvelous, lavish meals. Bob got fat. Still that was alright, because Gebo counted calories, and amid sewing for her children and making gorgeous homemade gifts for the entire family, she counted calories for Bob and laboriously cooked accordingly.

We heard nothing further from the Air Force. So we all continued a kind of super-low-key waiting. You know, you still function, but at a slower pace; things are in a kind of fog, and you tune out the outside world.

Aside from telephone calls to us, Gebo was emotionally isolated. She waited alone, she grieved alone, and pretty soon the little habits Bob had developed over the years made her mad.

Married since she was a college girl, she wasn't much of a woman of the world. She didn't have anything concrete to account for her new feelings about their marriage, but things weren't right. Their limited social life, for one thing, wasn't right for her. She wanted to go out but they never went out; she wanted more of a social life; but most of all, she wanted to have another baby.

Spike was gone, everything was beginning to go to hell, when their two-year-old daughter, Carol, became desperately ill. It started out as a fever and cold. It didn't let up, but grew worse until little Carol was in the hospital, slipping away. The general practitioner Bob and Gebo had on Carol's case wasn't able to solve her medical problem. Carol grew even worse. There were panicked calls to Mother in California; she left hurriedly for Phoenix.

Then, out of the blue, a young, established, exciting pediatrician dropped in on little Carol. He immediately diagnosed her illness as rheumatic fever, and the appropriate treatment was begun.

That was how Dr. Marty Berger walked into Gebo's life.

At Carol's first office check-up a few weeks later, Gebo mentioned to Dr. Berger that her brother had been shot down in Vietnam. Marty was interested and wanted to know more. Her story gradually unfolded. He was sensitive, caring, and emotionally moved by what she had to say.

She told him more; she talked to him about the feeling of limbo she was going through.

Gebo had needed someone she could confide in, someone to talk to about being all tangled up inside. Marty listened. They talked about her fears and her deep feelings of helplessness, and he consoled her.

Hypochondriacs

Today it was 'instant shit' for the whole cell block. Some of us got diarrhea, and some of the guys who had a weaker set of intestines got what we refer to as the 'screaming shits.'

John Brown got diarrhea first and instantly shit his dinner, Blevins was next, and then me. But it was no big deal; it happened frequently. In the middle of the night Art Cormier in the next cell got the 'screaming shits.' Art could get the 'screaming shits' worse than anybody.

In the morning we tapped on the wall, "What's the matter?" Fred Cherry answered, "Art has dysentery. He is shitting his brains out." Fred described his ailment as 'having the shits and the cramps.'

It wasn't an hour later when John Brown developed the 'shits and the cramps,' and he used the very same words.

A few weeks later, perhaps months later, who knows, the Gooks moved three men into the empty cell next door, Porter Haliburton, Paul Kari and J.B. McCamey. They had all been captured a year earlier, old hands.

They had just been moved in from the Briar Patch, a really primitive hole thirty miles from Hanoi which the Gooks had closed down for some reason.

Right away we started tapping on the wall to them. They wanted to know all the names of the men at the Zoo, how the treatment was here, and especially, when was the war going to be over?

Paul Kari had hundreds of questions for me. We had been stationed at the same base in Tampa, Florida, where I had met his wife. Paul's back-seater, Kurt Briggs, was rescued by a CIA helicopter the day Paul was captured. Kurt and I were good friends so I had lots to tell Paul. Whatever medals Kurt had gotten, Paul got too; I knew the status of all his friends, one from McDill had been killed . . .

Paul told me he had been part of the Hanoi March, on June 25, 1966. That was the day the treatment of prisoners changed from just hanging around in prison to shitty, right after we bombed the oil fields of Fu Chin, before they got me.

We blabbed on for weeks, because when you're tapping this way, information takes a long time to get through the wall. Pretty soon the word got around to health. From health the subject went to hypochondria, and we must have spent 87 hours on it.

Three POWs were famous for their hypochondria: John Brown, Mark Hart and Ron Kimball. I had one as a cell mate and one living next door. Most of their conversations sounded like "The Young Doctors." Hypochondriacs hate to have anyone else around who is sicker than they are.

One day Mark sent us a message describing how he was going blind. We questioned his blindness. Then he started describing his symptoms: he saw spots, had blurry vision, couldn't read or write anymore. Sometimes it was so bad he couldn't see to eat. Of course he couldn't peek out to watch for guards.

There was nothing to read in the cell anyway except the 'camp regulations' which were glued to the door.

The next morning there was Brown, one eye covered, squinting, moving back and forth, checking first one eye, then the other. He kept it up until Blevins (who is more sympathetic than me) said, "Well, what is it, John?"

"It's just like Mark said, I think I'm going blind."

I howled with disgust. "Oh John, Jesus Christ, if Mark Hart hadn't told us about going blind you'd never have thought of it. Last week you had the shits and the cramps because Art had them and now you're going blind! What next?"

(Why me, God?)

Birthday Wish

The family got together for Pete's twenty-third birthday. Grandmother Louise, Dad's mother, was there. After Pete blew out the candles on the cake, Louise said:

"And what did you wish for?"

He said in the smallest voice I've ever heard:

"I wished that Spike is all right."

The whole family dissolved into tears.

Feast

"John, did you hear that?"

"I think so."

"I heard it, too."

"Either I've gone nuts or there's a turkey gobbling."

"Let's get on the wall and ask Fred's room, maybe they know."

Brown peeked out the hole to make sure it was clear. I called up the next cell to ask about turkeys.

Fred tapped back, "Last Christmas the Gooks gave us a big turkey dinner, each guy got a big chunk of barbecued turkey, a bowl of good soup full of potatoes and beans, some fresh salad, a couple of pieces of candy, six cigarettes, and A GLASS OF BEER!!"

"Could you guys read Fred?"

"I heard the beer part, what else did he say?"

I repeated Fred's message, we were all drooling, "Jesus, real meat!"

"Wait a minute, Fred's back up."

"Last year Gooks gave us a big meal at Tet. Tet is Lunar New Year. Something called banchung. It's a big rice cake with beans and meat in it. Good! Beer too! September 2 is Gook Independence Day, big meal too. C.U.L." (See you later.)

"He's done, John."

"What else does he have?"

I told Blevins and Brown what Fred had to say . . .

"Hey, John, you were here September second, you didn't say anything about a big meal."

"I must have forgotten. It wasn't that hot, but compared to normal it was super."

"How was the beer?"

"Warm, flat, but good, reeeall good."

The winter of 66-67 was long and cold. I wore every piece of clothing the Gooks gave me. During the day I wrapped my blanket around my body like an Indian, at night I buried myself so my breath would keep me warm. When it was take a bath or rot, I'd take a bath, but only then.

One day early in December, Blevins asked Brown and me to help him to the window so he could peek out and get a look at some of the other POWs as they walked by to empty their shit buckets. We heard the cell next door open and the guard grunt, "Bo . . . Wash."
"O.K., John, watch close, Fred's gang will walk by in a second."
I saw 'em! Who's who?"
"Fred (Fred Cherry) has the nice tan, Pitch (John Pitchford) has his arm in a sling, and Art (Art Cormier) looks pissed off."
"Jesus, they're skinny."
"Have you looked in a mirror lately?"
"Am I that skinny?"
"Skinnier."

"Hey, you guys, look. I see a turkey."
"They look like buzzards, we grow pigeons bigger'n that in Louisiana."
"Jesus, John, you'd bitch if they weighed eighty pounds. Wonder where the Gooks got all those turkeys?"

"Merry Christmas, John."
"Merry Christmas, John."
"Same to you, Spike."
"Hope this is the only one we spend here."
"You think they'll let us stay here another year, shit no! The U.S. ain't gonna fuck around with these assholes."
"This is Alvarez's* third Christmas here."
"That poor bastard, bet he's loony as hell."

It was a real feast. The turkey was delicious, the soup was thick, fresh lettuce, candy, three extra cigarettes and a GLASS OF BEER.
"Hey, you guys, they're bringing something else."
"What?"
"It's something to drink, I can hear 'em asking for cups."
"Maybe the war's over."
The peephole opened.
"Cup! Cup!"

*Everett Alvarez, first POW in North Vietnam, shot down August 5, 1964.

"What is this stuff?"
"Tastes like orange brandy."
"Who gives a shit! It's booze!"

My cast came off in January of '67. I was expecting to see some neat scars under it. Not so. I couldn't believe my eyes—one huge open wound, red meat staring at me, twenty or thirty smaller wounds. Nothing had healed under the cast!

(Jesus, I hope the bone went back together.)

Every third day I was taken to the medic's shack to change bandages and dress the wounds. 'Novocain,' the camp medic, unwrapped the long ace-type bandages and threw them into a basket with other blood-soaked rags to be washed and re-used. Then he'd peel the scabs off with a big pair of tweezers, douse the raw meat with alcohol, sprinkle on a little sulfa powder and wrap me up again.

When the cast came off I couldn't bend my elbow or move my wrist. In sign language Novocain told me to try to straighten out my arm. I couldn't possibly straighten it out. It had all grown together and it hurt. When I'd try the wounds would start to tear open. One day Novocain got tired of my pussyfooting around, grabbed my arm and gave it a jerk. It ripped right open—from then on I had no problem with my elbow's movement.

My wrist was a different story; I had no mobility in my wrist or fingers. The shrapnel must have severed the muscle and tendons in my right forearm. Somehow after five months or so these things re-routed. As soon as the cast was off, I started exercising it. It hurt like hell but, what the hell, I had nothing but time. So, each day I wiggled it. I put it on the bed and started forcing it to bend a little bit, each day applying more pressure. Some days I'd actually be leaning on the bed pushing hard. It took five years to regain full use of my hand.

Pete

Up in Arcata with Carmen and the boys, toddler 'Little' Pete and infant Jeff, I think Pete began to go mad. Oh, just a little bit mad, but nonetheless he was enormously disturbed by Spike's untenable predicament. Pete started to go out a little too much with his drinking buddy, Warren Hitchcock. They were drinking, talking, ranting and raving, fists pounding, trying to come to grips with Spike's fate and whatever tortures he was going through.

Pete and Carmen were deeply entwined in a classic love-hate relationship and they both knew it. Madly in love at the age of fifteen, they could never get enough of each other. Pete, ruggedly handsome, and Carmen, whose looks took your breath away, appeared to be the perfect couple. They looked it and they might have been, but they had years of poverty and struggling ahead of them. Pete was enrolled in a tough pre-med program at Humboldt State when they married. He wanted to be a vet. Pete and Carmen had been married in his sophomore year. Nine months later 'Little' Pete was born, and just twelve months after that, baby Jeff came along.

It was when Jeff was in his infancy that Pete got the phone call from Paul Lee, the call that shook him to the depths of his being.

Life in Arcata was going at a frenzied pace, at least for Pete. He took seasonal work, unloading fish, sawing lumber and went to school during the day. Carmen was home alone with the two boys, poor as a churchmouse and lonesome, far away from her mother. The young mother desperately wanted more of Pete's patience and indulgence, but Pete had none to give.

Mostly he kept it all bottled up inside, except for the nights he went out drinking with Warren.

In his daily life it was as though a madness had overtaken him. Preoccupied with this horror and feeling helpless, his long-dormant violent temper began to surface. Pete knew he had a temper which he had kept well reined in before this. Now it was free to surface.

I'd only seen Pete's temper a few times in my life. You didn't push Pete too far. However, twice when he was a teenager and I was seven or eight, he was out back lifting weights, and he said something rotten to me, so I called him a name. He threw down his weights; I was terrified. Pete chased me down the street and proceeded to pound me with a stick.

Another time he was in a violent rage over something concerning a girl who lived down the street. Mother knocked him down with a two-by-four. End of scene.

Now, with Spike on his mind, some unfortunate bitched at Pete about his performance on his lumber mill job. Pete knocked his face in. Carmen's whining nearly drove him up the wall. But they hung in there through graduation. After graduation, Pete shit-canned the idea of becoming a vet. That dream no longer held its appeal. The day-to-day process of getting there wasn't important. It was insignificant.

Pete couldn't deal with the piddly things. He had no patience. He was a loving father, but he was frantic inside. You could feel it.

First Bath

John Blevins is a healthy little guy. Poor bastard, lying on his butt all the time in his huge Gook cast, waiting for the next day.

He washes once a month whether or not he needs it, which leaves the room smelling pretty good. He chose to wash once a month because we insisted. Every once in while we'd carry Blevins out to the well and wash him down the best we could. We had to carry him because of the cast. It wasn't that he didn't care about smelling; it was so damn cold, once in a while the water had a fringe of ice around it. After you wash, there's no way to dry off with these little tea towels we have. Blevins couldn't move around to warm up. He just froze his ass off for hours after bath time.

He's been healthy all along, he never seems to be very sick, just stinks a lot.

Blevins must have cast-iron insides. Brown and I get diarrhea from a bad dose of food, but Blevins stays solid as a rock. Then he got his, the worst case of the shits known to man.

Poor John turned grey, then white. I thought he was going to die, and he hoped he would.

After he had completely drained his body he shit blood and mucus, usually down his leg, because we couldn't get the bucket there fast enough.

Brown and I called the turnkey a hundred times.

"Bao cao! Bao cao! Bachsi! Bachsi! Doctor! Doctor!"

Three days later, Novocain opened the peephole and handed me a handful of white pills. Blevins took four with a cup of water.

"Bring the bucket, fast!"

Immediately he shit the sulfa pills, ping ping, right into the bucket. I don't know how long it takes a sulfa pill to dissolve, but it ain't long. I mean they didn't even look like they had been in him a minute. Blam, they came right out. Obviously they didn't do him any good.

Brown and I started yelling for the turnkey, "Bao cao! Bao cao!" The lazy bastard guard we had nicknamed A.B. (for After-Birth) came in, we pointed: "Bi,* mouth, bucket, pills." He accused us of throwing the pills into the bucket. We pointed to what was left of Blevins, and he could tell from the look on John's face that this was no joking matter.

Finally they told us the doctor was coming down to see Blevins. That was supposed to be a big occasion. The doctor arrived with an English-speaking interpreter. He asked Blevins, "How is your health? How is your shit?" (They always ask, How is your health? How is your shit?) Blevins opened his little grey eyes a slit, looked up and described the terrible time he'd been having. He'd been shitting pills.

Zorba** and the interpreter jabbered for a couple of minutes.

"Here is medicine for Blevins. Doctor say he okay soon."

For the next three or four days John didn't eat a bite; he took his pills, chewing them first, and survived. He spent perhaps a week bed-ridden, and another week when he didn't care whether he lived or died.

Finally everything healed. It took only eight months. Well, almost everything, the deep puncture wound in my right leg still had a way to go. But no more bandages, no more scabs.

It was bath day. Clyde came, opened the cell door and gave us the 'wash yourself' signal.

I walked down to the well in my shorts, carrying my tea towel, a chunk of soap and my tin cup. The ground was hard, damp, thought I'd freeze before I got there. With no more sores, I could finally take a real bath. With my cup I threw water over every inch of my filthy body.

I'll never forget how cold that water was, almost ice water. Froze my ass off.

It had been nine months for Blevins when the Gooks came into the cell and sawed the cast off John's leg. They were ecstatic, two mended bones in the same cell. John wasn't quite as thrilled as they were.

"It's crooked."

"John, you've still got a leg, the bone's mended! When we get home they'll be able to fix it."

"Jesus, it took these little dummies four thousand years of their glorious tradition to fuck up my foot . . ."

---

*Bi—the name the Vietnamese gave to John Blevins.
**Zorba the Gook, our nickname for a friendly old medic the Vietnamese called 'The Doctor.'

Summer started in mid-April, 1967. It was the longest, hottest, driest summer in Vietnamese history. By the first week in May, Brown had broken out with little red bumps all over his body. We had no idea what it was.

We tapped on the wall to Fred.

"Hey, what is this? What's going on with Brown?"

Fred tapped back, "It's heat rash, you'd better get used to it, it lasts all summer."

Fred was right. By the first of June, John was covered with red bumps from the top of his head to the tips of his toes. Brown thought it was terminal. (I wished it was.)

I never suffered much from heat rash, I just got a little bit in the crooks of my arms and backs of my knees. I was fortunate. The guys who got it were just driven nuts. It itched all the time.

It was no wonder almost everyone got heat rash. It was so hot that the slightest movement, such as eating, brought on an instant deluge of sweat.

It's hard to visualize this unless you were there. You probably will never sit down in a 125-degree cement cell and eat. Why should you, it's really dumb. But if you should, and if you eat anything hot, like a bowl of rice, it will maintain its temperature all day long. Why should it cool down? What happens is, when you put something hot into your mouth, all of a sudden all of your glands start running, your eyes, your nose, and your sweat glands. You have a bowl of hot soup (it's never hot in the winter, but it's always hot in the summer). You have to eat the food when it's hot because they come back in a few minutes to pick up the dishes; if you haven't finished, tough.

If you sat perfectly still all day long with a fan—we had little hand fans—and learned to fan yourself with just the tiniest of movements, just your wrist moving back and forth, you could stay almost dry. But if you should do any exertion such as get up to pee in the bucket, when you sit down you're soaked. You lie on your back after doing something and your eye sockets fill up with sweat.

From the middle of May to the middle of August, we lay on our beds with our bamboo fans. All we had the strength to do was lie on our beds, fan our faces, and let the sweat roll off. It drove me nuts lying there on my bed at night, eye sockets full of sweat, the beads of sweat rolling off my belly; I'd think it was flies or mosquitos. They gave us half a little pitcher of water a day. But we got dehydrated anyway. You didn't pee more than a teacupful a day.

We just lay there on the beds, looked at the ceiling and sweated. Each guy had a bamboo mat, two-and-a-half by six-and-a-half feet. By the end of the summer my mat had rotted through. There was a big hole where my back hit, a big hole where my butt was and holes where my calves touched it. I never unfolded my blankets that summer. I used them as a pillow. The sweat rolling off the top of my head and the back of my neck rotted two great big holes in the blanket.

It was very difficult to explain to the Vietnamese that following winter what had happened to my blanket. I finally did manage to get a couple more out of them. The summer of '67 had been the worst drought in the history of Vietnam, no rain for 69 days.

Ruth's Dream

Our neighbor, Ruth Lee, came over this morning only four days since the unexpected tragic death of her twenty-year-old daughter, Martha. Ruth sat down at the kitchen table across from Mom, sort of held her hand, ran her fingers through a disheveled tangle of dyed red hair. She bit her top lip and said, "Martha came to me last night, Spike isn't up there."

Bartlett's Story

Going through the mail one morning, Mother found a letter from a Captain in the Air Force. He introduced himself as Captain Russ Bartlett. He said he was the last person to have had radio contact with Spike.

Mom showed it to me. My God, we almost jumped out of our skins. Here was someone who knew what had gone on that day. Oh, there were a million questions we wanted to ask him.

His letter was short and to the point. He was back from 'Nam now, stationed at Nellis Air Force Base in Nevada. He said if he could do anything for us, we should let him know.

Let him know, we were about to burst!

Dad made arrangements for us to go to Las Vegas immediately. The three of us, Dad, Mom and me, didn't say much on the plane ride. We were just waiting to hear what Captain Bartlett thought.

Russ Bartlett met us in the Officers' Club. All very anxious to hear what he had to say about Spike's last flight, we sat down. You could tell that Russ was really nervous about how we would react. Russ was a member of Spike's flight and probably somehow felt responsible for what had happened. We had sort of an unspoken agreement among ourselves that we would try not to cause Russ to feel as though we held anything against him.

First Russ explained that he hadn't seen Spike get hit. He was not at all in agreement with the part of the telegram which said Spike's plane was last seen as a 'fireball falling to the ground.' Russ said he didn't know where they got that because no one saw Spike get hit.

Russ said, "Now I don't want to get your hopes up too much, but I have seen the letter the Air Force sent to you and I disagree with it. I think Spike and Ray's plane was damaged by a SAM and that Spike flew the damaged aircraft away from the ground fire, and then ejected."

For a few moments we were speechless. I got teary-eyed, and I had promised Mother I wouldn't.

Then we started asking questions. "Do you really think that could have happened?"

"Yes, a pilot of Spike's caliber would do just that."

We questioned and requestioned him about surviving a SAM hit. And, why hadn't they heard a beeper from Spike on the ground? The beeper thing really bothered us. Why hadn't anybody heard a beeper? Russ described a SAM missile.

"Hell, they are as big around as telephone pole and as long as the Officers' Club bar." Russ explained to us several times how vulnerable the Phantom's radio is, that it takes hardly anything to knock one out. About the beeper he said, "They are just plain unreliable. Don't worry about the beeper, don't even consider it."

When we were finishing up our talk, one of us said, "Now we don't want to put you on the spot, Russ, but you're a flier, you were there. What do you really think?"

Russ said, "If anybody could make it, Spike could."

This cements it for me. Spike is alive, he has to be.

JANUARY 23, 1968

The USS Pueblo, a Navy Intelligence ship, its
commander, Lloyd Bucher, and its 83 crewmen
were captured by North Korean patrol boats.

The Contest

For lack of anything else to do, we decided to have a little contest with the two adjoining cells, Dick Bolstad and Bob Lilly to the left, and to our right Rod Knutson, Chuck Baldock and Brad Smith. We've been having this problem with that insane guard, Clyde. Absolutely every time he opens the door, somebody gets belted for something. So we set up this contest: each man is to keep track of how many kicks, hits, slaps, smacks, bangs with the keys or with a shoe he gets from Clyde in a thirty-day period. It doesn't matter whether you get a hit, kick or punch, or smacked with his sandal, or a hit with a board; they all count as one point.

The Vietnamese are doing some construction. They are building another brick wall. They are always building walls to isolate us. When they build a wall they use these little tiny coolie ladies to carry bricks and cement in little wheelbarrows. These tiny little Vietnamese women are about four feet high. If you go outside and a coolie lady walks by, you have to bow to her.

It was close to the end of the month, the contest was about over and I was leading the pack. I had eighty-five hits, kicks and slaps. Of course you had to have verification of your count. You just couldn't report twenty-four whacks. One of your roommates had to count for you.

One day the three of us were walking to the bath area. Because of the construction somebody had screwed up. There was an American across a fence sweeping. We looked over at each other and smiled. That was our mistake, to look. I scored first, as Clyde threw his keys, hit me in the back of the head; we counted that a 'oner.' Then he went over and blasted John Belvins, but hurt his hand. So, he picked up a stick and smacked John Brown with it. The stick had a nail sticking out of it which stuck into Brown's head and drew a little blood. We gave Brown a score of two for getting a creative hit.

The contest goes on. I'm having a hell of a month. I've got the contest by the balls. And I'm really kind of proud of it. It's really no big deal, but it's the biggest thing going on for us right now.

By the 30th day, I was 17 hits, smacks and kicks ahead of Brad Smith, the closest guy. I had it made. That morning, through the wall, I go "tap, tap, tap, tap, tap, how did it go last night?"

The answer comes back from Rod Knutson, "Tap, tap, tap . . . nobody got nothing . . . fact is, Clyde was off yesterday, it was a peaceful day."

I tapped back, "This is the last day, baby, I got it, I'm gonna get that drink when we get out of this place."

The morning meal passed. Nothing happened; I even got a couple of scores while listening to the camp radio. When they play the radio, you have to sit up and pretend like you're listening. I was lying on my bed during the broadcast when Clyde popped open the window. Here I am lying down. God, he went berserk! He took his key, opened the door and told me to kneel with my hands up, which I did, because if you didn't, something worse was going to happen. Then he kicked me. John Brown was counting. He got me in the gut, was going for my crotch, got a good one in my throat. I got thirteen points right there. My lead was insurmountable.

Rod Knutson and Brad Smith, my competition from next door, hear this. They are incensed, because now I am way out ahead.

Rod Knutson has always been belligerent toward the Vietnamese. They never liked him. In the past they have really worked him over, broke his wrists, broke his arm, cracked some of his ribs kicking him, and he's spent months in irons.

Every day when our room is opened for us to go out and take a bath or pick up our food, we can count on getting blasted by Clyde. He doesn't even use his hand any more, he blasts you on the side of the head with his damn rubber shoe. That loosens your brain a little bit.

There are only a few hours left in the contest. After I caught the thirteen kicks, I thought I had enough to insure my win. I was ahead by thirty.

They didn't empty the shit buckets this morning, the afternoon meal passed, nobody had any more scores. The last thing to happen was when they came to empty our buckets and Clyde was back on duty. We empty ours, without incident. Clyde goes to the contest cell next to ours, I'm spying out this little nail hole. (You could see the guy walk by, flash, flash. That's the only visual contact we had with them.) I was peeking out, my score is 116; Brad trailing in second, 86. Just as he walks by our nail hole he looks in our direction as if to say, "I'll show you who's gonna win the contest."

At this moment a tiny lady walks by pushing a wheelbarrow of cement. She has on a hat and rags wrapped around her. She shuffles on and Brad just looks at her but he doesn't bow. He looks toward us like, "This ought to even me up." Brad is right in front of the peephole, I'm spying out. I hear Clyde yell at him, "BOW!" Brad just kind of looks at him and says, "Fuck you." I couldn't hear but I read his lips.

Clyde's on him like a wild man. He beats the shit out of Brad. I'm sitting there counting, "One, two, three, four, five, six . . . bam, bam, fifteen, sixteen . . . Shit, he passed me, the dirty bastard." I guess he was keeping track in his head, because pretty soon he bows. Clyde quit. Brad shrugged toward me as if to say, "Well, you came in second, asshole."

When Clyde put him back in the cell all beat to shit, he went over to the wall. The code to call up is, "dat, dat da dat dat," really quiet. But, Brad pounds on the wall, "bom, bom ba bom bom . . ." pounds out, "I WON!"

JANUARY 30, 1968

During the 'Tet offensive' the Viet Cong and North Vietnamese attacked more than one hundred cities and military bases in a major assault.

Red Peppers

Sometime in May of '68 the cell door opened.

"Van!" The guard called Brown's Vietnamese name and gave him the 'roll up your stuff' signal. Twenty seconds later he had his life's possessions rolled up and tucked under his arm.

"Good luck, John."

"Same to you guys."

After almost two years together I was glad to see Brown go; I'm sure the feeling was mutual.

Shortly after Brown left I stole two little red peppers from a pepper bush out where we dump the shit bucket. I gave one to John Blevins and I kept one. They were the real hot kind. If you aren't careful they set you on fire. I took mine, broke it into pieces, then used my spoon to grind one piece up against the side of my bowl. I mixed a few drops of water with it and made a little bit of hot sauce. Hot pepper sauce on rice! Delicious! We hadn't tasted hot pepper for a couple of years. That's one thing we don't have, spices of any kind. We haven't even had salt.

"Hey, Blevins, be careful, these are really hot."

Blevins comes back, "Well, don't tell me about peppers. I'm from Texas and I can eat these goddam things by the carton."

I shrug, "All right."

Next thing, John takes his whole red pepper, tears it up and throws big chunks of it all over his rice and soup. Then he eats like he always does, wolfing it down in the middle of the summer. Sweat running off him, nose running, eyes running. Amid all this, he naturally reaches up and rubs his watering eyes. All of a sudden his eyes turn bright red from the hot pepper on his fingers. He's on fire. This aggravates his nose and it really starts running. He reaches up, rubs the snot off his nose like he always does, and his nose is on fire. It's just like putting gasoline in his nose and lighting it.

It's just terrible. He's thrown down his food in about eighteen seconds. I'm just sitting down to start mine.

His eyes are on fire, his nose is on fire, and he gulps down all his water. I give him some of mine. In minutes he gets a terrible case of diarrhea. Then he wipes his ass and gets pepper on his ass. He's running around the cell with a burning ass, burning eyes and a burning nose, and no more water. The water the Gooks give us is hot anyway because they always boil it. It never cools off in the summer.

Blevins is in agony, running around the cell, really suffering, but he can't yell too loud or they'll open the door and kick the shit out of us.

I've been living with him long enough by this time so that I don't give a shit. I just chuckle about it.

A few days after Brown's exit, the cell door opened and in came A.J. Myers. A.J. was a big ugly guy with four teeth missing in front. A.J. came hobbling in with two crutches under one arm, carrying a bunch of crap under the other. We shook hands and started talking.

Big, tall, and ugly. His nickname was the Dancing Bear. It fit him. He looked sort of like a great, big, hairy bear. He was so damn big that he had a long way to go to get really skinny. In fact, he was always on a diet. He had a terrible weight problem, managing to gain weight on forty calories a day.

A.J. had one of the less-than-successful bone settings performed by the North Vietnamese. He had crushed his ankle when he ejected. The Gooks set it in their customary method, crooked, really crooked, thirty degrees crooked! They left a gruesome blue color about the scar where they cut and hacked around with some bones and messed it up even worse. We never could figure out why he wasn't healing.

One day A.J. said, "Hey, there's something coming out of my foot." We looked closely and I said, "Well, if I'm not mistaken, I think it's a stitch." When we went out to empty the shit bucket I found a little piece of glass and gave it to A.J. He brought it back and worked for an hour or so on his foot. Sure enough, they had left a stitch in him. But he still didn't heal. A year later another stitch came out.

A.J. never let that get him down. So what if his foot was crooked? He assumed that when he got back to the United States the miracle doctors would fix him up like new.

The summer of '68 wasn't nearly as hot as our first summer had been.

Instead of having a drought for sixty-nine days like we did in '67, it rained almost daily. We even had a flood scare. One night the guards had us roll up our mats, making us think we were going to evacuate the camp. We didn't.

A.J. turned out to be a dandy roommate. With A.J. there was never a dull moment. He was extremely smart, a real intellect, so I called him Professor. His head was full of academic information that was good for killing time. He decided that anything anybody else knew, he should know, so he wouldn't be wasting his time as a POW. A.J.'s vocabulary was incredible; he had memorized jillions of words out of dictionaries when he was young.

A year earlier when he had been living with Quincy Collins he had stolen an English dictionary. Somehow he got hold of a pencil stub and reams of toilet paper. He copied several thousand words out of this dictionary. A virtual pile of paper he had wadded up, stuck in his pants. He created a little dictionary of twenty-five-dollar-words which he committed to memory. There wasn't really a hell of a lot to do around the place, so I memorized them all. I, too, became a walking dictionary of twenty-five-dollar-words.

A.J. wanted me to tell him everything I had learned in college or anyplace else, verbatim. He was a philosophy major from Oregon or Oregon State. An interesting guy, he sure knew a lot of shit. We had lots and lots of interesting discussions. Of course, we theorized on every imaginable thing there was to talk about.

A.J. always conducted himself as a philosopher. He never would tell the Gooks yes or no, he always argued with them about everything. He must have created a lot of things to talk about, because the Gooks had him up so often for interrogation, trying to convince him he was wrong and they were right, yelling at him, harassing him, trying to get him to memorize speeches. The poor guy spent hours listening to Gooks who could hardly speak English, lecturing him with their prepared speeches.

That summer the Gooks came up with something else to harass us with, 'The Blue Book.' All the POWs were told to fill out this book with detailed biographies. Some refused and were tortured until they agreed to do it. Word was spread around camp by the senior man: "It's up to you. If you want to fill out your biography go ahead, put what you want."

The 'Blue Book' turned out to be something the Gooks used when we started getting mail a few years later.

If the name of your mother or wife wasn't in your 'Blue Book' and you received a letter from one of them, obviously it couldn't be yours. (Typical Gook logic.)

They withheld a lot of mail from men because they lied or put down that they weren't married, then all of a sudden in came letters from their wives.

When I got called up to do my 'Blue Book,' I had already been there a couple of years. I knew they were using the 'Blue Books' to check the mail, so I put down some real names: parents, brother and sisters. I had already broken the code of conduct as far as only saying name, rank, and serial number. Some of the men thought if they gave the real names and addresses of their families, the North Vietnamese would send them letters and put pressure on their families. I didn't think they would. Fact is, I was hoping they would. As far as I knew, my name had never been released as captured. I was getting to the point of trying to think of anything to do just to get my name out so my family would know I was alive.

Talking about hypochondria one morning, I was telling A.J. about Brown, what a hypo he was.

"Well, shit," he said, "you ought to meet Quincy Collins. There's the world's greatest hypochondriac. But the Gooks have cured him."

I said, "Oh, really, how'd they do that?"

"Zorba the Gook came in one day, when Quincy and I were living together. We both had broken legs. Both incapacitated, we wanted some medical attention, so we were yelling and screaming for the medic. Quincy was thrashing around complaining about some new thing he had when Zorba the Gook decide the cure for whatever he had was 'injection.'"

Zorba couldn't speak English, but he could say injection. Zorba, according to A.J., would bring in a huge syringe, about a foot long, a couple of inches around, filled with horrible-looking brown liquid, and shoot it into Quincy's ass. It took about a minute to empty the syringe. It did nothing for him. Quincy became convinced it was just dirty water they were using, but, curiously enough, he got over the ailment he had. The next time he thought about hollering he knew Zorba's only cure would be 'injection.'

(God, I roared when I heard that story.)

We spent most of the days during the summer sitting still, fanning ourselves with as little exertion as possible. It was too hot for the Gooks to do anything, either. Twelve hours at a stretch, sitting and fanning, developed calluses on your butt. Three little calluses, one where your tail bone sticks out and two where those little bones are in your butt.

When it was unbearably hot, I fantasized about being cool. Regardless of what I set my mind to, I could only think of cool things: swimming pools, snow in the mountains, an ice-cold drink dripping in my hand, a can of beer. I took every opportunity to escape by brainwashing myself into feeling cool. Even frying in the heat, drenched in sweat, I could always go to sleep. I would drift off into sleep. Sometimes I'd sleep twenty hours a day. It was so hot the guards didn't look in on us much, except when that infamous Clyde was on duty. So sadistic and cruel was he, if he caught you lying down, he'd get furious and put you on your knees for a couple of hours.

In the winter when it was cold, I'd close my eyes and imagine I was somewhere by a warm fire. Remember the Everly Brothers' song, "Dream, Dream, Dream . . ." When you hurt, you drift off into thoughts about not hurting. And, when I was hungry, which could be for months at a time, all I could think about was McDonald's!

It's kind of hard to describe how a day goes by like that, say when you are daydreaming. A day goes by and it takes an eternity. But, all of a sudden, 365 of them have gone by, and that's a year. I found it ludicrous that a single day takes so long and then all of a sudden a year had gone by. My theory was that the only reason a year on the outside seemed like a long span of time, was that a lot of things happened that year. Not a lot happens here.

One day in September of '68 the door opened and Clyde walked in. He called out in his sharp little snarly voice: "My, Bi," then gave them the 'roll-up-your-gear' signal. John Blevins and A.J. rolled up their possessions and split. We had excellent communications, so within a matter of a couple of days I knew that they had been separated and into exactly which two cells they had been moved.

Some more long days went by. It was a lot worse to be alone. Clyde caught me tapping to Fred Cherry in the next cell, then I really had some long days and nights. Clyde walked in, a set of leg irons in his hands. Talk about feeling helpless. He pointed for me to sit on my bed. I sat down. He slammed my feet into the leg irons, feet crossed. Then he cuffed my left wrist to my left foot. When he walked out, the sadistic bastard, he took my mosquito net away.

After a while with no mosquito net, it wasn't so bad. There got to be so many bumps on me, there was no place left to bite. Mosquitos are kind of particular, they don't like to take a bite out of a swollen spot. I watched them walking along on me looking for a place to poke, and my skin was such a mess they'd say, "Fuck it," and haul ass.

Mosquitos are not only particular, they're greedy. You know how dumb they are? A mosquito, if you don't wiggle—and you do get immune to the itch—a mosquito will fill himself so full he can't fly. If you try to kill him and you miss, he'll fly off and nail you again, a second hole. If you're smart, you'll let him fill up till he becomes purple, then you can just reach over and smash him, or better yet, just flick him off onto the ground. He'll fall over on his back helpless and die.

Family Waits

You call Mother to share, you call Mother to let her know you love her without actually saying it, but most of all you call Mother for her contagious enthusiasm. She's always positive, always ready to listen and her advice is right on.

Pete called from Arcata frequently.

"Do you think we're ever gonna hear from him?" he'd ask.

"Yep," Mom would reply, "we'll hear from him one of these days."

I called Mom from college in San Diego, God, almost every day. Sometimes I'd be so down I could hardly talk.

"Well, Mom, what do you think?"

"I think we'll hear from him one of these days."

I'd been crying all morning or all night, constantly bothered by these horrible dreams, all choked up—Rick's sympathy wasn't getting me out of it, but I didn't tell Mom that. I didn't want to make her cry; besides she knew what I was going through.

Mom heard from Gebo, too.

Gebo felt so far away from the family way off in Arizona.

Gebo never called collect like the rest of us; she had too much pride. She'd want to gab for a long time, kind of meander in and out and around about Spike . . . pumping Mom for something positive to hang on to.

We didn't call on Dad for those pep talks because he seemed to have made up his mind about Spike. He had been so devastated, we'd all been devastated, but Dad was unable to join in—even in the beginning—with our family talks trying to rally everyone's spirits. So Dad got left out of much of our sharing of concerns for Spike and our commiserating when Spike was MIA.

Gebo always came across stable and controlled on the phone, but Gebo was looking: looking away from her inner unhappiness about Spike and away from her husband who had somehow begun to annoy her. It was insidious at first, but she found herself no longer tolerant of a lifestyle that did not absolutely please her.

She loved her kids, loved her role as the perfect housewife and hated not knowing about Spike. She hated doing nothing about it, but was scared to do anything, as we all were. She resented her predicament in a life-and-death matter. She hated being helpless and impotent and found herself emotionally trapped by it all.

Then she looked at her husband. Everything she wanted to run away from: torment, frustration, circumstances that made her feel trapped in a real life-and-death situation.

She couldn't cope with the way her husband felt about his job. He worried, he felt anxious. She couldn't tolerate it any more.

Always the strait-laced, straight-forward lady in the past, she decided to break away. So she began. There was never any outward sign of trouble at home. The children were surrounded by a loving atmosphere. Even Bob didn't notice the changes. Maybe Gebo didn't fully realize what she was doing, but it was there.

She began to keep busy and got out of the house at night a lot. She took classes and worked hard on them. She received A's. She and her friend, Betty Lloyd, attended the opera, symphonies, supported the arts. Once in a while they stopped to have a drink with their friend, Dr. Marty Berger.

Irons

They came in one day and took off the leg irons. Couldn't move around much, but I could wiggle pretty good. Moving is all relative anyway. It hurt so good. I sort of straightened up, lay back . . . Nice.

Communications

Summer, 1968

Sometime after my punishment was over and I had recognized my mistake, the door opened and in walked a funny-looking, tall, skinny guy with a big nose.

"Hi, I'm Jim Pirie."

"Spike Nasmyth. How long you been here?"

"Since April."

"Of which year?"

"This year, how about you?"

"September '66."

"Jesus! You're an old one. Hope to hell I don't have to spend two years here."

Jim, a lieutenant commander in the Navy, from Bessemer, Alabama, was to be one of the best cell mates I ever had. He taught me how to enjoy prison life. Even though my life's motto has always been 'Thou shalt not sweat,' Jim taught me the true meaning of my motto. Whatever happened, he'd shrug it off and in his heavy Southern drawl say, "That's the way life goes; take it one day at a time."

In a nutshell, the only trouble we ever got into with the Gooks was when they'd catch us making too much noise laughing in our cell.

One day I'm sitting on the edge of my bed listening to a story Jim is telling. It isn't really a funny story, it's just the way he tells it. It's so terrible and so funny I'm consumed with laughter. Pretty soon I'm lying on the floor of the cell, holding my stomach laughing. I can't stop. A guard opens the window because I'm making too much noise. It's that psycho, Clyde. He thinks I'm laughing at him. This really pisses him off. Clyde jerks open the door and stomps into the cell. Clyde's standing over me, pissed off but I can't stop giggling. It's such a stupid story, I try to stop, Clyde kicks me in the stomach, I get it under control, look up at Jim, and start laughing again. This goes on for a few more kicks and slaps until Clyde gives me the punishment signal. Clyde's punishment is: on your knees, and hands up. He can make you stay like that for as long as he wants.

I'm on my knees, he kicks me, I look up at Pirie again and I'm convulsed. Incensed, now Clyde looks at Pirie and Jim starts laughing too. Even this lunatic can't be mad at Pirie. Clyde gets caught up with the contagiousness of the thing. This is the only time I ever saw that little bastard smile. He starts to smile and leaves.

He was back in two minutes, said, "Shit down!" My punishment was over.

You didn't have to do anything to get hit by Clyde; he was crazy. He'd use anything he could get his hands on: a stick, his ring of keys, or his favorite, his heavy rubber shoe.

We spent thousands of hours fantasizing ways to kill the little creep. My favorite was to hang Clyde over the open cesspool of shit where we dump our buckets. He'd be hung upside down by his feet, so that if he could bend his legs he could keep his head out of the pool. After a while, exhausted, his legs start to sag, his head slowly sinks into the muck. Clyde drowns, in a slow, smelly death.

Pirie and I are the dishwashers for our cell block, which is a good deal. We get out of the cell at least twice every day, even on Sunday when the others never get out.

The guards leave everybody's bowls and spoons just outside each cell, then Jim and I pick them up and go out to the well. It's something to do, but best of all there are the leftovers.

Some of the prisoners don't eat all their food. Maybe they're sick or they just can't stomach some of what passes for food the Gooks give us. Jim and I can.

It's an especially good deal for me when they bring in this rotten fish. I don't know what they do to it. It looks like they let it rot until it ferments. They serve it to us, black and mushy, bones and all. I'm not even sure it's edible, but I eat all I can get. Jim can't handle the fish; the smell of it makes him sick. He won't even pick up a dish with rotten fish in it.

"Jesus, Spike, how can ya'll eat that rotten shit? Jus think what it's doin' ta yer guts. Ya know a pig wudn't touch that crap!"

One benefit of doing the dishes is that from the well we can see the peephole in the window of cell number eight of the Office. We'd drop the bucket down the well, hoist it up full of water, then squat right there in the dirt. We'd scrape the dishes, rinse 'em off and once in a while find a message tucked in under somebody's leftover rice. Might say "Hi" to Ed over in cell number four, then go back to the doorway of our cell block. There's a little covered area there and two sawhorses with an old door on top. We'd stack the dishes here, right outside cell number four in the Barn, say 'Hi' to Brad, Charlie and Rod, then go back to our own cell.

Another interesting time of day is when we empty our buckets in the sewage hole. The hole's only thirty feet from our cell, but from there you can see right into cell number one of the Garage and say 'Hi' to the guys there. Sometimes we leave notes stuck around the sewage dump. It's always a little exciting to see if there's going to be a note stuck there, or to leave one without being caught.

Communications work like that. We all use the same sewer hole so we can pass a note to just about any cell. Of course, the next guy there after you is going to pick it up. Then if it isn't for him he can 'tap' it on or leave the note.

We have a good system for communicating visually. For instance, when Jim and I are out washing dishes, squatting there in the dirt we can signal something to the men in cell number eight of the Office. They send it around the Office, then to cell one of the Pool Hall. Two cells in the Pool Hall then pass it on; cell eight sends it on to the Stable and cell ten flashes it to cell two in the Pig Sty. It's almost impossible to get anything to the guys in solitary in the Auditorium. We use the sewer dump to get to the Garage and the Garage flashes to the Gate House.

It's a little complicated, but it works.

The Gooks helped us set up our best form of communication; of course they didn't know it. Every day they would have one of the POWs sweep the cement area around the pool and the hard-packed dirt in front of the cell blocks.

Anyway, Dick Bolstad, the crazy bastard, is credited with starting the sweeping-tap code.

Out there sweeping one morning, he says, "Hi!" That's: swish swish, pause, swish swish swish, pause, swish swish, pause, swish swish swish swish. Then he sweeps: "If you read me, cough."

The whole damn camp sounded like it had TB.

It's amazing how long we'd been there before somebody thought of sweeping in code, but the truly amazing thing is how long we swept in code before the Gooks caught us.

For the next couple of weeks, everybody who got the chance went

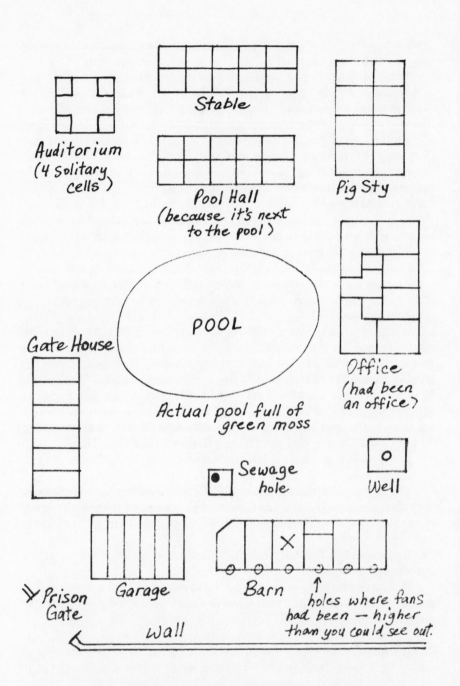

Plan of the prison camp; 'X' is Spike's cell.

out sweeping, "Hi, I'm so and so . . .." and endless other bullshit. It was crazy, and everybody signed off with 'Fuck Ho'—abbreviated FC-HO—which always got a round of coughs because everybody wanted it repeated.

Somebody figured this was a good way to pass news because everybody in camp could hear the sweeping. The Zoo was a small camp. I could hear somebody drop a tin cup in the Auditorium and I was in the Barn, clear on the other side of the camp.

It took a couple of months to set it up, but pretty soon we were organized. The whole camp could get the message at the same time. Important things, not just inept stuff, like Fuck Ho.

The North Vietnamese were always after information. They'd take two prisoners and torture them for what they wanted. Each guy'd end up telling a different story. Then they'd go after the rest of us to see which guy was lying.

The Gooks started all kinds of campaigns. One of their favorites was, "How do you communicate? We want to know how you communicate."

They might torture two guys for the answer or every man in the camp, one at a time. Another ongoing campaign was, "What order has your senior ranking officer given you?"

Now here's why sweeping in code was so important to all of us. If two men were asked the same question and if they both refused to answer, the Gooks might torture them until they talked. If they told different lies it was obvious to the Gooks that somebody was lying; then they both were in for a very rough time.

With the broom, Larry Guarino, our senior ranking man, could send out a message to everybody at once: "If asked—here's the lie we will all tell."

Maybe the smartest thing we ever did was to synchronize our lies.

Still MIA

The Nasmyths always come home for Christmas. Christmas is the most painful time. Three Christmas trees have withered in front of Spike's portrait and still he is not home.

Once a month for all these years, our family has been allowed to post one letter to Spike. Most often we congregate at the kitchen table. Each of us puts down two or three lines on the same single sheet of paper. I find these to be the most difficult and sensitive moments dealing with Spike, still missing in action. We have to write cheerful letters.

His twenty-sixth, twenty-seventh and twenty-eighth birthdays have passed, and still he is not home.

For the past three and a half years, our family has lived under a tremendous fear of incriminating Spike. The Johnson administration, backed by the Armed Forces, has given us heavy warning that NOTHING regarding Spike's missing-in-action status should be said or discussed outside the family. And, therefore, we have been living under a great silence.

During the first forty-two months of waiting, the Air Force approached us half a dozen times with pictures of unidentified prisoners of war. We all tried very hard to see Spike in a number of the pictures. There was one skinny, blond fellow with hollow eyes that we wanted to tag as Spike. But his head was thin and misshapen. It's hard to imagine Spike weighing a hundred pounds. Even at a hundred pounds, I think his head would still be round.

When the Air Force brought these unidentified photographs around, they would show us nine or ten pictures labeled unknown, each with a number. They were photographs of very skinny men, backs of head, profiles showing an ear, neck and shoulder or men at a great distance. If you thought you recognized your man, you would give his name and the corresponding number. Some numbers had as many as fourteen names. A couple of times we viewed foreign film clippings for identification purposes. We had no luck.

Around Christmas each year the Air Force would send out instructions for the Christmas package. We tried very hard to fill all of Spike's possible needs once a year in his six-pound Christmas package. We talked about medical, clothing and nutritional needs, made lists and then we changed our minds. Needless to say, it was impossible and frustrating. What was most important for Spike? What did he need? What did he want? What could we send that would say how much we love him? Should we have sent him medication for temporarily curing ringworm, malaria or dysentery, try to keep his feet warm, or send food which would feed him for two or three days?

Mother and I had spent endless hours shopping for the one little thing, which, if it reached Spike, would tell him, 'I love you.' One Christmas we settled on a green Vera scarf, because green is Spike's favorite color. Several times I embroidered handkerchiefs with 'I love you' or a Christmas tree.

Breakup

While I was still in my senior year of high school, Dad's job moved him to San Francisco during the work week. He commuted home on the weekends. It was a good arrangement, and it cut down tremendously on the friction at home. Dad, charming socially, an excellent businessman, was very difficult to live with.

He called Mom frequently to check on her whereabouts, but never once offered information on what he was doing in San Francisco, and Mother was damned if she'd ask. So even apart, the irritation in their marriage was growing.

One day after I'd been away at college for less than a year, when Dad was back home again permanently, Mom walked out. Troubled with Spike's life-and-death predicament, she had no patience for the flim-flam of her daily life. She had made up her mind that she wasn't going to spend the rest of her life with a man who was a workaholic, possessive and, in Mom's opinion, a pain in the neck to live with.

When Mother makes her mind up, that's it. It was over.

She moved into a motel at first and Dad stayed in the family home, which turned all our stomachs. Tough as Mom seems, we still wanted to protect her—at least a little bit.

From the motel she moved into one of the dinky little rentals she's always fixing up, and turned it into a darling little nest.

Dad, totally miserable as far as I could see, stayed at the old home still bucking pressure from all his children to move out. It just didn't seem right. Everyone knows the man gets an apartment, the wife stays in the family home. Besides, what would Spike think of all of this?

While Mom was living in the little house on Dorothy Street, Dad called to say he had a piece of information from the Air Force. A meeting had been called at Los Angeles Airport, a meeting called by the Nixon administration.

Roger Capen spoke to Mother and about thirty other POW wives, moms and dads. Capen said he knew that the families had been deluged with leaflets and propaganda from the Johnson administration warning us not to make waves. He was looking at the faces of people whose sons and husbands were mostly MIA. He cut the meeting short, the subject was so awful.

His final remarks were: "Since this administration (Nixon) does not agree with the past administration (Johnson), why don't you people do something?"

He didn't give one word as to what we should do.

Mom thought about it for a couple of days. In the back of her mind she could see Rick and me talking about going to Europe, and how much we'd made at garage sales. She made a beeline to San Diego to give us the go-ahead.

Packages

Christmas of '68 provided Jim and me with a couple of laughs. The Gooks opened up the cell Christmas day and took us up to visit the camp commander. He gave us each a piece of candy and a message: "If you continue to have the correct attitude, you will be released when the war is over and the United States finally admits its mistake and surrenders." Same ole shit.

The Gooks demonstrated their lenient and humane policy to the fullest: they took Art Cormier out of leg irons, on account of it being Christmas, to get a letter from his wife. They put him back in after he had read her letter. Merry Christmas, Art.

Tap tap ta tap tap . . .

"Jim, wait 'til you hear this! Some guys in the Pool Hall got packages from home today, and they say most of us are gonna get one."

"Hot damn, tole ya man, fuckin' war's bout over."

Everybody was pretty excited. Through the grapevine we heard who were the lucky recipients of these parcels from home and what they had in them. The stories coming down had us convulsed with laughter. Jim was lying there laughing while I had my ear to the wall, trying to listen to some guy tell about the junk he had gotten in his package.

"Nothing, just garbage." The guy tapping away on the wall was saying, "Boy, my wife doesn't have any brains at all. What a bunch of shit! Nothing to eat, just a bunch of worthless crap."

Well, hell, I'd been thinking about this package thing for a long time now. I told Jim, who was getting over his current laughing seizure, "If I get a package from home, I'll get a two-pound box of Swiss Miss chocolate, and two pounds of cashew nuts and chocolate bars, some hard candy, maybe a little gum, tooth paste . . . " "Yeah!"

Jim was looking off, getting into thinking about his dream package. "I know my wife will send good stuff. She has such a good head."

I knew just what he meant. "I'd kick my Mother in the ass if she sent me some of that junk, a handkerchief, underpants, a T-shirt . . . " We spent the rest of the day badmouthing these other guys, just lying there on our beds dreaming about all the things we were really looking forward to.

It was late in the afternoon when the cell door opened and the guard called up Jim. He got up off his bed, "Well I'll be . . . " With a cocky smart-ass grin he marched off to the office. He knew he was going to pick up his dream package. A couple of minutes later Jim was back. He had one package of gum, five sticks, in his right hand, and a miniature can of Planter's peanuts in his left hand. That was it. That was all. Of all the stuff his wife sent—it must have been pure junk—that's all they would let him have. We ate the peanuts on the spot.

The months from September '68 to April '69 flew by, because if you gotta be in prison, in a crummy Commi-Gook prison camp, and you gotta have a cell mate, Jim Pirie's a good one to have. He's a crazy redneck who's never been known to say a bad thing about anybody, he's got a million jokes, he can tell jokes about blacks, polacks, Jews and other rednecks twenty-four hours a day. He never repeated himself and he never told a bad one.

Very early in prison life, the cigarette ritual became the highlight of the day. In the early years they gave us one cigarette at a time. They were supposed to open your window and give you your cigarette and a light. Actually it depended upon your guard. If you had Happy, he was like clockwork. He'd give you three cigarettes a day and three lights. If you had Clyde or a turnkey we called A.B. (After-Birth) you'd be damn lucky to get a smoke. A.B. walked around camp stealing everything under the sun. He'd take the cigarettes, put them in an old can and toss them around till the tobacco came out. Then he'd steal the tobacco.

The worst thing though, the worst prison torture a man can have is to have a cigarette and not be able to light it. That doesn't sound rational. But Pirie and I sometimes became incoherent with rage at having a cigarette and not being able to get a light.

It's the worst kind of frustration with Clyde, though, because he does it on purpose. He doesn't smoke. He knows how we depend upon our one or two smokes a day. It's typical of Clyde to open the window, give us our smokes, light 'em up and then say, "Now go take bath."

You've got five minutes to take a bath. You can't smoke and take a bath, can you? God, he's a son-of-a-bitch. There's nothing you can do about frustrations like that. You can't have a tantrum too loud, they won't tolerate noise, but, "FUCKIN GOOKS!" I'd look at Pirie, clench my fists, "That fucking Clyde, I'd like to strangle him, crush his throat in my hands, dissect him . . ."

Sometimes Pirie would say to me—he was much more mature than me; he'd only been there a year—he'd say, "Really, it's not all that bad, we'll have two smokes next time we get a light."

So Jim and I came up with a plan: steal matches!

He was a great thief. Goddam Pirie, he should have been in the Mafia. He'd go up to interrogation and listen to their B.S. for a while. When he came back I'd say, "How was the interrogation?" He'd shrug, open his fist and there'd be a box of matches. Sometimes he'd come back and throw a handful of cigarettes at me. He stole them, right in front of the interrogator. They always have cigarettes there. If you gave a right answer, they'd tell you to take one. He'd take one and pocket four.

A.B. used to throw us the box of matches. I'd dribble three on the floor, take one and light our cigarettes, then give the box back to him.

Everybody in the cell block started stealing matches. We had a real match thievery ring going on. Pretty soon there was a huge store of matches hidden out by the shit hole. Besides matches, I think, of all the cells, we had the greatest cigarette supply. There were three guys next to us and none of them smoked. They'd take their cigarettes when the guards passed 'em out and stash them out by the shit hole. We'd pick them up along with some matches and smoke when we felt like it.

Jim and I began to refer to ourselves as 'The Unfuckables.'

MAY 10, 1969

The Paris Peace Talks officially began.

Paris

It has been a long time coming, the decision to do something, three years since the fateful telegram. Years of waiting and doing what President Johnson said to do—nothing. We had kept the whole mess a secret.

Rick and I, down in San Diego, had been dreaming up a plan to take off for the summer and hitchhike around Europe.

We were working on digging up the money for the trip, when Mom showed up at the front door of my beach house. Her lips were tight and straight. She had something serious on her mind. Right inside the front door, short-spoken as is her way, she said it only once.

Mom said, "Virginia, I think you ought to go to Paris and see the North Vietnamese, find out something about Spike."

Frankly, I felt a clamminess and surprise I didn't show. She was asking me to do something enormously important.

"You think I ought to do it, huh?"

"Yes, I do."

"Okay, Mom, I'll go."

We didn't speak another word about it. That was that. Spike's fate couldn't be talked about. It was too big a deal to talk about casually and the consequences too overwhelming to discuss.

Later, after Mom had left for home, I told Rick about our talk. He agreed we should go. We didn't talk about it after that, not one word. As a matter of fact, Rick and I didn't discuss what I might say to the North Vietnamese until we arrived in Paris.

We didn't talk about it, but I thought a lot about it and I was scared. Not scared to go to Paris or scared to talk to the North Vietnamese. Fact is, I'm not much scared of anything, but there was one thing I might find out that I didn't want to. I wouldn't have it!

Missing in action is bad, horribly bad. It's painful, it's nauseating, it's limbo, but it's not final. Even though he's MIA, we still have Spike.

We've got Spike and I didn't want to hear otherwise, wasn't gonna hear otherwise!

School was still in session, so we had a couple of months to prepare. Immediately Rick and I enrolled in Tulie McIntyre's conversational French class. I was her star student because I'm such a talker. Rick was great at grammar and spelling. Tulie was wonderful. We let her know we were going to Paris, even told her about Spike. She had us over to her house a few evenings for a drink and some practice speaking French.

Rick and I already carried passports, Rick from the summer past and me from two years earlier, but we were mighty short on cash.

It was my idea to go to Europe on garage sales. I love to collect junk. It drives Rick crazy.

Every Saturday, from the day we decided to go to Paris, we hit garage sales in La Jolla (high-class garage sales).

We'd walk up to families, always after noon, with all their junk laid out on their driveways and lawns and give 'em our pitch.

"Hi, we're college students putting ourselves through college. We clean up after garage sales, no charge. We'll haul away anything: books, clothes, furniture . . ."

We had as many takers as we could handle, every Saturday afternoon. In practice, they helped us load up our car right there on the spot. Most people were tired of the mess by about lunch time. We hauled their leftovers away on Saturday and hit the Sunday swap meet. Our policy was to take any amount for our wares; also, we only worked till noon on Sunday and never took an item home. At the stroke of twelve, when it started to get hot, we'd grab a kid and sell the whole mess to him for one dollar. It was a bonanza for the kid and we were off.

We made over $1,000 and were ready to go in June.

Two days before we were to leave, I discovered a couple of my shots for traveling abroad had expired. Now, I hate shots. I had to go alone because Rick was taking finals. I drove down to the health department and took one booster in my right arm, then had to turn around for another booster in my left arm—thought I was gonna faint. By the time I got home, both arms were paralyzed.

Now we were ready to leave.

June 10, 1969, the day after my last final, we said goodbye to Mom and headed out. We stopped off at Gebo's in Arizona to let her know what was going on. There, on her dryer, I left my carefully-faded, carefully-worn-to-look-and-feel-just-right blue jeans. We wore shorts hitching at first, so I didn't discover they were missing until it got cold in New York.

So we arrived in a wet, misty Paris, me without my long pants, and began immediately to look for Xuan Thuy. We knew we wanted to see Xuan Thuy, because we'd read about him in the newspapers. We wanted to go to the top North Vietnamese official, someone we were sure would have information about Spike.

We searched by ourselves on a hit-or-miss basis. We wanted no publicity. Scared that someone might try to stop us or that the press might get wind of our activities, we contacted no one in the American Embassy or the press services. We weren't sure our government would condone our interfering, and we thought we might even get into trouble.

We walked all over Paris, checking out various embassies, trying to locate Thuy, never letting on why we wanted to see him or giving our names.

We walked into one North Vietnamese office or embassy, the wrong one, only to find their display cases full of pictures and war souvenirs taken from dead Americans . . . Rick hustled me out. I didn't handle that one too well; it was hideous.

That finished us for day two. We went back to our campground. I was numb and sick to my stomach and awfully afraid of what I might see when I finally did get in to talk to Thuy.

After three days of searching, we gave up and contacted United Press International. They directed us to the proper North Vietnamese compound, no questions asked. They also told us that Xuan Thuy was in North Vietnam, expected to return to Paris in August.

We did not want to forewarn the North Vietnamese of our coming, giving them time to decide against seeing us. Nor did we want to see a flunky and get nowhere. So, planning to return in August, we hitchhiked out of Paris, south to North Africa, through Morocco, Algeria and Tunisia, then up to Italy, over to Greece and back to Paris.

It was a wild trip. We fought in every country, made up in every country and pretty well decided we couldn't live without each other.

I wrote Spike from every country.

Back in Paris in August, it took me two days to get up the courage to look up Thuy. I raised hell with Rick and had a terribly emotional morning before setting out.

We decided that it would be more effective if I went alone. I wore the dress I had taken on the trip, wore my hair long and prepared a letter for Spike which I had in my handbag.

Xuan Thuy and his Peace delegates occupied an old school which had giant walls surrounding it and numerous guards. French police patrolled around the entire compound.

I walked up to a tiny door and in feeble French asked to see Xuan Thuy. No one had ever done this before. The guards didn't quite know what to do with me, so they invited me in out of the rain. Once I was inside the compound, they decided to let me see Xuan Oanh.

Oanh was the interpreter or English-speaking aide for Xuan Thuy. Oanh was just a little bit taller than I am and he weighed just about as much as I did. I entered a lounge, we shook hands and I sat down. He had skinny little hands. He asked me to sit in a chair closer beside him. I wondered if they were photographing me. I told Oanh that this was strictly a personal visit. I assured him that all I wanted to do was find out if my brother was alive. Before I had been allowed entrance at the compound gate, I had written out my purpose on a card. I'm sure Oanh knew all about Spike's status before he entered the room. Oanh asked me over and over, at least four or five times, if I was sure I had not heard any news of my brother.

"No," I told him, "I've heard nothing."

Xuan Oanh gave me a new address at which to write Spike. He said that as far as he knew the only letters delivered were via this new address, that is via Moscow. I copied it down.

I asked him again and again about Spike, but each time he was evasive. He would only generalize about things, giving me no concrete information at all. During our conversation, he asked me if I had any other brothers and whether or not they were in the military. I told him that my younger brother was not in the military; that he is a husband and father. Oanh wanted to know what Spike thought about the war. I told him that Spike looked at being a pilot as a job. He said he understood. Oanh said that he had suffered personal losses in this war and that he could understand how badly I wanted to see my brother. I asked Oanh why they didn't send the prisoners home. He said that the people of North Vietnam were suffering from this war, that every family had lost at least one son. He said that the North Vietnamese wanted the American people to feel this war too. I asked Oanh if there was anything I could do to get my brother back. I said that even though I had never heard anything, I was sure he was alive. I hinted around about money, but I wasn't direct because I did not want to insult him. Oanh said that soon he would write me a letter, telling me of my brother's status.

Finally, when I could sense the interview was about over, I reached into my purse and clutched my letter for Spike. I held out my letter. Oanh stood, and took it from my hand. "This is for Spike," I told him, in a voice from deep inside me, "It says 'I love him.'"

"I will see that your brother gets this letter," Oanh said.

Somehow I made my way out of the North Vietnamese compound. Hurrying down the street through the rain, I wanted to talk to Rick. I was thinking about what had just happened and about running on the wet street. I had to talk it out with Rick.

At the end of the block I could make him out, wet, straining, looking for me.

"Oh, Rick, I'm not sure what happened."

He held me in his arms, "It's okay, baby, slow down."

"He didn't even mention the possibility that Spike might be dead."

"Who?"

"Oanh, and, he had a twinkle in his eyes when he talked about 'Your brother, John Nasmyth.'"

I collapsed onto Rick, "I'm so terribly, terribly relieved he just didn't say, 'Oh, he's dead.'"

We walked and talked and I felt sort of strange and tingly, very, very relieved. He didn't give me any definite news on Spike, but he didn't give me any bad news either.

The North Vietnamese are surely a different culture. I don't think they understand our kind of love. They have a different sense of values. And yet, Xuan Oanh somehow seemed sensitive to me. I felt that I had reached him in some way.

Later in the afternoon, Rick and I made our way to the American Express office, which we did in each city, to check for mail. There was a telegram waiting for me.

"It's from Dad!" We opened it and read it together.

VIRGINIA SPIKE'S STATUS CHANGED TO POW STOP CALL HOME IMMEDIATELY STOP DAD

"Oh my God!" Rick read it to himself then reread it to me.

We made the call immediately and got right through to Dad. From six thousand miles away, Dad told me that three prisoners of war, Seaman Hegdahl, Captain Rumble, and Lt. Robert Frishman, had been released from Hanoi. It was after their debriefing that Spike's name turned up.

They're wild at home, we're beside ourselves with joy.

Apparently Spike has never been seen by these men. His name was on an old memorized list. Officially, the Air Force could only say that at one time Spike had been alive in a prison camp in North Vietnam.

This information, coupled with what Xuan Oanh told me today, that he will see that my brother gets my letter, clinches it! Spike *has* to be alive.

Rick and I headed for home. I had the feeling Spike would be there when we got home.

By Myself

Everybody is skinny now. I weigh about one hundred and twenty pounds; some weigh a lot less. We're just not getting enough to eat. Treatment has been the same since I've been here—miserable. It's just that they get after you for everything, every day. When they want something, they torture people for it. The bowing bullshit is still going on; every time you see a Gook you have to bow.

Living with Pirie somehow made it tolerable. I really liked the guy. In the spring of '69 when the cell door opened and the guard said, "Pe, ugh," I felt a twinge, I kind of hated to see him go.

Jim turned and looked. "See you around, pal," he picked up his things and hauled ass.

I don't know how many times I moved, but that's about all the warning you ever got. The door would open, a grunt from a guard and you were gone.

Once again I found myself alone for a while. I didn't like to think of it as solitary. There were always guys in the other cells to tap to. It didn't help the smell of the cell any to be alone. It still smelled like shit whether you were with somebody or not, just different grades of shit.

A couple of weeks later a guard comes through the door.
"Ugh."

I gather up my stuff from the cell I've been in for three years and follow this skinny-necked Gook across the camp towards another cell block. He opens the door to cell number three of the Office. Leaving the sunlight behind, I walk into my new, dim cell. There are two guys sitting there looking me over. As soon as the guard splits I find out they're Henry Blake and Jay Jensen.

Billboard

Early in September Pete, Mom, Rick and I went to hear Robert Frishman speak to about one hundred family members of prisoners of war. After this briefing we wanted to get his personal opinion on what we should do. We also wanted to personally tell him 'welcome home.' We set a date, and a week later met Bob for coffee. We talked for three hours, then moved up to the bar. After five hours of hard, sincere talking, we came to the conclusion that secrecy was doing our men no good at all.

Rumble, Hegdahl and Frishman's experiences, impressions, and opinions broke the camel's back on secrecy helping the prisoners. When they were designated to be released from prison camp, some of the fellows told them to sing, and they did. The men left behind want the world to know what's really going on.

Would this have gone on for so many years if the people of this country knew what was going on in Hanoi?

All these years of silence have allowed this disgusting turn of events to occur.

After hearing Bob's story, all of it, firsthand, the family took two weeks to digest this new knowledge and hash things over. We carefully considered the pros and cons of making the prisoner-of-war situation public knowledge. We took the positive approach and decided that by campaigning we could get the prisoners out, or at least get the ball rolling. It was because of Bob's opinion and the messages Hegdahl brought home from other prisoners that we decided to actively start campaigning.

Our first move was to get Spike's story into the newspaper. Mom did that. She called the local paper and they came out and did a small story. Interest was stirred. We all sat around and got drunk one night and the idea of a billboard came up. We set a date, located a site, sent out news releases and went to work.

Pete designed an 8-foot by 12-foot billboard with a message on each side. Pete spent two days setting 4-by-4's in cement and building the frame. A fellow Spike grew up with, Jon Dahlstrom, a commercial artist, did the lettering. The site we chose, donated by a neighbor, was on the corner of San Gabriel Boulevard and Delta Street, the street we lived on.

October tenth, at ten o'clock in the morning, we erected one side of the billboard for an ABC camera crew. At two that afternoon we erected the other side for the other networks, radio and various newspapers. Our billboard had a white background.

In large red letters it said: HANOI
In large black letters it said: RELEASE JOHN NASYMTH

The billboard shall remain until Spike comes home and takes it down himself!

The first billboard, homemade, on Delta Street, with Pete holding 'Little' Pete, Carmen, Mom, me, and Dad.

About one hundred neighbors, old friends, and teachers of Spike's were present for the event. We passed out petitions reading:

"Attention President Richard Nixon: As concerned citizens of the United States of America, we would like to enlist your help in bringing home Capt. John Nasmyth of the United States Air Force and his comrades who are at this time Prisoners of War in North Vietnam."

We had bumper stickers reading, 'Hanoi Release John Nasmyth,' and lists of important people to write on a card table under the billboard.

Our press coverage was excellent. For the next weeks we circulated petitions like mad. I sent copies of all our news coverage to Xuan Oanh, special delivery. Prior to this, I had sent Oanh a letter telling him that our government had informed us that Spike was alive and a POW.

On October 22, I received the following letter from Oanh:

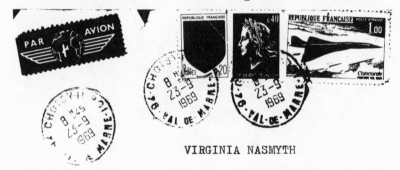

VIRGINIA NASMYTH

                              Choisy Le Roi
                              France
                              September 22, 1969

Dear Miss Nasmyth :

    Thanks for your letter.

    I am glad you got the news about your brother.

    I will think of writing you in the future if any other information reached me here.

    With my regards to the rest of your family.

                              Sincerely,

                              OANH

On October 23, we erected another homemade HANOI RELEASE JOHN NASYMTH billboard in front of State Senator Jack Schrade's San Diego office. The press was there, along with Jack Schrade who had flown down from Sacramento, and had a police escort to the sign-raising. We also had a few Sigma Alpha Epsilon members from San Diego State, Spike's fraternity alumni, a few friends and the family.

While the press was interviewing me, I showed my letter from Xuan Oanh to reporter Bob Dietrich of the San Diego *Evening Tribune*. He said it was important, very important. I had no idea of the significance of the letter. It made our story go national.

According to Bob and the Pentagon, no one has ever received a letter of this kind from the North Vietnamese. This letter definitely confirmed that Spike was alive!

Tapping

Henry Blake and I never did hit it off too well. Kind of hard to say how we hit it off at all, because he didn't say much, just a grunt now and then. But Jay was a gabby dude; he talked a lot.

We hadn't been together all that long when they opened the cell door, pointed to Jay, "Ugh," and Jay moved out.

I'd already gotten the message about Henry from Jay. Jay used to talk about Henry all the time; Henry wouldn't say yea or nay. Jay told me, "You know, I used to think Henry was crazy since he never talked to me. Then after a while I guess it really didn't matter, I'd just talk to him whether he answered me or not. It was somebody to talk to."

Jay was right. Henry made a grunt every now and then. Sometimes he'd really be a chatterbox, say three or four things a day. Like, "How's it going?"

Jensen was gone a month or so, leaving Blake and me in this 8-foot by 10-foot cell, when they moved five guys into the cell next door: Tom Browning, Reed McCleary, Dave Carry, Bill Bailey and Harry Monlux. I spent my time talking to the new guys next door.

There had been an escape attempt in May of '69. My new neighbors had been in the same camp as the escapees and they filled me in on the details.

John Dramesi and Ed Atterberry had planned it very thoroughly. They planned to escape on the first Saturday night that there was a thunderstorm. They figured that during a good storm everyone would be inside, giving them a better chance of making it over the wall.

For weeks Ed and John and their cohorts made all sorts of things to be used when the time was right. They stored the supplies in the attic of their cell and waited.

The storm hit and they went over the wall. A few hundred yards from the camp a Gook dog smelled some non-Gook people. The guards caught them early that morning, tortured Atterberry to death and messed up Dramesi pretty bad, but he survived.

We knew the Gooks had been torturing somebody that morning—screams could be heard all over, and now we knew why. Usually they took guys off to the Hanoi Hilton when they were going to torture them real bad, but not that time.

There are a lot of men in solitary. We can get to them as long as there is somebody in the cell next to them. General bullshit about when the war would be over, good jokes and new prisoners' names got to everybody sooner or later.

We're passing information back and forth while Blake, totally disinterested, ignores it all. And I ignore him.

Spending my time tapping to the five guys next door, I tell them, "tap, tap, tap . . . t h i s   c e l l m a t e I've got over here is flipping his cookies. He lies on his back looking at the ceiling all day long. Never says a word." Once in a while he'd swing around off his bed, get up to pee; didn't look at me, didn't talk. Nothing.

Now I start spending hours talking through the wall. We develop a new way; instead of tapping, we actually talk through the wall. Don't ask me why somebody didn't think of it years earlier. We each have a metal cup. You wrap a little towel around it, put your mouth into the metal cup, hold it up to the wall and shout into it. The guy next door puts his ear up to the wall. You can hear as plain as day, but no one can hear it from the outside. It works perfectly. We just talk the hours away. I become good friends with Reed McCleary and the others.

NOVEMBER 15, 1969

    The largest anti-war protest in U.S. history took place.

Official List

Just a month after receiving the letter from Xuan Oanh, the day before Thanksgiving, we were busy in Phoenix, Arizona, erecting the first of several dozen commercial-size billboards. Gebo had contacted Carl Eller, of Eller Outdoor. Upon hearing her story, he took on what he called his 'Hanoi Release John Nasmyth Project.' He put our billboards up all over the country. We also had billboards available reading: Hanoi Release The Prisoners, Hanoi Release My Father, Hanoi Release My Husband, Hanoi Release My Son, and Hanoi Release My Brother, plus others with any POW's name available by special order.

That afternoon, after meeting the press, giving interviews and passing out information on the prisoners, we returned to Gebo's home to see how it all looked on TV.

Rick and I got there first. We turned on the news just in time to see our story come on. Directly after showing our family putting up another billboard, the news commentator said: "It is with great pleasure that I make the following announcement. Today the North Vietnamese have announced their first official list of Prisoners of War held in North Vietnam. John Nasmyth is the fifth name on the list!"

"Oh my God! Did you hear that, Rick? Hooray, we did it! They admit they've got him. Oh God, I'm so glad."

We called the station. "Hello, this is the Nasymths, we just heard what you said on TV! What about a list?"

Jubilant, a man in the newsroom relayed the flash amid our jumping and squealing in the background.

"We've been looking for you all day."

"We've been out putting up a billboard."

"The list contains one hundred and twenty names; according to our records only two are new."

"Oh thank you, thank you so much."

"Congratulations!"

We called the Air Force, the Pentagon and the State Department. The United States Government said, "Yes, the list is for real." Heaven only knows how happy we were.

Invigorated, we arranged to have three hundred more billboards put up by professionals. These were scattered across the country. Mom, Gebo and I and friends and people we'd never met were daily cutting out clippings from newspapers and magazines of Spike's story and the others. We collected them at Mom's house for our mailings. I kept sending Xuan Oanh stacks of our clippings.

Every month now, Mother, Gebo and I each get out a mailing. We send each Senator and Representative and a long list of foreign editors a personal letter and a fact sheet or a news clipping. It's amazing how little our representatives know about the POW-MIA situation.

December 3, 1969

Dear Sir:

My brother John Nasmyth has been a Prisoner of War in North Vietnam since September 4, 1966. My family has never been allowed any communication with John. Only two months ago did we learn that John is indeed alive and a POW.

I am appealing to you because of your influence with the public. Thousands of families have been suffering for years because they do not know the status of their loved ones.

I cannot see the reason for the North Vietnamese keeping secret the names of the prisoners nor do I understand why they have not released the sick and wounded.

Sir, please help me and thousands of women and children just like me. I want to see my brother again. I cannot bear the thought of my brother suffering much longer.

Please tell your public of this painful situation and ask them to please appeal to Hanoi for humane treatment for our prisoners.

I am appealing to your compassion and respect for mankind. Please help me.

Very truly yours,

Virginia Nasmyth
Virginia Nasmyth

United States Senate

COMMITTEE ON FOREIGN RELATIONS

WASHINGTON, D.C. 20510

Dear Friend:

I wish to acknowledge your recent communication concerning American prisoners of war.

I share your concern about the problem and I have done everything I know how to be of help on it. You may be interested to know that the Committee on Foreign Relations and the full Senate have approved a resolution concerning the plight of our prisoners and I enclose the text of it for your information.

I appreciate your taking the trouble to let me have your views on this issue, and I apologize for having to resort to a form letter but the mail has been particularly heavy in recent weeks.

Sincerely yours,

J. W. Fulbright
Chairman

Enclosure

ISN'T THAT A BUNCH OF BULLSHIT!

Our Congressmen have waited around until it is politically expedient before taking a stand or even expressing an opinion on the POW situation. Most of them are still waiting around. Their attitudes are deplorable.

When a man is shot down over Hanoi, about one dozen people's lives back home are drastically affected. Another couple of hundred people are slightly affected, depending on the man's circle of friends and distant relatives. Our United States representatives have not been affected at all over the past six years. The average citizen has no idea how many POWs there are or what to do about them. Most people don't want to think about the fifteen hundred missing men. When asked if they care, they say yes. But this is only because they don't want to sound cold-blooded. Really, they don't give a damn until it happens to them or their best friend; or the teary-eyed little sister of a POW approaches them, challenges their self-image and asks them to do something.

After receiving hundreds of say-nothing-do-nothing form letters, I sent a second letter to nearly all of our U.S. Congressmen.

> Dear Sir:
>
> I am pleading with you as a leader of this country to please help me. My wonderful brother has missed three Christmases with his family. He is working on his fourth year as a prisoner of war in North Vietnam. How much pain do you, the leaders of this country, think the 3,000 half-crazy next of kin of the prisoners can take? You guys may mess around for ten years before you bring home the men we love. How much do you think the men themselves can take? You just might bring home vegetables.
>
> Come on, Representative, get human. Every day I think of my wonderful brother rotting away because of this country's inaction. How would you like to be a skinny little 20-year-old girl and know that your big, handsome, alert, smart brother weighs just about as much as you do?
>
> I don't see how you guys can sit around debating much longer. My God, it's been over six years for some of these men. Think about people, will you?
>
> I'm sick of being reasonable. The leaders of this country must be the most unconscious, shallow things that inhabit this earth if they can't get up the courage to do something for a bunch of suffering people: men they sent to war. Really, waiting until the American Public forgets about the prisoners stinks.
>
> I've done more to inform the country about the POW situation than any so-called leader.
>
> Please, for my sanity and the prisoners and their families, don't give us more resolutions, GET THE PRISONERS HOME!

You, the representatives of the United States, have shirked all responsibility for the lives of the men of this country. I'm not proud that the strongest country in the world is waiting around for world opinion to do its job. Hanoi didn't negotiate in Paris, did they? How ridiculous to wait for them to become culturally sophisticated enough to SUGGEST humane treatment for the POW's. You have really taken the easy way out.

I am informed about the prisoner situation. If signing a resolution can relieve your conscience and grant you the privilege of dropping these men, then you are not much of a leader.

Sincerely,
Virginia Nasmyth

I received fewer than a dozen replies to the second letter.

Six-line Form

On October 18, 1969, something of insurmountable importance happened: the food ration doubled, the cigarette ration became a real ration, something you could count on, and guards no longer had the authority to do anything they wanted. They had to get permission. Now we could tell a guard to 'go get fucked' and he had to get permission from an officer before he belted you.

Rabbit sent a guard for me.

"The Camp Commander allows you to write a letter to your family."

"You're kidding."

Rabbit gave me a six-line form. "Write only on lines and write nice or it won't go. We will even give you a stamp."

(Something's up! The war must be over!!)

Back at the cell I got to thinking about it. Why are things getting better now? First, something must be going on back home, or something we really know nothing about has had an effect on the Gooks. Suddenly the Gooks, to their surprise, have become aware that each of us has a great value to somebody. They have been smart enough to figure we could be used in barter come the day of our eventual release. Whatever is going on back home, it has genuinely increased our value. I'm convinced this is going to save a lot of people from dying, from just plain starving to death. All of a sudden we're worth keeping alive. Not because they like us, but because they are going to be able to trade us.

Second, Nixon has been President almost a year and they are convinced he isn't bullshitting.

And third, on September 3 Ho Chi Minh died.

September 2 is Vietnamese Independence Day; September 3, 1969, Ho Chi Minh died; and September 4, 1966, I was shot down. Three great days in history.

First Letter

Friday morning, December 23, 1969, Dad hung around the house instead of going to work. By 10 a.m. when he was ready to leave, the mailman had already been by. Dad walked out to the mailbox and picked up the dozen or so letters which had just been dropped off.

"My God!" he thought, "There's a letter from Vietnam."

Standing in the front yard, Dad unfolded the paper, which was more like parchment. It was addressed to Mr. and Mrs. Nasmyth. There were two cancelled Vietnamese stamps clinging to the corner. He began to shake, his eyes watering so he couldn't read any further. He did make out the signature though; it was signed Spike!

Dad was sobbing so hard that he tried to read the letter but just couldn't focus. He ran to the phone and dialed Mother at work. Dad was so choked up he could hardly get the words out.

"We got a letter from Spike."

Mother threw down the phone, rushed out of the office, leapt into her car and drove home. She was crying all the way, driving like mad. She pulled her car up on the lawn and rushed into the house to see the letter.

Mom and Dad sat at the kitchen table and read and reread our first wonderful piece of news from Spike in over three long years.

This time Mother was able to function. She phoned Gebo and read the letter over and over while Gebo copied down every word. She phoned Pete's office but he was out to lunch. She had Allied Chemical page him at his luncheon meeting, her message: "Emergency, phone home, Mother."

Pete finally got her message. He didn't even have to phone home, he knew what had happened. He knew we had finally received a letter from Spike. Pete headed for home.

Mom called me and read Spike's letter over and over. We were both crying so hard.

"How's he sound?"

"God, he sounds great."

"How's his handwriting?"

"It looks wonderful."

"I'm coming home."

I attempted to dial Rick at work. After four tries, I hit the correct numbers and got Rick on the line.

"Hello, Rick, we got a letter from Spike; I'm going home."

Blam, down with the receiver. I ran out of the house barefoot with my car keys and made the ninety-mile drive home in just over an hour. Almost crashed the car when I flew into the driveway. I ran into the house to find everybody crying and laughing and reading not one letter from Spike, but three!

In his excitement, when Dad first sorted the mail, he missed two more letters from Hanoi!

Dear Mom Dad and Family How's everyone? I am in excellent health and still retain my optimistic outlook on everything, so don't worry a bit about me. The food and treatment here are very good. I got your packages, they were great. I think about you all much of the time and look forward to being home soon. Love Spike

NGÀY VIẾT (Dated) 9 October 1969

GHI CHÚ (N.B.) :

1. Phải viết rõ và chỉ được viết trên những dòng kẻ sẵn *(Write legibly and only on the lines).*

2. Trong thư chỉ được nói về tình hình sức khỏe và tình hình gia đình *(Write only about health and family).*

3. Gia đình gửi đến cũng phải theo đúng mẫu, khuôn khổ và quy định này *(Letters from families should also conform to this proforma).*

26 November 1969

Dear Mom Dad and Family

I recieved your previous packages (first time on
15 February 69, second time on 30 September 69).

I've been informed by the camp officers that this
year the DRV Government will again allow families of
U.S. captured pilots to send Xmas packages.

In order to help packages arrive fast and in perfect condition - no breakage or spoiling due to transportation or weather
you should follow these procedures.

1- Everyone is allowed to recieve only one package and
not exceeding 3 Kg (appro 6.6 lbs).

2- Following items are allowed: Dried food stuff, tonics in pills
tablets or capsule, tobacco together with pipe (no cigarettes) Personal articles,
Soap, tooth brush, paste.

3- Food and medicine stuffs must be packed in hermetic and solid
containers. Tonics must be packed in original containers from manufacturers.

Attention - Above procedures should be strictly followed
otherwise packages will not reach.

Love Spike   John H. Nasmyth

-117-

Dear Mom Dad and Family. Happy birthday Gebo and Dad. Now Mom Gebo and I are all twenty nine. (Ha) The Camp Commander gave me a nice birthday party. This package send cans of nuts, jam coco, all kinds of hard candy, cool aid, p-nut bars etc. How am I doing financially? Would like some pictures of all. I am in good health and spirits. Say hi to everyone. Love Spike

NGÀY VIẾT (Dated) 1 December 1969

GHI CHÚ (N.B.):

1. Phải viết rõ và chỉ được viết trên những dòng kẻ sẵn (Write legibly and only on the lines).

2. Trong thư chỉ được nói về tình hình sức khỏe và tình hình gia đình (Write only about health and family).

3. Gia đình gửi đến cũng phải theo đúng mẫu, khuôn khổ và quy định này (Letters from families should also conform to this proforma).

We read the letters and touched the letters and cried on them and smeared the ink. What a miracle, what a Christmas!

Thirty minutes later Rick walked in, delayed by a cop who had given him a speeding ticket.

I called Gebo and we bawled about the good news.

The Lees came over, and two or three television crews showed up and filmed our emotional, disorganized joy.

I guess we called just about everybody we knew. Deep down the letters seemed like a good omen. Things were happening so fast, surely there would be a release for Christmas.

We read and reread his wonderful letters, and they are wonderful letters, about forty times. We all sat around looking at them, holding them and talking. We talked mostly about how Spike's handwriting looked, the spacing and the fact that he signed his name Spike. We have always been

-118-

super careful to refer to Spike as John Nasmyth. Somehow we attached importance to using his formal name. It is really something to see old Spike's name after all this time.

I'm afraid that for days Pete and I were each independently, though willingly and happily, caught up in searching for a code in his letters. I tried everything I could think of, reading only the capital letters, reading diagonally, reading backwards, asking myself if the funny question mark meant anything. "Hey Pete, do the 'T' crosses point to something?" This went on and on!

There was something really 'heavy' about Spike's long letter. He made no mention of any need for clothes or medical supplies, but he underlined the word *food*.

Boy, that really zonked us. The distress caused by this was evident, although no one dared utter the unthinkable, i.e., Spike was slowly starving to death. Boy, that starving to death stuff started gnawing away at us, made us feel pretty anxious, made me cry thinking about his asking for food.

The Air Force had informed us that starting in January, 1970, we would be allowed to send one package every other month, meaning six five-pound packages a year.

Spike said in his long letter, "I received your previous packages on 15 February '69, second time on 30 September '69."That meant he hadn't gotten any of our packages for two and a half years. The two packages he did get were about one-half medicine and one-half food. We decided to change that.

Together Mom and I drove up to the local market. We took Spike's underlining very seriously as we walked back and forth through every aisle. There have never been two more intense shoppers. We must have picked up and discussed every single canned item in the store. We settled on over a pound of chocolate, semi-sweet, Planter's peanuts, a little tin of beef, some gum, a huge bottle of vitamins and some hard candy to make it exactly five pounds.

Next day, Mother turned two of Spike's letters—along with an old sample of his handwriting—over to a team of experts to verify our theories.

"Our experts feel that the letters were written by your son. The analysis further revealed that while he is naturally an active, lively, outgoing and expansive person with a lot of drive, he appears to be slightly uncomfortable and gives the impression of being somewhat tense and a little irritable; however, this may be due to the lack of stimulation and activity. Overall he is handling himself quite well and doing as best he can under the circumstances."

We didn't think much of this analysis, since it said absolutely nothing we hadn't already figured out.

After we'd become exhausted from our search for a code, which turned out to be futile, we all got to analyzing and studying Spike's letters as a whole.

These wonderful, heaven-sent letters were in Spike's handwriting, there was no doubt about that. Although the handwriting seemed a little light and weak, maybe that was from fatigue. We had seen letters from other prisoners of war in Hanoi. Some of his phrases like "and still retain my optimistic outlook on everything . . ." seemed to be an attribute of form letters. So we figured he was not writing freely; they were probably telling him what to say.

In his third letter, Spike's crack about Gebo, Mom and him all being twenty-nine is a family joke. We were always kidding around about how nobody in our family ever got older than twenty-nine. I guessed that Spike put it in his letter because we had mentioned it the last time we wrote. This was so important to us. I had been keeping a folder with copies of all the letters we have ever written to Spike, so we could keep track of what we've told him.

His sentence, "The camp commander gave me a nice birthday party," could be a response to a letter we wrote to him a couple of months ago. On November 14, 1969, we threw a giant birthday party for Spike, in absentia. Three hundred people came. We sold drinks and made $1,000.00 for our 'Hanoi Release John Nasmyth and His Fellow POWs' fund. I thought Spike might be saying that he knew about the birthday party, he knew what we were doing.

"How am I doing financially?" That was another family joke. Pete had always written how Spike's money was piling up in his part of our letters to Spike.

We tried to be objective when we read these letters. We wanted terribly for Spike to have heard from us. We wanted so badly for him to know that we know he is alive, but we might have been seeing feedback which wasn't really there. I hoped not. I hoped the instances of mutual references were not just coincidence.

More Breakups

The sign, our 'Hanoi Release John Nasmyth' billboard, did more than launch our campaign for Spike; the sign saved Pete.

Living in Los Angeles now, away from his drinking buddy, Warren, Pete didn't have anybody to talk to. He became enormously uptight and couldn't talk about it with any of us. Pete's violent temper, which he'd been pretty good about controlling as an adult, began to surface. Frustration on the job and frustration at home just made him madder.

I'll never forget one morning when Mom and I went over to visit Pete, Carmen and the kids. Carmen met us at the front door.

"Hi, where's Pete? Where are the boys?"

With a straight face she said, "Oh, they're out back in their hole."

So, we went out back and sure enough there were Pete and the boys busy digging a hole in the backyard. Hell, the thing was already six feet by six feet and almost that deep.

Pete put his shovel down and, with a stupid grin on his face, explained, "When I get sick of the bullshit in the house I say, 'Men, let's go out and dig.' "

And they dug. The boys for fun, their father furiously!

It wasn't long after the hole episodes began that Pete went to work for Allied Chemical by day and selling roofs at night. He was gone all the time. He was busy all the time. He was turning himself into a workaholic.

But it worked. It got him through emotionally. Instead of blowing up, he worked his ass off. It worked for Pete, but it sure left Carmen alone a lot. He felt he was really providing for his family, but she felt neglected—trapped with two small kids.

And when our billboard went up, any attention Pete might have had for Carmen, outside of the bedroom, went into talking about and brainstorming for the *campaign!*

To drive by that damn homemade billboard, knowing it was gonna stay up until Spike took it down, gave us all something to hang on to. It saved Pete, for he dragged himself up and out of his depression to do something for Spike. For me, it was a symbol. It ignited unstoppable energies in me:

A news release once a week—out to 200 important news media people around the world.

Daily phone calls to the Air Force, Pentagon, State Department—trying to stir them up.

Rick and I were on the road to L.A. two or three times a week for strategy meetings, to put together mailings, or to rant and rave about our representatives. But mostly to be home, because it looked like there would be a token prisoner release for Christmas.

Breathless and wild about that possibility, we raised all the hell we could. Maybe the North Vietnamese would get sick of the Nasmyths and send Spike home to get us off their backs.

As Christmas approached we watched the news. Other moms and wives were flocking to Paris trying to see Xuan Thuy, looking for anything, any word about their men.

The tension the day before Christmas was incredible. We expected a message, a call. I expected Spike.

He wasn't home for Christmas; he wasn't home for New Years. Just like all the years before, Spike did not come home in 1969.

Our intensive campaigning slowed down in January. I guess we were depressed.

What has this awful mess done to us after three and a half years? Today I was hit with a mood of depression so deep, so total, that I was immobile until the tears came. The realization that I am only 20 years old and have been torn apart for the past three years is unbearable. I want to be 20 and I want to act 20. At this point, I feel that the only way I am ever going to be able to relax and live just one unhaunted, happy day is when the whole world gets behind me and my family.

If I don't think about it, I want to sleep and just let the time pass until I can be happy. When I do think about it, I cry. I have adored my brother my whole life. For over three years he has been a prisoner of war in North Vietnam. Every night for three years I've dreamt of the horrible things that might be happening to him.

Our men are at the hands of merciless guards. The guards must be merciless, if the North Vietnamese delegates are any example. These men are subjecting the families of 1,500 men to the constant terror of doubt and fear. If diplomats will let American women and children suffer so . . . what must it be like for Spike at the hands of these animals?

I swear I would do *anything* to help our men. Because this war has touched me personally, I can recite the facts about the POWs. I'm tired of reciting the facts. We need the world's help. I find horror and revulsion in what the North Vietnamese are doing to human beings. The rest of humanity must be made aware so that they too will feel this same revulsion. As human beings, we must bring to a stop these atrocities against human lives.

Gebo and Bob split up New Year's Eve, 1968. She simply explained to Bob that she could no longer be happy living with him and would he please leave. Bob moved out that same evening.

Mom's and Dad's divorce finally got rolling. Dad moved into a nice apartment, and immediately he seemed much happier. Mother moved back home and we kids felt much happier. It was good to have our parents' lives straightened out.

About the time we got Gebo, Bob, Mom and Dad all situated, Carmen walked out on Pete.

The romance to beat all romances catapulted into the divorce of the ages. It was war: Carmen was furious; Pete was bitter. Being their mother, Carmen took her boys, Little Pete and Jeff. Pete was devastated. He literally barricaded himself in their home and suffered. He quit his job that day. He was served with divorce papers the following morning. Soon he slipped into a massive, deep depression.

Pete visited Mom at the family home every day. He'd sit down in the deep comfortable green chairs in the kitchen, forehead in hand, and just sit there. A half hour would pass, an hour. Pete would look up and say,

"Do you think we'll ever hear from him again?"

"Yes, Pete, I sure do."

He'd slip back into that position, head bent, forehead cupped in his right hand. Later in the morning he'd get up and leave, go back to his own place.

Ants

Now Blake was spending his time lying in the fetal position, but on his back, right on his back with his knees drawn into his stomach, holding on to them, staring at the ceiling all day. I never looked close enough to see if he was blinking his eyes. I was kind of hoping he wouldn't blink, that he'd be dead. I didn't give a shit. I just wondered how and why I should have such bad luck! (There must be a couple of good guys in this camp somewhere. How come I got stuck with this nerd?) And then when the dumb fucker did talk, he was so goddam stupid. He usually said things that were so fucking dumb you wished he hadn't said them at all.

One afternoon in January of '70 the squawk box came on: "All the criminals who show the correct attitude will be allowed to receive package from their family."

One day shortly after the announcement the door opens, the guard comes in and gets Henry Blake. He leaves. A few minutes later, he comes back carrying a little cardboard box. In it he's got a bunch of shit from his family: candy, peanuts, all kinds of stuff. Henry is the kind of guy who saves everything. If he got something good to eat, he'd rat-hole it and eat it later. All of a sudden he has this bunch of junk, and some of it has to be consumed instantly or it will rot. But he's also got a bunch of hard candy, lemon balls, lifesavers. He wraps them in a little rag and hangs 'em from this string where you hang your mosquito net. Henry hasn't spoken to me in ten days, give or take a day. Whatever, he doesn't speak very often. Of course, I wouldn't have considered having a piece. It was his. I had plenty to do talking to my friends through the wall.

Of course, he's crazy. I'm almost as crazy as he is at this point, there's no doubt about it. I don't want you to think that I'm the only sane person in this situation. He ain't talking to me, but I ain't talking to him either.

I used to justify that by telling the guys in the next cell about him.

I'd be talking to Tom Browning, and Blake wouldn't even pay attention to what I was saying. Shouting through the cup, I'd say, "I'm not going to say another word to Henry. We'll see how long it takes him to say something to me." Every day they'd say, "How's it going with Henry?" My reply, "He ain't said shit."

One day Henry said, "What's going?" I said, "Nothing." He said, "Oh." It had been fourteen days. Twenty-two days later he said something.

"Hey, there."

"Yeah."

Anyway, he's got this candy hanging up. Every day he's eating one piece. Now, if you take about five rolls of lifesavers and a bunch of other things and eat one piece a day, it'll last a year. I think he had it figured out so it would last exactly one year. I asked him one day if he wasn't going to eat more of his candy. He said, "Well, when I want to."

Something happened and he quit eating the stuff, left it up there for a long time without touching it. I probably caused it. Then I start noticing ants in the cell. There are jillions of ants. The ants must smell the sugar. They are going nuts, running up and down the walls, four hundred miles an hour. Finally one ant finds this string and zings down it. Next thing there are three of them. The scouts run in. Whatever ants do, they run in to check it out, the scouts run back to the nest, then the soldiers come. It looks just like somebody has taken a black ink pen and drawn a line. Zing, zing, zing. I'm watching this. Shit, they are running up and down this string for about three days. Then they stop coming.

I say to myself, "Well, shit, that stuff must be packed good. They couldn't get to it."

A couple of days later Henry opens his bag and here's a paper wrapper of livesavers and it's hollow. They have eaten it. I mean to tell you those little critters have cleaned him out.

Blake was aware I had noticed the ants, because I'd stand there and watch them by the hour. He wouldn't allow himself to notice them, since I had noticed them first. We were a great pair.

While this was all going on, the treatment was getting better. They began tearing down most of the solitary confinement cells, and communications busted wide open. I started standing at the window, yelling at guys out at the shower and things like that. They knew we were doing it. Our new interrogator was the Rabbit, who was a lot less cruel than Dumb-Dumb.

When he'd call me up for a quiz, I started telling him that I could hear the sounds of the changes in the prison camp.

"I want a cell mate. I'm going crazy living in solitary confinement."
Rabbit retorted, "You're not in solitary confinement."

"Yes, I am. Blake doesn't ever speak."

I had absolutely no more patience with Henry. Besides putting up with a non-roommate my wisdom teeth had started bothering me. They were always there, gnawing away at my mouth, flaring up once in a while, hurting like hell and making it impossible to eat.

It just all sort of built up until one day up at the quiz I told the Rabbit that if he didn't move me that day, from that cell, I was gonna kill Blake that night.

They moved Blake out, less than an hour later. Left me in solitary.

Now, this isn't what I had in mind. I'd been in solitary for months even with Blake there. To demonstrate how desperate I had become, I went on a starvation diet. I stopped eating everything, demanding that I get cellmates like the rest of my fellows. Not eating for days helped put a wild look in my eyes. The Gooks continually caught me standing up on my bed, looking out my window at the five guys next door. I was yelling at them and not getting any crap for doing it. There had been a big policy change. The torture stuff had stopped. Guys were doing all kinds of shit. I yelled at the guys next door and anybody else I could get glimpse of. Laughing, looking out the window all day long, a loony grin on my face. I couldn't see why I was all alone. So, I stayed on a hunger strike for a lot longer than I had planned to.

It went on for 25 days, and I got pretty skinny. Of course, you can't really get too skinny when you only weigh 120 pounds. But I got down to 110 or so.

During the days of my fast I pretended I was dying. I lay on my back staring at the ceiling. When they fed me they opened the cell door and put my bowl inside the door. When they came back, they took the untouched food away. I felt starving, ravenous. When you're crazy you can always think of something to be mad about.

"I'll show these little yellow-bellied bastards, I won't eat their food. They'll be sorry."

I was flipped out in the head. How loony can you get? Loony is loony. Oh shit, whenever I'd see anybody I'd climb up on my bed, look out the window at everybody, yelling, an uncontrollable grin on my face, "Hi."

The Vietnamese never touched food that an American had touched. Once in a while they'd give us a small loaf of bread. You could tear it in half from the bottom, take the guts out, eat that, then put the shell of the loaf back. We watched them by the hour. They never touched it. Then the guys who came to wash the dishes would take it and throw the leftovers away.

The other guys said, "Hey, Spike, this is kind of loony." But what the hell, I had nothing better to do. I wasn't gonna kill myself. I drank water, and the guys passed me food.

This really sounds dumb. I'd throw my food away and they'd leave a little bit of food out by the place we dump the shit buckets. I'd throw mine away. They'd pick it up when they washed the dishes, take my food and hide some of theirs for me.

It was really insane. When I think about it, I was starving anyway, hungry as hell on the regular diet, and here I was not eating anything.

On the twenty-sixth day, they called me up to the office. I sort of floated up there, I'd been on a perpetual buzz anyway. Rabbit was sitting behind his table, and he said, "Because of the humanitarian policies of the Vietnamese people toward the American war criminals in the Democratic Republic of Vietnam," (Jesus have I heard that before or what!) "we have decided to allow you to live with some of your fellow criminals. Return to your cell."

(Ha, it worked, they really think I'm crazy.) I got my ass out of there before he could change his mind.

Man, I flew back to my cell. The five guys from next door had already been there, rolled up my stuff and laid it out in their cell. They put me in with Crazy George McSwain, Art Cormier, Dick Ratzlaff, Art Black and Bill Robinson.

New Tactics

It's kind of funny. When Spike was missing in action we were really tortured. There was constant pain and worry. I got so I could put him out of my mind, though. Sometimes I would go for hours and he wouldn't even enter my thoughts. Now that we know he is alive and in one piece, his image never leaves me. It's the same with the rest of the family. Now we're constantly worried about his health and his thoughts while he's wasting away over there. Now that we've got him back from the dead, I just can't bear to lose him again. We just want him to make it, no matter how long it takes.

The weak handwriting in Spike's letters has really bummed us out. We kept talking about the fatigue he must be experiencing.

After a few weeks of talking and thinking about this, we've pretty well convinced ourselves that he is in solitary confinement. The image we've conjured up is scary, a guy just sitting, alone in a cell yet suffering from fatigue. That fatigue really gets us. We hope it doesn't mean he is sick.

The North Vietnamese have admitted they've got him. That's life insurance. We're pretty sure now that they won't actively knock him off. But if this fatigue thing means he is sick, they may be passively letting him die.

When we started campaigning, our ultimate goal was to get Spike out. Now that we've been working on it for a while, we realize we had some secondary objectives:

One, we had to get the North Vietnamese to admit that they were holding Spike. They have done so.

Two, they've got to keep him alive until his eventual release.

Three, we're going to do everything we can to get them to improve our guys' living conditions. It they are going to hold the men we love captive, they've got to allow them to live with some semblance of dignity. They must allow our men to write and to receive letters, to have roommates and decent places to live.

In December we laid the groundwork for going to see the North Vietnamese in Paris again. We were pretty down-in-the-mouth about Spike still being in Hanoi this Christmas, so we put off leaving.

We weren't making any headway through the first of the year; just sort of floundering around in January.

Then on January 20, 1970, Mom found another letter from Spike and a Christmas card in the mailbox. God bless the mailman.

Dear Mom, Dad, Gebo, Bob, Pete, Carmen and Virginia. Merry Christmas and Happy New Year. Larry, Carol, Pete Jr. and Jeff, when Uncle Spike gets home we will have a real big party to make up for the 4 Christmases I have missed. I will be thinking of you all at Christmas. Have one for me New Years Eve. Love Spike

NGÀY VIẾT (Dated) _11 December 1969_

GHI CHÚ (N.B.) :

1. Phải viết rõ và chỉ được viết trên những dòng kẻ sẵn (*Write legibly and only on the lines*).

2. Trong thư chỉ được nói về tình hình sức khỏe và tình hình gia đình (*Write only about health and family*).

3. Gia đình gửi đến cũng phải theo đúng mẫu, khuôn khổ và quy định này (*Letters from families should also conform to this proforma*).

FROM: John H Naomyth
Camp of Detention for
U.S Pilots Captured
in The Democratic Republic
of Vietnam

NHA XUẤT BẢN MỸ THUẬT AM NHẠC HANỘI — NHÀ MÁY IN TIẾN BỘ

To: Mr. and Mrs. John H. Naomyth
1238 North Delta Street
South San Gabriel
California, U.SA.
Dear Mom Dad and Family

Merry Christmas and
Happy New Year. Have

One for me New Years Eve

Love Spike

HOA HỒNG
Ánh Dương Tiến

Like the first time, Mom and Dad called everybody. Overjoyed (to put it mildly) we all rushed home and began holding, reading and examining his letters.

It is inconceivable how important these little scraps of paper were to us. We were wild to hear from Spike. Again this letter and card were our inspiration.

Maybe he has finally heard from us, and that's why these letters sound so much happier than the last. His handwriting looked much better.

We'd had an injection of energy. Now we were all pumped up for that trip to Paris!

Mom called me in San Diego on March 3. She said, "Get packed, we leave Wednesday, March 11."

I told her, "It's wet in Paris. You'd better take something besides your Indian moccasins."

Mom said she'd get another pair of shoes.

"When will we be back, Mom?"

"Well," she said, "I figure since we're going all the way to Paris, we might as well keep on going. We're going around the world. Be back in six weeks."

"My God, I'll need more shots."

"You'd better get busy."

"I will."

We were busy, too. Mom was back in the family home. She didn't want to leave the place vacant, so Pete moved in to mind the house. It was good for him. He'd been out of work and out of sorts for three or four months. He moved into the house, watched for the mail, pruned the trees and enrolled in real estate school. And he had a good, stable place to bring Little Pete and Jeff every other weekend when they were visiting him.

Dad was great about the trip. With Mom back in the old homestead, family tensions cooled.

They were utterly divorced, no doubt about that, but when it came to doing something for Spike or having anything to do with Spike, they were together and enormously cooperative. Besides, we felt it was important to present a united front to the press. We didn't want the folks' breakup to interfere with our campaign or our appeal. When it came to Spike, we were still one family.

Going Crazy

The POWs who were captured in my era, 1965 through 1968, all went a little crazy after a while. All of us did loony things. A starvation diet— can you imagine that in a prisoner-of-war camp? Here we were not getting enough to exist on, and A.J. Myers went on a diet. A.J. was always on a diet, worried about his waistline.

Other guys wouldn't speak to each other for months. Or they'd get violent. Some really got pissed off. Take Bob Lilly—instead of hitting his cell mate, Bob slugged a two-brick-thick wall as hard as he could. We heard the crash and figured somebody had been murdered. But no, he broke three knuckles, and no doctor. That's stupid! His hand could have developed gangrene and fallen off. But, Lilly and Dick Bolstad had been cellmates for four years, just the two of them, in an eight-by-twelve-foot cell. Can you imagine that?

Everybody had his own little way of going crazy. The degree of craziness varied from just a little 'wacky' to the real thing.

Three of the toughest prisoners were also three of the craziest. They got into an unspoken competition, didn't make sense to us, but it made sense to them. In other words, you and I are competing but we will never admit we are competing. Their competition? To see who could resist torture the longest.

It started out when the Gooks wanted something from one of them, say, a confession or making the guy get off his bed or bow. First they tortured one man for three days before he would comply. The next guy lasted three and one half days. This went on until they were holding out for weeks at a time. Tough mothers. They went through unbelievable months of torture, resisting. After virtually months of out-enduring one another, Tom Weston actually held out for a full forty days on the stool. It was like a little milking stool. They strapped him to it. Wouldn't let him off, wouldn't let him tip over. He couldn't, or they'd hit him with a gun.

What those three went through because of their unspoken competition cost two of them their lives. The two who didn't make it got so skinny they came down with pneumonia; still they resisted. Then they each regressed to a point where they curled up into balls, like fetuses. That was the end, they didn't make it.

Around the World

Got up this morning at 6 a.m. My cat Petit was so worried last night, he licked me awake at 3 a.m. He spent the whole night on my pillow.

Mom was up and ready to go at seven on the dot.

I would have been on time, but Bob Dietrich of the San Diego *Evening Tribune* called. He took information for a story and I gave him our itinerary. He asked if we had any indications of success. I reminded him that when I went to Paris the first time on August 25, 1969, we had had no word of Spike. Because of that trip and my pleading with Xuan Oanh and our heavy publicity campaign following the trip, we have received four letters from Spike. We think Spike's letters were a direct result of that trip.

Mother and I have talked it over. We will do anything to get Spike out. We have a loan, immediate withdrawal okayed, waiting in the Bank of America. If we can buy Spike out, we've got that money ready and we figure we can scrape it up in three days if we need it. All of Spike's and our friends are willing to pitch in if we need more money.

Pete drove us to the airport; rather, he tore to the airport sure that cars were letting him pass because of our "Hanoi Release John Nasmyth' bumper sticker.

While having coffee in the airport coffee shop, Virginia Nasmyth was paged. (That meant either Mom or me, as we have the same first name.) I answered the phone and got a message to call KABC radio, the Michael Jackson show. While I was taking down the message, another radio station called and I did an on-the-air interview. I responded optimistically. That was the only way to go at this. After KTLA I called Michael Jackson and did a long on-the-air interview with him. He wished us luck. About that time KTTV showed up. The interviewer asked the same questions: Where are you going? Whom do you hope to see? What about the petitions? Are you optimistic? Will you go to Hanoi? What's our government doing?

We arrived in Washington. The plane ride was fine.

March 12, 1970
Washington, D.C.

Up this morning and on the phone making all kinds of arrangements. We left off petitions containing 15,000 signatures with a White House aide. He assured us that President Nixon would see them and that Nixon's press secretary would probably say something about them next Thursday morning at his press conference. He did not.

March 13, 1970

By noon Mom and I were off to the Pentagon to see Colonel Work. Colonel Work's brother-in-law has been missing since November, 1967. His attitude right now is also optimistic. Work told us in a roundabout way that he'd strangle us before he would let us go to Hanoi. He implied that nasty things might happen if we were to end up there. Mom and I are inclined to disagree.

Mom got her last two shots and Colonel Work had her health card stamped. I contacted Senator Alan Cranston's and Senator George Murphy's offices. Senator Cranston is in Los Angeles and his staff showed no interest whatsoever. Senator Murphy's assistant, on the other hand, took down our itinerary and said the Senator would send telegrams to the places we're going and have someone there expecting us. He was true to his word.

Got hold of Frank Sieverts of the State Department again. He gave us a comprehensive list of things to do in each place we visit.

Called Jeb Stuart Magruder's office back and he again assured me that President Nixon would see the petitions.

Called Pete at 9 p.m. He was so excited I could hardly understand him. He says we got good publicity in the Los Angeles *Times*.

Can't wait to get out of Washington and get going. There's nothing else we can do here. We sure could use snapshots of ourselves. We've had dozens of requests for them from the press.

March 15, 1970

I just called Audie Murphy, World War II hero, now a resident of North Hollywood, California. (You'd recognize his voice anywhere.) I told him of our projected trip to Algiers and said that United We Stand, Ross Perot's organization, suggested we seek his advice as to whom we should see in Algiers.

Audie Murphy adamantly warned us not to contact anyone in Algiers, explaining that he has a connection there and that our visit might blow it. He also said, "Stay away from the press. Going to Algiers would be a waste of time." When I mentioned that the Pentagon advised it, he said: "That's because the Pentagon doesn't know what we're doing there. The Algerians don't want to talk to our government officially. The Algerians are so sensitive that they might close up shop if families descend upon them like they have in Paris."

Mr. Murphy will be going to Algiers in three weeks. He said, "I can't promise to get Spike out, but I can get the most up-to-date information on him."

Our talk would have been deflating except that we're used to this kind of reaction.

H. Ross Perot, the Texas computer billionaire, plans to pull off something big in the next month, or at least by summer. Audie Murphy thinks he can get some information through his contacts in three weeks.

(You know, a few months ago a fellow wrote me a note that said, "I can get your brother out if you'll meet me in a coffee shop—alone." I threw that letter away and avoided that coffee shop. I wonder if that guy really thought he could do some good?)

We've listened to Perot because he's a successful businessman. We've listened to Audie Murphy because he's a war hero. We would listen to anyone who was halfway sane.

The Pentagon says it can get the POWs out in the long run via a bunch of complicated dealings. One of the wives in particular wants them to get out through her dealings. The President wants Hanoi on its knees and then the prisoners sent home. Is it possible that all these people's egos are so involved that they only want the prisoners back on their own terms?

What a vicious game! Oh well, if all these people keep trying their own things maybe our POWs will get out one way or another. I'm sure these people are really sincere, but we just feel a little desperate at this point.

If we had taken everybody's advice, we would not have built the first billboard, never written the first letter, never gone on TV, never gone to Paris. Consequently, Spike would still be listed as missing in action, and he wouldn't have received our packages nor communicated with us.

March 15, 1970
New York City

Short flight to New York.

Headed on down to 365 42nd Street. This is a crummy-looking neighborhood, full of dirty pictures, books, peep shows, and on the street—

ladies galore. We were seeking a peace group, whose door was locked, dirty and had a piece of paper stuck on it which said 'Committee of Liaison.' We stood outside writing a note and an old bum told us to ring. A few minutes later a tall, dark, hairy girl answered the doorbell. She showed us up a narrow flight of stairs into a big, partitioned, dirty, messy room with papers strewn everywhere. It looked like a combination whorehouse and hog pen.

We said hello to a greasy, strung-out-looking blonde who ignored us. Then we sat down and talked with the brunette.

Mom told her we had come up to thank them for bringing us a letter from Spike. The girl said she recognized our name from having forwarded his letter.

I asked her if any of her group had plans for a return trip to Hanoi. She said that in a month or so someone planned to go and that person would carry any letters they had on hand to the prisoners. I asked her if we should write one and leave it with them. She and the blonde looked at each other and she said, "No, not just now, it might be lost or misplaced before the trip." I found this a most difficult moment. Here was the 'peace group' I had heard so much about and they were so disorganized that they couldn't hold onto a piece of mail which might prove to be a man's only word from his family in four years. Certainly the letters this group claims to have delivered are the very first communication many of the three and four-year POWs have had from their families. I thought I was going to cry and felt like throwing up.

We asked about the six-line forms. That's one thing the peace group people had. They gave us a half a dozen. This is the new rule imposed upon the prisoner-of-war families by the North Vietnamese. In order to write prisoners of war you must obtain and use their prescribed letter form. I asked if they could check through their connections about Ray Salzarulo, Spike's co-pilot, and a couple other fellows whose families we know personally. She said they only did that on special request of the families. I made a note to write Sandy Salzarulo, Mrs. Fitton and a couple of others to relay this message. I looked over at Mother. Her jaw was set, her mouth made a straight line, and she didn't utter a sound. I said I thought I was going to cry and that we ought to leave.

Walking away down the street we watched the hookers proposition various men, shaking our heads in disbelief at the dirty, disorganized— and uncaring—scene we had just left.

March 17, 1970

Got up, wrote out five telegrams, although I discovered it would be better to send them from Paris. Called ABC and UPI. ABC wants to meet us at 4 p.m. We shall try to make it; however, we must leave for Kennedy Airport by 4:30 p.m. There's a St. Patrick's Day parade on Fifth Avenue, just to complicate things.

Waited till 4:20 p.m. for ABC, as they weren't sure they could make it through the parade traffic, and they didn't.

Hopped in a cab and set off for J.F.K. Airport. Prior to catching our flight, we had an in-depth interview with Mr. Veccio, a UPI reporter.

March 18, 1970
Paris

We landed in an overcast Paris. It's 8 a.m., that's 3 a.m. in the States. Needless to say, we're dead tired. Mom was so excited she couldn't sleep on the six-hour flight over.

Checked into Le Grand Hotel and decided to rest just a minute, but we woke up at 6 in the evening. Still exhausted, we climbed out of our beds, dressed in warm clothes and headed for the Sorbonne. I was very anxious to show Mom the places Rick and I discovered last summer, while we were chasing down Xuan Thuy. I showed Mother the hot dog stand, the crepe place, the Regent Hotel, a shishkabob bar, flower stand and darling little restaurant. We ate in the cozy restaurant.

March 19, 1970

UPI called last night, wanted to know what we had done on the 18th, told us that Thursday was Paris Peace Talk Day and not to bother trying to visit the North Vietnamese as they would be at the meeting. The UPI man also told us about POW wives Mrs. Hanley's and Mrs. Dennison's adventures of the day.

It seems that these women, after days of attempting to meet with the North Vietnamese—with no success—had finally received word that the North Vietnamese consulate had a letter for them. They raced out to the meeting, expecting some word on their husbands—only to receive a note instructing them to inquire about their missing-in-action men through Cora Weiss and the Committee of Liaison, 42nd Street, New York. The ladies had the press with them. They tore up the letter, threw it in the street and demanded an audience with someone of more authority than the French secretary who had delivered the letter. Dennison and Hanley said they would not leave unless they were received, at which point the French police threatened them: leave or be physically ejected. They left.

We haven't told the press about our plans in Paris. We want a crack at the North Vietnamese at Choisy alone, like last time, before we go out to the North Vietnamese Embassy.

Late in the afternoon we met with Colonel Gorman at the American

Embassy, a man deeply and emotionally involved in the POW situation. Colonel Gorman's personal opinion is that POW families should do anything and everything they can or want to do. I agree with him.

As for traveling to Hanoi—Gorman says we should go to Hanoi if we get the chance. Unlike the very careful people we have talked with in the past, Colonel Gorman thinks if we get a toehold we ought not to let go for anything.

We discussed the 'Dove' and 'Hawk' Senator situation. Our consensus: one way to reach the North Vietnamese is to get the 'Dove' Senators to speak out, to make public their feelings about POWs. That's one of the projects we have to work on when we get home: see and get statements out of Senators McCarthy, McGovern and Fulbright. Senator McCarthy had dinner with Xuan Thuy in Paris two months ago, so we hoped he'd take the lead in campaigning for our men—but he didn't.

We asked Colonel Gorman every conceivable question about his knowledge of our POWs, where he gets his information, how they keep records, contact families and so on. In an effort to show good faith, so to speak, Colonel Gorman excused himself from his office to get the 'The Book.' Shortly thereafter he returned with a cumbersome, very secret-looking ledger. As a matter of clarification, the Colonel wanted us to see just what the records said about Spike.

We opened up 'The Book' to the N's and located: Nasmyth, John Heber, Serial Number FR3120117. Date MIA status became effective—September 4, 1966.

(Yes, that corresponds with the information we have.)

Status changed to POW-1967. 1967! We looked again. We had Colonel Gorman look. "Yes." he said. "The government officially changed Spike's status to POW in 1967." We were stunned. "Are you sure?" Colonel Gorman was sure. "Well, why didn't they tell us!? We weren't told about a status change until August, 1969." Colonel Gorman thought it must have been an oversight.

Some oversight! Do you realize what we went through all those years, desperate for news . . . Mom and I were so shocked we let the subject drop right there. Had we had our wits about us we would have looked up Salzarulo, Fitton, Hardy and some of our other missing friends.

I wonder how many other oversights there have been?

That evening we sent off letters to some of our MIA-family friends. We urged them to get a look at 'The Book' in Paris.

March 20, 1970

We were at the American Embassy doors when they opened and escorted right up to see Ambassador Habib. Habib doesn't look like a pushover. First thing, we handed him the January, 1970, issue of the *University of Idaho Alumni Magazine,* (U of I, his alma matter) which featured: Spike, a POW; Donald G. Waltman, father of a five-year POW; and Philip C. Habib, chief negotiator for the POWs at the Paris Peace Talks.

Like Colonel Gorman, Ambassador Habib urged us to do anything and everything for our men. As for the Committee of Liaison peace group bringing out names and letters, his only disappointment was,"They are so disorganized." The Government's position: "We don't care who the hell gets information, the more information, the better."

Mr. Habib explained that over the past three years the Government has been trying quiet tactics. Only for the last six months have things begun to pick up due to 'new tactics.' He would not discuss them with us so as not to put us in a position where we might make public something we should not. (I'm not sure what I think about that.)

As we left, he assured us that Spike would live through it.

We were escorted downstairs to the Embassy Commissary. We were escorted everywhere on the second floor, even to the bathroom. I suppose they didn't want us poking around.

At the Commissary we put together another box for Spike, six chocolate bars, caramels, a bar of soap, and a wash cloth, and then went up the street to purchase vitamin and protein pills for him. We put these things, along with the fungus ointment, hand cream and pictures from home, into a small box, added some citrus-flavored candies until the weight was exactly six pounds, and wrapped it. This took all morning.

It's such an intense and futile feeling putting together these packages for Spike. We want him to get them so badly!

About two o'clock we got back to the room, cleaned up and summoned up our courage for our trip to Choisy. It took all we had to get up the guts to go out to see the North Vietnamese. To top everything off, we took the wrong metro. Finally we got back across town.

On the way we decided that I should go in alone, so Mom walked up the street and had a cup of coffee. I went down to the Ave. General Le Clerc, past the police, up to the compound gate and rang the bell. The same French guard who was there last time (1969) let me inside the guard house and asked why I had come. I gave him a note written in French which gave my name, stated I was a friend of Xuan Oanh, and I had a letter and a box for my brother who is a POW. I said I wanted to talk to Xuan Oanh. Boy, was I surprised at how my French came back when I needed it.

The guard went into one of the buildings and I suppose presented my message to Xuan Oanh. However, Oanh refused to see me. I had in my purse—in case this happened—a formidable-looking stack of newspaper clippings, about thirty of them. The guard told me that I must take the box and the letter to the Vietnamese delegation at 2 Rue LeVerrier. I told him I was here to thank Xuan Oanh and Xuan Thuy for the letter I had received from my brother. When the big boys said they wouldn't see me, the guards at the gate tried to hustle me out. I said, "Un moment," stepped back into the guard house, sat down and started writing a note on the back of our book of clippings. This made the guards terribly nervous. We had previously decided to deal with Xuan Oanh in a most genteel way. While the guards were fluttering about I wrote, "Monsieur Xuan Oanh et Honorable Xuan Thuy, Je desire a dire merci pour la lettre de mon frere. Merci."

At this point it didn't look as French as that so I asked the guards about the spelling of *dire* and how to say "from my brother." They quit fluttering and helped me out.

They really acted anxious when I started to write again. In my schoolgirl French I tried to convey to them that they could get some favorable publicity if they would only cooperate . . . .

They wouldn't let me finish; they were making a terrible racket so, after making them promise to give my message to Xuan Oanh—one guard said he would, the real nervous one said he wouldn't—I put the clippings in the hands of the one who said he would and left.

I met Mom at the coffee shop, told her what had happened. We took the bus and metro back to the hotel and both fell asleep from pure nervous exhaustion, still dressed. We didn't realize until 8 o'clock the next morning that we hadn't had a bite to eat all day.

March 21, 1970

I wrote a letter to President Nixon from our bathtub in Paris this evening.

Dear President Nixon,

I am on a trip around the world, seeking information, relief, and the release of prisoners of war of the North Vietnamese.

We're in Paris now. On this trip the North Vietnamese have acted unduly hostile toward us.

Yesterday I went to Choisy to visit Xuan Oanh. He refused to see me. I left a collection of thirty newspaper clippings about Spike for Xuan Oanh and Xuan Thuy. I will try again Sunday or Monday to see Xuan Oanh.

At Choisy they would not accept a letter I was carrying for Spike, nor a regulation six-pound box containing vitamin and protein pills, fungus ointment, chocolate candy bars and nuts. They told me to see Mai Van Bo at the general delegation headquarters.

Today Mother and I went to see Mai Van Bo. We rang the buzzer. The meanest, nastiest woman I've ever seen, a Vietnamese, answered the door. I said, 'We have a package and a letter for my brother who is a prisoner.' She told us to go away. I asked if there was anyone there that I could talk to. She said, 'Wait.' We waited. She came back and said, 'No,' that everyone had left. She slammed the door.

We rang again several times. She answered the door saying in a very nasty voice that they were closed and that everyone had left. I asked, 'How about tomorrow?' She said, 'No.' 'How about Monday?' 'No, never!'—Slam!

Four French policemen were right there. They were very kind and sympathetic, especially when we showed them the package of medicine and food for Spike. When we left they were saying, 'She only had a box of medicine and food for her brother.'

It's been a pretty lousy few days here.

Mother and I saw Ambassador Habib yesterday. He and Spike are both graduates of the University of Idaho. Mr. Habib outlined his procedure in carrying out the peace talks. Cruel as it sounds, at the peace talks yesterday, the North Vietnamese did not even use the word 'prisoner' when the Ambassador directed questions to Xuan Thuy regarding the prisoners. Xuan Thuy replied, 'In regards to that issue refer to our previous statement.'

In New York on the 16th we ran into another sad situation. We went to 365 W. 42nd St., New York City, to see the Committee of Liaison. Staffed by two kids, the place is a messy dump. While we were there, we asked if they had any plans to send someone to Hanoi in the near future.

A staff member said she thought someone would be going over in six weeks or so and that they would take letters from the prisoners' families. We suggested that we leave a letter with them for Spike. She said, 'No. We would probably lose it.'

It's sad to think that they are so inefficient that they could lose one of our letters—the only word from home a man might ever get. One wonders how many of the prisoners' letters have been misplaced.

I'll let you know what happens in Moscow.

AP and UPI have been very helpful.

Mr. Nixon, we are behind you, no matter what you have to do to get these men home. The North Vietnamese are not a Western culture. They are not responding nor reacting like a Western culture and I think that it's about time we stopped negotiating with them as though they are a Western culture and started treating them like the spoiled children they emulate. When a child is bad, he is disciplined. First you warn him, if he is bad again you spank him. I suggest that we try these tactics. I think the United States would gain more respect if we were to start acting like the big strong nation we are. I find it extremely disheartening that I, a 20-year-old sister of a prisoner of war, and his family have gained more results than our government has in 3½ years. I find subjecting my Mother to these torturous people an impossible situation. To think that we have to travel 40,000 miles, spend $15,000, undergo extreme emotional distress and harassment for one letter from my brother Spike, one ray of hope that he is still alive.

Virginia Nasmyth

March 22, 1970

I spent some time writing in the diary I'm keeping, then Mom and I wrote the POW families who wanted information on Paris. Later we got out the notebook and outlined what I still have to do. I wrote Rick a massive, depressed letter about yesterday's disappointments. I had a nightmare about spiders.

March 23, 1970

Checked with AP and UPI. We arranged to meet both press services, a reporter and cameraman each at 2 Rue LeVerrier. Mom and I took the Vavin Metro, then walked five or six blocks to the embassy headquarters. We arrived at exactly 11 a.m. The reporters took many pictures. We told them that Spike is one of the longest-held prisoners and that informed sources have indicated that he is suffering from malnutrition. We had with us our package of food and medicine and a letter addressed to Spike. I had previously written to Mai Van Bo requesting information on Spike. Friday the people out at Choisy told me to deliver my package and letter to this delegation.

We told the whole story to the reporters: explained to them the runaround we've been getting, pointed out that the North Vietnamese are absolutely not living up to the Geneva Convention, and emphasized that all communication between the prisoners and their families has been cut off.

We then proceeded to try and make contact with the North Vietnamese. After ringing the bell, we didn't get any further than the French secretary at the door. She would not accept the package and threw the letter back at us. After a brief argument she shut the door. We rang again telling her that we had written for an appointment. I slipped the letter in the door. In French she ripped through several reasons why we could not be seen. I missed much of it, but then two of the reporters stepped in and argued with her. She said that the North Vietnamese wouldn't see us because "the other ladies have been incorrect" and that we should understand.

The reporters took a few more pictures of us, defeated, standing in the damp street by a giant closed door, holding medicine for Spike. By now there were a half a dozen policemen gathered around. The reporters left, we walked around the corner and away. I cried.

Seek News of POW

Mrs. Virginia Nasmyth watches as daughter, Virginia, rings bell at North Vietnamese delegation building in Paris.

PARIS, March 23 (AP)—An employe at the North Vietnamese delegation threw a letter back at two American women inquiring about an American prisoner of war today.

The Americans turned away were Mrs. Virginia Nasmyth of San Gabriel, Cal., and her daughter Virginia, 21. Mrs. Nasmyth's son, John, 29, an air force captain, is a prisoner in North Viet Nam.

The women brought a package with them, asking that it be forwarded to Hanoi for Capt. Nasmyth. When the employe would not accept the package, they asked to have a letter forwarded, but the employe threw it back on the street. The Nasmyths plan to fly to Moscow tomorrow to try to see North Vietnamese officials there.

Right around the corner the police had parked a paddy wagon with four more policemen in it. As we walked away a police van pulled up carrying another twenty-five or thirty policemen. Later we were told that the French officials expect some kind of violence as time goes on and the POW families get more desperate.

We went straight back to the metro, made two changes and got off at Choisy. Caught the bus to Choisy Le Roi and walked up Ave. General LeClerc. Mom went to the coffee shop and I went up to the Delegates' Committee gate. The French guard who had let me in twice before and delivered the messages to Xuan Oanh peeked through the peephole and disappeared. Three French security guards opened the door and stood in the passageway as if to block my entrance. This time, besides the letter and package for Spike, I had a letter for Xuan Oanh describing a proposition I wished to put to him. The Frenchman said he had gone back to Vietnam. This was not true. I said, "Okay, deliver it to Xuan Thuy." Still they said, "No."

I made various suggestions, translated the letter for them showing that it was *tres gentille*. But I got nowhere. They had strict orders not to let me in, nor to allow me to communicate with the North Vietnamese in any way. I hassled with them for twenty minutes or so, told them the same things I would have told Xuan Oanh, hoping that one of them was the North Vietnamese PR man. One of the important things I told them was that the North Vietnamese had received much publicity that morning. I told them that if the North Vietnamese would bend some, then I would have good things to tell the press. They said that wasn't important. They asked if I wanted peace in North Vietnam, I said yes, that all Americans wanted peace but that they thought badly of the North Vienamese for their maltreatment of the prisoners. This sent them into a tizzy. They told me that this was not true, that it was American propaganda. I said I hope so, started crying and left them saying, you tell Xuan Thuy to be good to my brother. I walked away crying but regained my composure before reporting to Mother.

We expected this, but found that we weren't really emotionally prepared to be totally shut down. We decided then to report back to Colonel Gorman and let him know firsthand what had happened.

March 24, 1970
Moscow

Emotionally beat, we had an uneventful flight to Warsaw. Nearly missed our flight to Moscow. A man from the hotel picked us up and deposited us at the Hotel Berlin.

March 25, 1970

First thing in the morning we had the lady at the service bureau write out 'American Embassy' in Russian. We walked over to the Hotel Metropol where a Russian fellow hailed a cab for us. It's difficult to determine which are cabs here and which are not.

First off, we went to the American Embassy. We went there for any advice they might have and we needed the addresses of the North Vietnamese Embassy and the Red Crescent Society. The people at the American Embassy are also the only people we can talk to. We met our representative there, a nervous redhead. (I think he'd seen too many spy movies.) He was appalled that we were there alone. He warned us that we were probably being watched, and we got the distinct impression that he wanted nothing at all to do with our goings-on. You might even say that our goings-on terrified him. Anyway, after an hour and a half we got two addresses and a phone number out of him. Then he thought he should at least insure our safety back to the hotel. His only option here was to stick us into an embassy car. When he saw us climb into the big black chauffeured car he shuddered and sneaked back into the confines of his office. I think the embassy people here are overcome with fear of being watched, bugged and sent to Siberia. If it's really that bad here, I'm glad we don't know enough to be scared.

Once back at the hotel, we met with a UPI reporter. This gentleman met us at our room, then drove us to Red Square to take some pictures. (The story appeared in the U.S. papers the next day.)

After the photo session at Red Square we drove across town, through the snow to the Embassy of the Democratic Republic of Vietnam, UL Bolshaya Prigogvski 13.

The reporter waited in the car. The North Vietnamese Embassy was very forbidding in appearance on this cold day. There was frozen snow piled up all around, the trees were bare, and a big Russian guard was posted at the gate. The embassy itself was a big white building, with steps leading up to giant wooden doors, and there was a solitary red star hanging over the entrance.

Mother and I walked up to the front doors and knocked. A North Vietnamese came out of a building on the side of the compound and waved for us to come in. We entered. He spoke French. I introduced Mother and myself, told him that my brother was a POW and that I had a letter for him. I also had a letter addressed to the North Vietnamese Embassy:

Gentlemen of the Embassy of North Vietnam, I humbly request

that you use your influence on your comrades in North Vietnam. I ask that you send John Nasmyth, nearly a four-year prisoner of war, to a neutral country as provided for in the Geneva Convention, so that his family can visit him, tend to his medical needs and take him home.

This is purely a humanitarian appeal. We appeal to your generosity and understanding of brotherly love.

Virginia Nasmyth

The gentleman to whom we were speaking identified himself as 'a person of the embassy.' He received this letter, promising to deliver it to his Vietnamese comrades. He would not take Spike's letter, but he suggested that we mail it from Moscow. We shall. He also said Spike could receive one package every other month and would be able to write us regularly.

Our discussion went on for about an hour. We all sat down at a table in a chilly room. There were always a couple of North Vietnamese men standing around listening; however, they said they didn't speak French or English.

One of the first questions I put to this man was: "Why can't you, the North Vietnamese, separate the prisoner-of-war issue from the war and military matters? I think the prisoners of war are a humanitarian issue."

Our man skirted this question by saying, "The prisoners are treated humanely. Your brother is healthy."

"Do you know my brother?"

He said, "No, but all the prisoners are in good hands."

During the course of the hour, we went over this question three or four times. He answered it the same way each time. He wasn't about to get down to the real issue.

The next thing I brought out was that some people in the United States sympathize with the North Vietnamese, and many haven't decided. "The people in the United States would think better of the North Vietnamese if you were to do something good, like release the prisoners or release John Nasmyth."

This issue we discussed a good many times. To this he very meticuously explained, using my French dictionary and drawings: "The United States has no right in Vietnam, Vietnam didn't enter your civil war, 'Mister Nixon' is responsible to and for your family now."

I said, "But the POW issue is separate from the war, it is a humanitarian issue." He replied, "The prisoners are being treated humanely." To which I said, "Why not have impartial inspection of the camps?" A question which he did not answer, because he was lying.

Next, I explained very carefully that there were many North Vietnamese prisoners in South Vietnam. It would be a very good thing to trade these men for the pilots in the North Vietnamese prison camps. The first time I brought this up he just stared off into space. I let it go for a few minutes but very carefully explained the same thing—restated the prisoner trade proposition—three more times. Each time he avoided the issue by changing the subject. The third time he said he didn't understand, but our communication was good. I said something to the effect of "oh, come on now," he sort of laughed it off and changed the subject anyway.

I didn't even bring up the Geneva Convention, because any mention of it to the Vietnamese in the past has caused belligerence and hostility.

Our discussion went on. I told him how badly I wanted to see Spike and how hard it was on my Mother.

He said, "Nixon is responsible."

"Can I go to Hanoi and see my brother?"

He answered, "No, it's dangerous there."

Right before we left, twice more I explained how good it would be for the Vietnamese if they were to release my brother. We ended up by suggesting that they move Spike and the POWs to a neutral country where we could take care of them. As we were leaving he offered his and Vietnam's condolences to Mother for her suffering.

The trip to Moscow has been a success because we were able to reach the Vietnamese. Part of our mission is to make this issue more human. We want the Vietnamese and the people of the world to stop thinking POWs and start thinking human beings, young men caught up in an untenable situation with suffering families back home, most of whom aren't even sure whether their man is dead or alive. For those of us who know our loved one is alive, we can't help but think of the *waste*. Most of these guys are in their twenties. Our men's suffering is beyond comprehension. But just standing by while they endure a decade of imprisonment—because our government is tangled up in rhetoric—is a terrible thing to live with.

I said our visit to Moscow has been a success. I mean that, because after just such a meeting with Xuan Oanh, the North Vietnamese delegate in Paris in August, 1969, we received confirmation that Spike was alive and a letter from him followed. The North Vietnamese work through complicated channels. We hope that the personal approach may trigger some sort of human reaction from those we are reaching on this trip.

Back in the hotel room, both Mother and I noticed our bags had been gone through. I wondered out loud if we were being bugged, too. It really didn't matter. Our discussion was interrupted by several phone calls from reporters. We gave them the facts about our visit. AP called; I told them that UPI had taken pictures and had done a pretty good story. The AP staff said that they, too, wanted a photograph. I told them that we were on our way out to the Red Crescent Society, the Russian branch of the International Red Cross. AP wanted the picture there, so I suggested that their photographer drive us out, which he did.

The photographer was a Russian named Vassily. We didn't pronounce it well and figured out that his name was Bill in English, so we called him Bill. He thought this was hysterical.

Driving out to the Red Crescent Society we got lost twice. At last we arrived, and Bill took our picture. We went through a French-speaking secretary and were received by an English-speaking member of the Society who handled local affairs. We explained what we wanted to do. In turn, he explained that the gentlemen handling international affairs were out, but that he would be glad to deliver our letter. The letter read:

Gentlemen of the Red Cross and Red Crescent Societies of the U.S.S.R.:

I humbly request that you as a humanitarian organization use your influence and intercede in the prisoner-of-war situation in North Vietnam and grant my brother, John Nasmyth, relief and release. John Nasmyth has been a prisoner since September 4, 1966. We fear that he is suffering greatly from malnutrition.

This is purely a humanitarian appeal. We appeal to your generosity and understanding.

Virginia Nasmyth

Mr. Koustki accepted the letter and we left. We went back to the Hotel Berlin and sat down for our first meal of the day. Mother had chicken kiev and I had beef stroganoff. It was different, served unattractively, but we liked it. The Russian wine was good, and they really know how to fry potatoes.

Mother and I prepare to present our plea to the Moscow branch of the Red Crescent Society.

Took a cold bath (boy, was it cold) and ABC called. A TV crew picked us up and our morning was spent shooting a story in a local snowy park. At eleven o'clock, Mother and I started looking for a place from which to mail Spike's package, the package we had put together in Paris.

First we went to the huge post office at the Hotel Metropol. After thirty minutes of gawking at the package, the clerk there wrote down the name of the proper post office in Russian. Only one post office in Moscow handles parcels going out of the country. We caught a cab, drove for twenty minutes across town, and were deposited at the International Post Office. For an hour we sat in a small waiting room with half a dozen scared-looking old people. We were waiting for the chief mail inspector, but our time was running short. The mail inspector arrived, and via sign language he directed us down the street to the main inspection station. We had been waiting in the 'inspection of incoming parcels' section!

In this large, busy building dozens of people were filling out forms, unwrapping their packages, re-wrapping them and waiting in long lines. The clerks didn't know what to do with us. Finally, I found an inspector who spoke French. After explaining that we wanted to send a package to a man in prison camp in North Vietnam, she called another inspector, translating our message into Russian. He didn't know what to do, either. He said that this had never happened before. He got out two big rule books, then went upstairs to his superior to decide what to do. Twice we called him down through the French-speaking inspector, telling him that our plane was about to leave.

While I worked on the package, Mom worked on mailing Spike's letter. Mom asked the clerk to mail the letter, and the girl looked at it and insisted that it be sent registered mail, 'to be sure it would be delivered.' "Besides," she said, "if it gets lost we can trace it."

Still waiting for the inspector, we decided that sending a package to Spike from Moscow was more important than catching our plane. Of course, we didn't know what would happen if we missed it, but we stuck it out with the post office inspector until finally he produced the right forms and started inspecting our package. He opened the package and checked everything, he even opened the sealed can of nuts and inspected each nut. He rewrapped the package, then we paid ten dollars postage, filled out five forms in triplicate, and ran out of the building.

There was a cab out in front. We hopped in, said "Hotel Berlin," and zoomed our hands around like airplanes. He got the message and the normally twenty-minute drive back to the hotel took only five minutes.

We were quite late. The Russian taxi assigned to make sure we caught our plane was waiting. We grabbed our bags and set off for the airport. That was another twenty-minute drive, and flight time was in twenty minutes. Everything went swimmingly until we ran out of gas.

Upon arriving at the airport, each with one little bag in hand, they waved us through inspection and put us on the airplane. I'd say we had about a minute to spare. God knows what they do to rabble-rousers when they miss their plane in Russia.

We flew on to Paris, waited there for two hours and boarded a terrible little Air Moroc plane for Casablanca.

March 27, 1970
Casablanca

Arrived at the Casablanca airport at 2 a.m. Exhausted, we hailed a cab and were deposited at the El Mansour Hotel.

We woke up at 1 p.m., went down to the restaurant and ate couscous for lunch. Then we walked around Casablanca and did a little shopping. We had a very leisurely day. I'm glad we decided to put a few places on our itinerary which were just for fun. The strain of running around Moscow was tremendous.

For the next three days Mother and I slept and then took the train from Casablanca to Marrakesh.

While we were Morocco my sister, Gebo, and her husband, Dr. Martin Berger, were visiting North Vietnamese embassies in Prague, Budapest and Moscow. They had gone on a medical convention, but Gebo pursued her mission with the same sense of urgency as Mother and I had. Marty and Gebo arranged an hour's audience with Kim Lan, second secretary at the North Vietnamese Embassy in Moscow. Gebo reported that he was sympathetic, said he would try to get a letter and some pictures to Spike, and try to find out what became of Spike's co-pilot, Ray Salzarulo. Lan said that although there would be no mass release of prisoners until U.S. troops are withdrawn, there will be small releases from time to time and surely one more this year. Gebo and Marty told him that since Spike was one of the first captured and had been there for over four years, he should be among those released. They got nationwide news coverage from AP and UPI.

The American Embassy tracked them down in Leningrad the following day, excited about inquiries they had received from POW families who had read about their talk with Kim Lan. When they got home they learned from the Shivelys, another POW family, that a group of families on the West Coast had sent copies of newspaper articles to Kim Lan, saying they hoped that what he said was true.

At the North Vietnamese Embassy in Budapest, they were flatly refused an audience; however, a cooperative secretary there helped verify a rumor they had heard from a Bulgarian journalist. At a bar in Kiev, the journalist had vividly described a movie on POWs. They finally learned that the movie *Pilots in Pajamas* was East German, had been shown two years ago on television in the Communist countries, included ten Americans (but not Spike) and had been shown to their families in the United States. Marty and Gebo bought a book with pictures of the men and the complete text of the movie from the East Germans.

In Prague the North Vietnamese informed them that they were much too busy to talk to them, that they should have made an appointment two weeks in advance.

March 31, 1970

We got up at five, added three new bundles to our original two pieces of hand luggage, and headed for the airport. We gave ourselves two hours and were glad of it. Boarding a plane at a Moroccan airport is quite a struggle. The plane flew directly to Algiers. We spent the night at the Hotel Saint George, mapped out plans for the next day and I wrote to Rick, another detailed letter which he in turn turned over to the press.

Dear Rick,
    Since our talks with the North Vietnamese and seeing the people we've seen, I'm not sure any more what our best tool is, as far as the North Vietnamese are concerned. Unfortunately I think it may finally be up to the U.S. Government to get tough. Talking to the North Vietnamese is like talking to a belligerent spoiled child. They've got their backs up to a wall. This stuff we've read and heard about them not understanding the value we place on our men's lives is poppycock. I am convinced that the North Vietnamese are simply enjoying this sadistic power they hold over the Americans. They want this country to crawl, and we're doing it; sadly, it's turned out to be a more disgusting situation the deeper we delve. The more I think about it the more real and horrible it becomes. It's too much to ask, our family has had to go through too much, just to be half-way assured that one package *might* get delivered to Spike. Spike was a dead man for three years. Then our family bared our hearts and went out and campaigned for him. Now we fear that when our energies or resources run out, communications with Spike may stop. This situation is too much to bear.
    Perhaps some families and wives aren't this strong. It's wrong that our government has abandoned these men. Our men have been held prisoner in North Vietnam longer than anyone in a modern war.

Our government should be and is responsible for these men. The U.S. sent them into this war. They ought to bring them home.

Our family is one example of a tool sadistically battered by a world power, the U.S., and a would-be world power, North Vietnam. This situation is utterly disgusting and I am sick of it. I am so terribly disillusioned with and ashamed of our government.

In evaluating the whole situation and really taking things for what they are worth, I see that I am only a twenty-year-old student and Mother is just a housewife. How much can this twosome really accomplish in world affairs? Isn't it ridiculous to think of the two of us traveling around the world negotiating for the life of my Mother's son? It's not the principle of the thing, it's the lack of government principle that got America into this ungodly mess.

Only for one year (as of next month) has the U.S. Government been actively appearing to move on the POW issue. You know all this hush-hush negotiating that has been going on. The U.S. isn't really negotiating for the men, we're asking for a list of names of prisoners.

Can you picture this—the United States of America asking a tiny little country like North Vietnam for a list of 1,600 missing men, men who have been in prison for as long as six and one half years and it took a bunch of wives and children, mothers and fathers, brothers and sisters, to stir this government up enough to bother asking for their names.

Virginia

April 1, 1970

We got up early, had coffee and then went downtown to the Swiss Embassy. A gentleman there directed us to the American section back up on the hill. There we met with Mr. Galante, a very efficient man. He immediately arranged for a more convenient hotel, located in the heart of downtown Algiers. We got the address of the North Vietnamese Embassy in Algiers and the Red Crescent Society. Mr. Galante suggested that he arrange a meeting between Mother, myself and a representative of the Algerian Ministry of Foreign Affairs. We agreed. He arranged for a car to move us from the St. George to the Hotel Suisse. This we accomplished by 1 p.m., and about 2:30 p.m. we set out by cab for the North Vietnamese Embassy unannounced. At the embassy we were very courteously received; however, the gentlemen we wished to see were not there. We arranged to phone ahead tomorrow morning and meet with the North Vietnamese Ambassador at that time. From there we went to the Red Crescent Society to meet with Dr. Balhouane, the president. He

-154-

was on his way out, so we set up an appointment for tomorrow afternoon at three. We took a long walk up and down the fascinating streets around our hotel, bought some pastries to eat and went to bed.

April 2, 1970

At ten o'clock sharp, we were at the iron-grilled gate of the North Vietnamese Embassy. They were expecting us. To our surprise a North Vietnamese walked down the embassy steps, greeted us with a smile and cordially invited us in. We were greeted by two North Vietnamese Ambassadors, who asked us to sit down in a comfortable lounge area. They served us Arab coffee and laughed about the amount of sugar one of them used, seven lumps.

We explained our situation: "Spike has been a prisoner of war for four years."

The North Vietnamese on my right corrected me, "Not prisoner of war, captive of war." He also said, "It is not a war, as WAR has not been declared."

I suggested the North Vietnamese send Spike to a neutral country. We were told, "The POWs will not be repatriated while the end of the war is only partially settled. The POWs will be repatriated when Nixon declares that all U.S. troops will be withdrawn." (He's talking about sending them home!)

"You should send letters and packages to your brother."

Many times they said we should send medicine. We went over and over the idea of sending Spike to a neutral country, as Americans are bigger than Vietnamese and cannot subsist on the average Vietnamese diet. The Vietnamese across from me said, "We know Americans need more food and we take that into account."

They didn't even react to the idea of trading POWs.

During the course of our conversation for over an hour, they offered us chocolate, coffee, and English cigarettes. While we were there they were courteous and acted understanding. I used my little French dictionary. We had some vocabulary problems, so one of the North Vietnamese brought out his huge Webster's type dictionary.

Through me, together they told Mom, "We understand your suffering, we are sorry, and the North Vietnamese are sorry."

Both men reacted strongly when I told them that I cried every day and that seeing my brother and knowing that he is well would be terribly important to me.

"I would like to go to Hanoi and see my brother."

They said, "Not now."

Many times I suggested that they send the prisoners to a neutral country, and many times I told them that Americans would think better of the North Vietnamese if they sent the prisoners home, that the war would stop sooner.

The head ambassador's comment was, "Nixon is responsible for the war, Spike, your Mother, and you."

We walked away from the North Vietnamese Embassy feeling sure that Spike will come home someday.

They had been very definite when they promised that no matter what, Spike will be sent home eventually. They will certainly have to keep him alive if they are planning on sending him home.

Walking down the hill towards Algiers, Mother and I agreed that the personal approach is making progress. Inch by inch they are bending. The North Vietnamese no longer refer to the POWs as war criminals as they have in the past. And they are talking about their eventual release.

We hailed a cabbie who let us off at the Red Crescent Society for our 3 p.m. appointment with the President, Dr. Balhouane. A tall, distinguished looking man, he was waiting for us with his interpreter. First off, the interpreter read our prepared letter:

Dear Dr. Mouloud Balhouane:

I humbly request that your use your influence as the president of a universally known humanitarian organization to appeal to the North Vietnamese for relief and release of my son, John Nasmyth, nearly a four-year prisoner of war.

My daughter and I have traveled to Algiers to personally contact the North Vietnamese and to ask your organization to intervene in the prisoner-of-war situation. We ask that you advise the North Vietnamese to move my son—and his fellow prisoners of war—to a neutral country where we can tend to his medical needs as well as his mental health needs.

Please help us.

Mrs. Virginia Nasmyth

After our brief meeting yesterday, Dr. Balhouane said he had already started looking into the matter.

The interpreter explained to us how tomorrow morning at 10 a.m. Dr. Balhouane will meet with the Algerian Foreign Ministry regarding Spike. The Algerian Minister who heads communication with North Vietnam will be there. Then in the afternoon he is meeting with the President of Algeria.

Dr. Balhouane says he has been anxious to do something for our POWs, that he has only been waiting to be asked. He told us he will do all he can to help us get Spike sent home. The Algerian Red Crescent Society and the President of Algeria will appeal for Spike to the North Vietnamese.

Mother and I could hardly breathe. Algeria is very friendly with North Vietnam. The North Vietnamese might just grant this favor to Algeria. Dr. Balhouane will also try to send a Red Crescent representative to visit Spike.

In concluding our meeting, Dr. Balhouane had us write a letter to Spike which he will attempt to deliver. He asked us to arrange to stay over in Algiers an extra few days, just in case. Then he sent us off into the streets of Algiers to prepare a box of food and medicine for Spike.

My God, somebody is doing something for us. I was jubilant, even giddy as we went from shop to shop, from pharmacy to food vendor, preparing what might be the last box of food and medicine destined for Spike.

Our box was exactly six pounds. After delivering it to the Red Crescent Society, we walked around the steep streets of Algiers and talked about Dr. Balhouane. God, this time I really believe something's going to happen.

We stayed over in Algiers the extra day. Hardly got any sleep last night. Split my shin on the bed. Got up at the crack of dawn. Waited around very excitedly until the appointed time when we left to see Dr. Balhouane. When we arrived at his office, Dr. Balhouane was unavailable. His assistant simply told us that he was sorry but, "Nothing came of it."

"Nothing came of it? You've got to be kidding!" Disappointed, hell, I'm crushed. Just like all the times before, "nothing came of it."

It has been a very depressing morning, plus I feel terribly foolish getting my hopes up like that. I guess I let my guard down. I sure did, but Mom wasn't shook; quite pissed but not upset.

Mom hadn't been as talkative about Dr. Balhouane as I had been. In fact she'd been a little quiet.

I asked her about it ten whole years later. Mom said she knew the Doctor and his staff were a bunch of lying bastards, they were hanging us out on the line to dry. She did not believe that old lying Red Crescent guy, because Balhouane had never once looked her in the face. When he asked us to change our itinerary by a few days Mom said to herself, "Okay, we'll change it by one day." After one day she was really going to be mad at Dr. Balhouane if he was still screwing around.

I asked Mom, "Why, if you had those vibes and felt that way, didn't you tell me?"

Mom said, "Virginia, I knew you'd get the picture. If I had sprung it on you any sooner, if we hadn't spent the extra day, you might always have had doubts in the back of your mind about what we should have done."

She was right, of course, but I had bitten hook-line-and-sinker and I was bitterly disappointed.

We were supposed to see Mr. Galante at the American Embassy at 10 a.m. An English news reporter interrupted the rest of our morning, so we arrived just before noon. His secretary had gone home and he was lost without her. We had a few problems for Mr. Galante.

Yesterday afternoon Mother and I had spent all of our Algerian money gathering items for Spike's package. All of it. We have eighty cents left, and the money-changers are closed on the weekend. It takes six dollars to get your visa, which we can't pick up because we have no money. There was a mixup. Our cab waited outside the embassy for thirty minutes, then the cabbie demanded nine dollars cab fare. The Egyptian Embassy closed at noon and they had our papers. Mr. Galante's man had a driver pick up our visas, Mom paid him with a check and another embassy driver took us to a place that would change money on the weekend.

We had forty-five minutes to get to the airport.

The Hotel Saint George had sent a telegram from Rick back to the main post office. Our driver took us downtown to get it.

The Hotel Suisse couldn't figure out our bill. Mom waited for the bill while I hailed a cab, loaded it with our four suitcases and one bundle.

Halfway to the airport the cab broke down. We managed ten miles per hour to the airport, arriving late.

In the hustle of getting our tickets validated, a Tunisian man butted in line, I called him a jerk, but he spoke English and got mad and caused a scene.

Then, a slow customs agent didn't believe that I travel with only $100.00 and didn't change any money in Algiers.

But they held the plane for us.

I forgot to take the hand luggage through customs. Disgusted, the customs agent sent us through anyway.

The money changer was out to lunch. We had to smuggle a little money out of Algeria. Finally we made it.

Algiers to Tunis: they fed us tons of sweets.

Tunis to Tripoli: they fed us lunch.

Tripoli to Cairo: they fed us dinner.
We're tired and glad we made it, which we almost didn't.

April 6, 1970
Cairo

We rested in Cairo, pretty depressed over that Algerian mess.
Unfortunately, I tasted Egypt Airlines special jellied tongue sandwich.
Dysentery has begun.

April 8, 1970
Beirut

All I remember about Beirut, Lebanon, is dysentery. However, while
at the Hotel Phoenicia we received a letter from Rick with an enclosure
from Governor Reagan's office. My appointment with the Governor had
been confirmed for late in March. Rick phoned the Governor's appointment desk and asked them to postpone it a month or so. When Mother
and I get home, we will see the Governor and give him the personal side
of the prisoner-of-war issue. It is time to get the State of California moving.

April 10, 1970
Tehran

We arrived in Tehran, Iran, at midnight. An American Embassy couple, the Wilsons, met us at the airport. Mr. Wilson brought a telegram
from the American Embassy in Phnom Penh, Cambodia. We have been
advised not to go on to Phnom Penh because of the war situation there.
They have nothing definite to say about Vientiane, Laos; however, I don't
imagine the State Department will want us stomping around there either.
We're staying at the Semiramis Hotel. Both Mother and I find ourselves
totally exhausted. I'm sick.

April 11, 1970

We had an early morning appointment with Colonel Wilson at the
American Embassy. There we met with several gentlemen and talked
about the POWs for an hour. Then we went over to the Iranian Senate
Chambers. Here we met with His Excellency, Vice President and Executive Director of the Red Lion and Sun of North Africa (their Red Cross
counterpart). We talked to His Excellency for about half an hour. He was
sympathetic, interested and rather uninformed. The meeting proved to
be fruitless.

After our meeting with His Excellency, we proceded to the Foreign
Ministry, where we talked to Mr. Tehrani. Mr. Tehrani was as warm and
sincere as he could be. The Iranian government will approach the Red
Lion and Sun urging them to take up the humanitarian issue of the
American prisoners of war. Mr. Tehrani took us out to lunch, where we
talked for four more hours.

We returned to the hotel at 6 p.m. and held a press conference with representatives from AP, UPI and several local papers.

Picked up a letter from Pete. He says that some 'Peace' group has notified him that a letter from Spike is on its way! We are wild to go home.

April 13, 1970
New Delhi

Arrived here at 2 a.m. Slept. At two this afternoon, we met with the U.S. Ambassador's second man, as the Ambassador was away. After hearing his views on the situation, we went on to meet with the Indian Foreign Ministry. We met with a very unimpressive man. He skirted the issue and kept saying, "You can understand our position." It seems the Indians feel that one day Hanoi will rule and at this time they don't want to do anything that might irritate Hanoi. It looks like North Vietnam is becoming a buffer between India and China. It's all politics and understandable, but still very frustrating.

After our meeting, Mom and I went shopping and enjoyed it. I received a letter today here in India, of all places, from a missing-in-action man's wife. After four and a half years she has received a letter from her husband. That's one happy lady. It was sure good to read her note.

April 14, 1970

My God, Rick called this morning. First the phone in the room woke us up, and the operator said it was a call from San Diego, California. I got on the phone and said, "Hello, hello . . ." The connection was bad so I had to shout. I could hear Rick shouting, "Hello, honey," on the other end, but he couldn't hear me. Finally the operator had me go downstairs to the main desk. I went flying down to the hotel switchboard in my nightgown. It was great hearing him, but everything I said the operator in Sidney had to repeat to Rick. He couldn't have found me any further away; I'm halfway around the world. For forty dollars I got to hear him say he missed me and he got to hear an operator say that I said I loved him. It was really crazy.

This afternoon we met with the Red Cross of India. We presented them with a letter requesting that, as a humanitarian organization, they become involved in the prisoner-of-war situation. The Indians haven't been terribly interested in becoming involved.

We drove out to the North Vietnamese Embassy here in New Delhi. A North Vietnamese male secretary met us in the outer office. We presented him with a letter explaining why we had come and asked to meet with the Ambassador. He motioned for us to wait, walked through an open door into the inner office where we could see the man with whom we wished to speak, sitting behind his desk. The male secretary returned after a brief conversation with his superior, leaving our letter behind, and told us that no one was there. We looked through the door at the official behind his desk (who wasn't supposed to be there) and left.

April 15, 1970
Thailand

Flying into Thailand, we looked out over the same terrain Spike must have flown over. Steep, angular mountains, a deep dark green—very wild, and very angry-looking.

Mom and I were both quiet, looking out at the ridges, fingers of them reaching northward. We were sharing quite a feeling of closeness to Spike, but quite a helpless feeling, too.

On our stopover in Thailand, we contacted the Thai Red Cross. We were exhausted. The heat in India and here in Thailand has almost done Mother in, and I fear I shall never get over that Egyptian sandwich.

After spending a couple of days in Thailand, which we would have enjoyed if we hadn't felt so lousy, we flew on to Hong Kong, where we had no appointments. Then on to Honolulu. We basked in the sun for a couple of days in Waikiki, then caught the last leg of our flight to Los Angeles. In flight, Mother and I got down to seriously discussing what we should do when we get home and what to do when we meet with Governor Reagan. We also noticed that I have an incredibly bad burn from the Hawaiian sun.

Arriving at the airport was different that I had envisioned. Pete and Rick were waiting for us with open arms and terrific grins. I flew into Rick's arms and then felt the terrible pain of my sunburn. There was so much to tell them, but first we were all just glad to be together. Pete looked good. He'd been busy holding down the campaign at home while we were gone. He looked more like his old self.

Mother and I were physically and emotionally worn out. I don't think I've recovered from having our hopes dashed by Dr. Balhouane in North Africa.

Throughout the trip I had imagined our homecoming press conference, another good chance to sum it up, get in some licks. We just didn't have the strength, though.

APRIL, 1970

American troops crossed the border into Cambodia.

A total of 115,000 troops have been withdrawn by President Nixon, and he announced plans to withdraw another 150,000 over the next 12 months. President Nixon's plan for Vietnamization of the war has begun to be implemented.

Crazy George

George McSwain is belligerent, an asshole, a prick, but kind of an alright guy, as long as you are a pilot. Dick Ratzlaff is not a pilot. He is what they call an RIO, which means Radar Intercept Officer. He was a back-seater in a Navy F-4. That means his job was to look at the radar scope and tell the pilot what he sees. His pilot was rescued, but Ratzlaff came within three seconds of being rescued. He was on the beach; his pilot was a hundred yards out in the water. The helicopter picked up the pilot and hauled ass. But they couldn't get Dick, the Gooks had him.

George McSwain is a pilot. He drove an A-4, a little tiny fighter, a one-man plane. And George McSwain does not believe that navigators or RIO's have any brains. Art Cormier and Art Black are both sergeants, paramedics, Bill Robinson is a helicoptor crew chief. Dick Ratzlaff outranks George McSwain, but Ratzlaff is not a pilot and George McSwain will not listen to anything that has to do with rank from anyone other than a pilot.

The day I walked into this cell to join them, they were all fit to be tied, I could feel the tension in the air. I shook hands with George and Dick, Art Cormier and Art Black, and Robbie. We decided to call Art Cormier by his middle name, John, so we'd have only one Art in the cell.

It was obvious after I'd been there for about two minutes what all the tension was about. The Gooks give everybody a light for their smokes at night, and here are four men huddled around the only tiny window in the room, smoking. George is standing at the other end of the room; he does not smoke. Here are four guys smoking around a tiny window because this asshole says, "Smoke around me, I'll kill ya." I walked over, sat down on my goddamn bed, lit up my butt.

George and I came to an immediate understanding. I'm the high-ranking man in the room now. I outrank George and I am a pilot. I think pulling rank in a prison situation is a crock of shit, but it boiled down to this. I didn't say anything in front of the sergeants.

George is very much a military man. After my smoke I went down to the end of the cell and said, "George, this is obviously what has happened. You are terrorizing these guys. You have completely destroyed Ratzlaff's credibility as the high-ranking man in the cell, regardless whether he's a navigator or not." I looked him right in the eye. "Look, asshole, I'm the ranking man and this is the way it is. And if you don't like it I'm going to beat the shit out of you right now."

Now, I probably couldn't have; he's a husky bastard. That occurred to me, so I went on. "You know something? I've got four people in this room who are going to help me. I hope I don't have to call on them, because we'll bust your fucking head. If we understand each other, we'll get along fine. If we don't, that's what we're gonna do. And we'll do it right now if we've got to."

We had an understanding. From that time on, we all got along great. The tension broke, it really took the load off. After we got that straightened out, when someone did dumb things—and believe me we all did dumb things—I'd say something about it, like, "Why not move the shit bucket to a place in the cell where it doesn't really smell up the whole cell? There's a place you can put it where it doesn't stink up everybody, especially if you've got bad diarrhea."

Can you visualize this? If you're pissed off at somebody and you've got diarrhea and it really stinks, shit in the wrong place and you'll get them all, but, shit at the other end of the cell and only one guy has to move, it won't be so bad, the stink will go out the window.

Every now and then a man developed an annoying little mannerism: say, walking the wrong way. Here are three guys walking clockwise around the race track—the space where we walked and jogged hour after hour—and the other one goes counter-clockwise. Or he might stand right in the middle of the floor looking out the window, cutting down space for the guys who are walking by two whole steps. Petty? Maybe, but infuriating. In another case, I might be teaching Art Black the Spanish I know when another man starts telling a story close up and loud . . . get the picture? Six men can fuck up each others' heads easy. The only thing easier is two men messing up each others' heads.

Everybody's crazy after they've been in jail for a while. How menial a task, solving the problem among McSwain and the four others. But how big that was in our lives! One little incident, smoking by the window, it was really nothing, no big deal, but they wanted to kill the bastard and the miserable bastard was too big to kill.

It wasn't long before the six of us became friends, sort of. We all started studying. I knew Spanish and all those dictionary words from A.J. Myers. Art Black retained some Spanish from college. We stole a pencil, and we fixed a brick with a hole in it, a place for our notes. We wrote Spanish dictionaries, English dictionaries, and 'Ratz' wrote poems. After a little education, we spent hours conversing in our very own brand of Spanish.

Everyone turned out to have incredible stories from their 'shoot downs' and their pasts to tell.

Ratz' 'almost' rescue was a spine-tingler. He told it over and over. Art's 'first piece' disaster story kept us howling for hours.

John had spent two years locked up with Fred Cherry and John Pitchford, two of the world's all-time liars; he knew a million of their tales.

Robbie came from some town in South Carolina, and his stories sounded like 'Tobacco Road.' Every idiot and weirdo in the South is related to him. I can't believe one family could have that many strange people in it.

Even Crazy George joined in. He turned out to know a hell of a lot about mechanical things. With our stolen pencil, he drew a beautiful diagram of a V-8 engine. George also came up with some really funny stories on himself. When he was in college he didn't get much action, but telling the yarns we could all see that some girls had thrown themselves at him. He was too dense to get the picture. George would finish the story where he'd almost been raped, then had blown it. He'd hit himself in the head: "Christ, I must have been blind, that broad was trying to get into my pants."

We did all kinds of 'clever' things: for instance, we had an arm-wrestling contest. George McSwain is built like a bear, a bear with hate in his eyes. Art Black, one of the para-rescue guys, is in great shape too, built like a wedge. Dick Ratzlaff is put together like a coil of wire. Robbie, John and I aren't too much of a threat.

This arm-wrestling contest had been going on for a couple days. Serious business. They wrestle for blood. About seven o'clock, just before dark, Art Black and McSwain were going at it. And I mean they were really into it. McSwain's almost got him. God, they're straining, grunting like a couple of sows, the sweat's pouring off them. Out of nowhere we hear this piercing blast, "KA BLAM!!!" Sounds like a gun shot. "Holy Shit!" George McSwain's arm had snapped. It just flopped, all distorted, and he turned white. Cormier and Black, the medics, grab him and start pulling and twisting on his arm. We all start yelling for the guard. Sunday night there's nobody around, George looks terrible, and we're all yelling. Finally a guard comes in, takes a look and leaves. McSwain is turning grey, his arm is already swelling up, turning purple. Cormier and Black have their feet on his body holding him down pulling his arm straight out. The twisting action when it had snapped had turned the bone clear around. They held him all night. The next day the Gooks looked him over again. They decided to take him off to a hospital. George was really lucky it happened late in the war, when treatment was better. They operated on him, cut him open, put his bone back together and put a stainless steel screw through it. Three years earlier, the Gooks would have said, "Tough."

The Gooks got so mad at George McSwain for breaking his arm they moved him out of the cell. He never came back. They put him in solitary next to us. He took his own cast off when he thought his arm had healed. He hated them. Nobody has ever hated the Gooks worse than Crazy George McSwain.

We had a reason for calling George McSwain 'Crazy George.' Every man had his own method of not doing what the Gooks wanted. Paul Kari went blind, others resisted to the point where every time they did anything the Gooks had to hurt them so bad the Gooks knew that whatever they did was because of torture.

Some guys went 'crazy.' George McSwain went crazy. Unfortunately for George, he picked the wrong time to go crazy. He was living with Tom Browning and Bob Wideman. He briefed them one morning. "Look, I'm gonna go nuts and get these fucking Gooks off my back. Just pretend I'm a crazy man. You guys play along and they won't ask me to do anything, confessions, that kind of bullshit."

So, McSwain goes crazy: he curls up in a ball in his cell, won't eat, won't wash, won't do anything. Tom and Bob go along with it. The guards ask what's going on? "Shit, we don't know, the crazy bastard just flipped his cookies." They're playing the game. They're giving McSwain some of their food; he's not eating any of his own. When the Gooks are watching he really plays the role well, lies underneath his bed doing loony stuff. George had them convinced, some of the Americans too.

Unfortunately for George, Dramesi and Atterberry made their short-lived escape attempt. The Gooks went nuts. They tortured a bunch of guys. Then somebody they tortured said McSwain was faking it. Poor George didn't know he'd been found out. A bunch of guards were sent for George. They hung him up over a pole like a tiger, tying his hands and feet over the pole. Then they hauled him out to the torture room and whipped him, kind of like they whipped Colbiel until he died. If George had really been crazy, they'd have killed him.

The Gooks were terrified by McSwain. Any time they ever did anything to George, they had to take him almost to the end before he'd give in. The Gooks respected his ass, because when they tortured him they really had to do a number on him before he'd cry uncle.

They whipped his ass till it was bloody and raw like a piece of hamburger. I'm not sure he ever admitted that he wasn't crazy, but at least he came around and pretended he was coherent.

He really hated Gooks after that go-around, more than before, if that's possible. When he broke his arm he blamed it on the Gooks, 'Fucking Gooks,' for not giving him enough calcium.

Anytime a Gook came into the cell, George had a 'fuck you' look on his face. The man can say 'fuck you' with his eyes perfectly. Even the Gooks who don't speak English understand it. They hate him. They used to beat the piss out of George before they had the hands-off orders. When they got the hands-off orders, they had to go ask the boss if they could beat the piss out of him. The boss usually said "Okay," so they'd come back and beat the piss out of him. He'd look them right in the eye, 'Fuck you,' every time they hit him.

George hated them from the day he got here until the day we left. He had interesting discussions with some of the Gook officers. The Rabbit used to come in and say, "What is your fondest wish?" Everybody would say, "Oh, the war will be over and we'll go home." The Rabbit nodded, "Very good." Then he'd ask George, "And what is your fondest wish?" George said, "I would be flying my airplane over Hanoi with a nuclear bomb." The Rabbit recoiled, "Return to your cell, you foolish criminal." They understood him perfectly, they always hated him.

They hated some other guys, George McKnight, Orson Swindle, Rod Knutson, Fred Flom and Wes Schierman, to mention a few, all masters of 'that look.'

I don't know why, but I missed George. He was and still is a belligerent S.O.B., but if I named the five POWs that I consider true friends he would be on the list. Two and one half years later, just prior to our release, George shocked me with, "Spike, you're one of the two people in the world I consider a friend."

I was flattered.

The Championships

A few days after George left, a new cell mate walked in, Mike Brazelton. Mike was captured the summer of '66, about a month before me. He was a science fiction nut with an incredible memory. We spent hundreds of hours listening to his version of *War of the Worlds*, *The Day Worlds Collide* and on and on and on.

With the arm-wrestling contest over, we had to come up with something else to do. They have been feeding us a decent amount of food for about a year now. We set up a physical fitness contest with the guys next door: Tom Browning, Harry Monlux, Dave Carey (all-American wrestler from the Naval Academy), Bill Bailey, Reed McCleary, and John Borling. Championships were at stake for the most pushups and the most situps. There would be a cell block champ, but more important would be the winning cell block in each event. The cell whose men averaged the most pushups would get the others' cigarette ration for one day, same for situps.

This is war!

We gave ourselves a month to prepare, then there was contest week. We had a whole week to send in our scores, because you couldn't do sit-ups if you had diarrhea that day, you'd shit all over the bed, and you had diarrhea two or three times a week. A lot of things you wouldn't ordinarily take into consideration when you're thinking of a Mr. America contest; or maybe that day your wisdom tooth is inflamed, and you're spitting pus. Another guy gets ready to do situps and he shits a quart.

Mike Brazelton started doing situps one morning during contest week. By the time he reached three thousand, his ass was bleeding profusely, I mean it was squirting out. We made him stop. The bone in the bottom of his ass came through his hide. He had to quit. A couple of days later the other cell's scores came back. He didn't win. Reed McCleary bettered him by 800.

Tom Browning, their champion pushup man sent down his score, he did 101. A day later I did 102. It was great to win by one. Of course, weighing in at 110 pounds, you know, that's not much to push up.

Sacramento

Those first few days back home after our trip, we sat around the kitchen sharing opinions about what we had done and whom we'd seen. We talked about what to do next and looked over the stacks of press clippings Pete and Rick had saved. The newspapers really followed us around the world. Our best coverage came from the confrontation we had with the North Vietnamese in Paris over mailing Spike the box of medicine and letter. The Moscow story was good, too.

More exciting than the clippings were Rick and Pete's stories of the television coverage. The story NBC News took in Red Square, Moscow, got a lot of attention here. It's not easy to get national news coverage when you are abroad.

I wish we had the energy and organization to keep somebody in Paris all the time. Not just our family, but the others too. I'd really like to keep the North Vietnamese shook up and log some bad press for them too.

My God, we're all tired and numb from this thing.

Four days after arriving home from our big trip, we opened up the mailbox to find another letter from Hanoi, Spike's fifth letter.

What a wild letter. Look how good his handwriting looks! And, oh my God, he says he may be home in 1970! Does he know something we don't? We are jubilant, we are inspired all over again. God, if he can hang in there with spirit like this, we can sure as hell get on the stick here!

Dear Mom, Dad and Family. Happy New Year. We had a big turkey dinner here for Christmas. I got your last package. Send another with p-nuts, cool aid, coco and candy. Send pictures along with a letter, not in package. The new year finds me in good health and spirits. With any luck I'll be home in 1970. I must be rich by now! Love Spike

NGÀY VIẾT (Dated) *17 January 1970*

Got an invitation today to go to a gathering of the clan. The National League of Wives and Families of MIAs and POWs in Southeast Asia has called a meeting. You are invited to be a member when your loved one has been shot down, captured or is missing in action.

Up until now the League hasn't done a whole lot, but has been studiously careful not to step on anybody's toes. Now, finally, they are getting it together.

About seventy-five of us, the Southern California group, had a meeting of people anxious to let it all hang out with somebody else who could understand. Since our family has been so active, we were asked to speak.

We told them of our story, how Rick and I had gone to Paris and met with the North Vietnamese. We told them of our mental struggles and brainstorming which resulted in the 'Hanoi Release John Nasmyth' campaign, and that after we started campaigning we finally received our first letter from Spike. Mom and I told about our recent trip around the world, emphasizing that campaigning is definitely helping the prisoners. I told them about my coming appointment with Governor Reagan and about our plan to get him to speak out for our men. Four wives who had just traveled around the world told their stories. TV personality Bob Dornan, in his flamboyant style, practically ordered us out into the streets: "Get out and work for your men."

Our success story, combined with Bob's pep talk, fired us all up so much that everybody decided to go see Governor Reagan. After some more discussion, we decided that we wouldn't just see the Governor but spend a day in Sacramento demonstrating, picketing and getting the word out to the world.

We've been forced to take our problems to the streets. The news media has politely dropped the POW issue. We had good press coverage for six months, but after Christmas the POW families you saw on TV were saying the same old things about the same old POWs. We just can't get media attention when it's not something new and exciting. We've got to try and find ways to keep the press interested. Demonstrations in Sacramento and meeting the Governor should do the trick, and we want to start a nationwide trend of getting state and local governments involved. Publicity is the surest way to get the ball rolling. Publicity has been responsible for some relief for our men and the release of a few. Our job, then: to get publicity.

We set up a project meeting for making the picket signs, passing out press releases, fact sheets, solidifying the flight arrangements and so on.

Dad handled booking the flight, Rick got 'Hanoi Release the Prisoners' signs printed. I took care of press releases and fact sheets, Mom did the mailing.

A bunch of nervous, excited and expectant folks met at the Los Angeles International Airport. Everyone's hands were full of things to carry, signs, pictures, and literature to pass out. Every single person who signed up for the flight showed up. All had sent out their press releases, and there were reporters milling around everywhere.

When they called our flight, fifty moms, dads, wives, children, brothers, and sisters of POWs and missing men boarded the 'Hanoi Release the Prisoners' flight #448 for Sacramento.

We arrived at the Capitol at 10 a.m. In a wave of determination and sincerity, we assembled our pickets and moved to our hired conference room. At 11 a.m. the press showed up. There were more reporters and TV crews than we dared to expect. Over thirty reporters were looking us over while we held our first formal press conference.

The atmosphere in the room was tense and electric—no chattering or smiling among the family members.

For the first time we were expecting a hostile press. This is because the demonstration we were putting on was contrived. We were actually picketing our government for action. I might add that the National League was very down on our trip to Sacramento. For most of the family members, this was their first press conference. Their adrenalin had been building up through the weeks of planning, preparation and the long trip. Although they would not be the spokesmen, they were nervous and anxious as to how we would be received.

The idea that the press might be against us was heavy on my mind when I looked out at the dedicated expressions on the families' faces and the noncommittal looks of the reporters.

Rick observed that for the entire forty-eight hours prior to this event I was so single-minded that come hell or high water, come bad press or whatever, we were going to get the job done! We were determined to put on a good press conference and get to Governor Reagan.

I went up to the podium, waited while they adjusted microphones and opened the press conference with a plea to the media and to the American people.

We are the families of American prisoners of war and missing in action in Southeast Asia.

Our purpose in Sacramento is to give the spokesmen for the people of California first-hand information on the tragic prisoner-of-war situation. We are asking our representatives to inform the public so that the public will have the opportunity to demand the release of their servicemen who are being held prisoner in North Vietnam, Laos, and South Vietnam. For the past six and a half years our men have been subjected to extreme physical, mental, and emotional stress.

It is time that the American public, press and our representatives demand our men's immediate release from their cells in Hanoi and bamboo cages in Laos and South Vietnam.

Our men have suffered terribly. Their families are also suffering. The children here today carrying homemade signs and pictures of their fathers urgently need their fathers at home. The pure anxiety of not knowing whether or not your husband, son, or brother is dead, alive, or dying is totally incomprehensible. We have traveled to Paris, Sweden, Russia, Algeria, India, Southeast Asia, and Washington, D.C. to ask the people of the world to help our suffering men. Now we are asking your help.

Our people have traveled, petitioned, billboarded, conducted letter writing campaigns, appealed to the radio public, the television audience, the U.S. Red Cross, the International Red Cross, and the North Vietnamese themselves. The North Vietnamese have told many of us that they do not go along with the U.S. Government but that they will listen to the American people. PLEASE, AMERICAN PUBLIC tell the North Vietnamese in every way you know that we want our men home. They're your men too. Make it possible for the North Vietnamese to humanitarily release our men.

I stepped down, then for the first time many of the parents and wives of POWs spontaneously went before microphones and television cameras and with open displays of emotion began telling stories of sons who hadn't been heard from, of children who had never seen their fathers, who don't even know whether their fathers are dead or alive.

The reporters became involved. They asked questions. They filmed bewildered-looking children. They were hearing terrible stories of the torture our men are going through right now and of the torture the North Vietnamese are putting the families through, by not telling us which men they are holding.

Senator ProTem Jack Schrade went up to the microphone to throw his support behind our cause. Then we marched around and around the Capitol carrying our homemade signs, 'Hanoi, Release John Nasmyth,' 'Hanoi Release Jack Hardy,' etc. State Senators and Assemblymen came out to hear our stories and offer their support. When citizens in the area picked up our signs and marched with us, it made some of us cry.

While all this was going on, I checked in with the Governor's office to make the last-minute arrangements for our meeting.

Apparently Governor Reagan expected to meet with just me. This hardly seemed possible, since I had been on the phone with his executive secretary at least a dozen times, reporting on what we planned to do, how we were coming, and so on.

I'm afraid some politicians' secretaries think it is their job to be battle-axes and screen out everybody who wants an appointment no matter what is at stake. Governor Reagan's secretary certainly outdid herself.

She became an obstacle when I told her that fifty family members and a few TV cameramen were waiting outside his office. She said I could choose three representatives from our group, that was all. Now, she and I had been discussing this meeting by phone for over a month. She knew that fifty of us were coming to Sacramento and we weren't going to be turned away. She didn't notice the rage I was feeling. Nobody stops us from helping Spike. I asked her which door the 'four' of us should enter. She indicated where we should enter and said we should be ready in five minutes.

I explained the situation to the group outside and said, "Don't worry, we're all going in." I asked the family members to bunch together and, when the Governor's door opened, not to stop. Pete and Rick would make sure the door stayed open. The media people were 'gungho' to help too.

At 3 p.m., when the outer office door opened, we all very quietly and steadily streamed into the Governor's office, the cameramen taking up the rear.

We entered the 15-foot by 20-foot conference room, positioning ourselves around the long center table.

It was a gaggle of people. It was hot and crowded. We were all excited, and we felt so right about what we were doing. The atmosphere was thrilling.

The children and I were positioned right up in front to the left of where the Governor would make his appearance.

Governor Reagan opened the door. Where another man would have been taken aback, he calmly began to assess this mass of people. A group of a dozen children to his left, flanked by women, men, reporters and cameras in the back. The room had been roaring. When he walked in, suddenly there was absolute silence.

I had arranged this meeting with the Governor but had never really thought about what I was going to say. After a pause, I realized he wasn't going to speak to us. He was waiting for us to talk to him.

I talked to him in a fairly quiet, mild tone of voice. I said: "Governor Reagan, we are the families of American prisoners of war and missing men in Southeast Asia. We are here to tell you our story and to ask for your help in bringing our men home."

The Governor looked over to his left and appeared to be surprised. I realized later why he was so astonished. I'm only five feet tall and I was standing among the children. He must have thought a child was the spokesperson for all these people.

He then realized who was talking. His manner became warm. He made a brief, almost fatherly, statement to us and to the press. He told us that he had been following our story and that we could rest assured that as Governor he would do whatever he could to gain humane treatment and the release of our men. He said it as though he were having an intimate conversation with us, and he was true to his word.

Patty Hardy, MIA Jack Hardy's wife, reminded the Governor that over 400 Californians were either POW or MIA. The meeting ended when Carol Hanson's little son, Todd, pulled on the Governor's sleeve and asked to go 'potty.' The Governor scooped him up in his arms and said, "I think we'd better take care of this right now."

Governor Reagan pledged his support to us for our men and presented us with a proclamation.

As we filed out of the Governor's office, we picked up our pictures and signs and moved on to the Capitol steps. Here more family members made speeches to a small crowd. A couple of elected officials came out and addressed us, also pledging their support.

We picketed the Capitol for the rest of the afternoon before heading back to the airport.

$\mathfrak{State\ of\ California}$

GOVERNOR'S OFFICE

SACRAMENTO 95814

Once again I want to appeal to all those in public office to join in urging the repatriation of American prisoners of war in Southeast Asia.

The continued imprisonment of 1,600 brave men-- more than 400 of them Californians--in violation of international law is the concern of all Americans and it should be the concern of people everywhere who believe in freedom.

Their release is a matter that transcends politics and differing points of view on our involvement in Southeast Asia.

We must make it clear to Hanoi that we are speaking with one voice when we ask for the release of these prisoners.

I am writing to our two United States Senators and our California Congressional Delegation to ask that they support this cause.

RONALD REAGAN
Governor

Picketing the state capitol: Steve and Carol Clapp, their friend Marcia Haugen, Pete, Rick Loy, me, Dad, Mom, Jack Hardy's daughter Mary Pat and wife Pat.

At the airport lounge we caught the early news. They were doing a story on the National League. We were furious. We thought the League in its paranoia had pre-empted us by calling a press conference of its own today. But our Sacramento rally was on next, and the press was very kind to us. The broadcasters said that we had chastized the press for letting the POW issue slide.

We cheered and patted each other's backs, listening to some of our new campaigners telling their stories on TV.

Our flight home was riotous. Again at Los Angeles Airport we caught ourselves on TV. In the midst of the smiles and cheering, someone had the brains to pick up an evening edition of the *L.A. Times.* Our story was already well covered, in the evening edition, no less. We can expect it in the morning papers, too.

For these fifty families in California, this marked the beginning of organized, active campaigning for their sons and husbands. We had more activities on the fire; we were just beginning to pick up momentum. Other groups had formed all over the country and were campaigning for our men too.

We all rushed home from the airport to our TV sets.

At Mother's house we sat around drinking beer, talking about what we had accomplished, what jerks some of the legislators we had met were and what we should do next. We were all exhilarated and exhausted.

The coverage was good, we were on the 'top' of the news.

We planned to pick up a dozen copies of each of the newspapers in the area, cut out clippings and mail them off to our slow-to-move Representatives in Washington.

Governor Reagan must have been turned on by our rally in Sacramento. Since we met with him, he has been speaking out to influential groups in California. Now we've got government at the State level talking about POWs!

The following: Excerpts of Remarks by Governor Ronald Reagan; American Legion State Convention, Sacramento, June 26, 1970.

. . . A few days ago, we had another demonstration at the State Capitol.

It was somewhat different than many we have witnessed in the past. The participants were for the most part women and children. They had not come to shout insults, defame the Nation, or to raise the banner of the Viet Cong and they did not challenge America's sincerity in its search for freedom and peace. But their purpose could be summed up in a four-letter word—HELP.

They were the wives and children and other relatives of some of the 1,600 American servicemen known or believed to be captives of the Communist government of North Vietnam.

They came to Sacramento to dramatize the fact that hundreds of brave Americans are being held by Hanoi under inhumane and illegal conditions. Millions of Americans must share their sorrow and weep with them.

Led by a 21-year-old girl whose brother is missing and believed to be a captive, they came to see me. Perhaps some of you saw the picture or the TV coverage of the little three-year-old who informed me he had to go to the bathroom. There was no coverage of later, however, when he motioned for me to bend down and then whispered in my ear, "Will you help bring my Daddy home?"

His father is an airman who was shot down and is one of the 1,646 Americans, 400 of them Californians, officially classified as missing and believed to be prisoners of the Communists. Another 1,016 are missing and may also be alive and imprisoned. As Governor of this State, and as just a plain American citizen, I want them released. I want them back home.

In the meantime, we have a responsibility to demand that Hanoi cease its violation of the 1949 Geneva Convention and give our government a complete list of the prisoners it is holding.

Hanoi also has repeatedly refused to guarantee or provide humane treatment of these brave men. They have failed to live up to the Geneva Convention's requirement that prisoners of war receive adequate food, clothing, shelter and medical care. And as a final measure of inhumanity, the Communists have refused to permit many of these men to write even one letter home and to tell their loved ones that they are at least alive.

The reason we know the plight of those who remain prisoners is because Hanoi and the Viet Cong forces, for propaganda or other reasons, have released a total of 31 men. These men have told of the hardships which American prisoners of war in Vietnam are now enduring, and the story is an ugly indication of the North Vietnamese and their claims to political legitimacy.

Under the Geneva Convention signed by more than 120 nations, a prisoner of war is guaranteed the right to correspond with his relatives. Yet Hanoi has taken delight in communicating with some of the noisy anti-war groups in the United States—using these prisoners as pawns in a sadistic game to further their own aims. Under the Geneva Convention, which both the United States and North Vietnam signed, nations involved in armed conflict are required to immediately release or offer to release sick and injured war captives. It requires impartial inspection of prisoner facilities, a complete accounting and identification of all men held prisoner, and it prohibits the use of prisoners of war for political propaganda—either through coercion or in any other way that violates the individual's rights or is injurious to human dignity.

Those who came to the Capitol asked me to join their protest and to speak out—along with other public officials—against Hanoi's barbaric refusal to live up to the Geneva Convention. I have made reference to this on a number of occasions including the continued reports that some Americans are still held prisoner in North Korea these many years later. But that tragic little group reminded me we must all do more.

Some of you know from personal experience the hardships of wartime captivity—and the agonizing anguish this experience causes for loved ones back home.

You have given strong and sustained support to efforts to secure and guarantee humanitarian treatment for the American POWs in Vietnam. Last month, we declared a National Day of Prayer in California and asked the people of our State to join in praying for the safe return of these brave men. Members of the American Legion, the National Jaycees and other veterans and civic groups have joined to support similar efforts to dramatize the plight of the POWs in Southeast Asia.

Still we haven't managed to create the national voice that will tell a savage and barbaric enemy we intend to muster world opinion. If those who have been so vocal in denouncing this country and its military effort in Southeast Asia are really concerned about the brutality of war, they can participate in this without compromising their anti-war credentials. To insist that the Communists in North Vietnam start living up to civilized standards of conduct is singularly appropriate for even the most dedicated advocate of peace.

A country that forgets its defenders will itself be forgotten. It has been said 'the deterioration of a nation begins with the abandonment of the principles upon which that nation was founded.' Ours was founded upon the idea that each one of us could call upon the Nation's collective might to insure the protection of our God-given rights wherever and whenever those rights were threatened.

[NOTE: Since Governor Reagan spoke from notes, there may have been changes in, or additions to, the above quotes. However, the Governor stood by the above quotes.]

Ingenuity

During the summer of 1970, time quit being such a big factor in prison life; mainly because back in October of '69 they had stopped torturing people for every little thing. Before October '69 it was drastic—if they caught you with anything unauthorized in your cell, you were in for an ass-kicking.

After the treatment change we began to make all kinds of stuff. We made homemade pens, homemade ink, using spare toilet paper to write on. We started taking extra chances passing notes, notes containing just nothing but information to pass the time. All summer we got gigantic notes from guys who were versed in Spanish and French. We passed them back and forth. Little classes sprang up. We made up new vocabulary lists and dictionaries and hid them in every conceivable place we could find. If a brick had a little hole in it we'd roll up our notes, stick them in the hole and cover it with bits of cement. We made it look perfect whenever we figured we were going to have an inspection.

Not only did we spend a lot of time studying and learning stuff, we spent most of our time preparing it, hiding it and taking it out of hiding.

We found lots of ways to make ink. Men were receiving packages, and Kool-Aid makes a beautiful ink, also coffee makes a good ink. You can make ink out of cigarette ashes and sugar and water. We made pens out of sharp pieces of bamboo or the end of a toothbrush, filed down to a point. Time began passing much more rapidly.

Some of the greatest 'pussy' stories ever heard were told in Hanoi. We screwed every woman known to man. Each man described in incredible detail probably every episode he'd ever had and some he didn't have, but would like to have had.

Art Black was only nineteen when he was captured. His stories were always disastrous: one stroke, then panic.

"Oh God, don't be pregnant."

Ratzlaff never got into much detail, sort of a private person. Not me. I'd lay it all out in minute detail; nothing was sacred.

Some 'pussy' stories became famous throughout the camps. Years would go by, you'd change cell mates several times: "Hey Spike, Ratz says you got a great story."

"Oh yeah, what about?"

"That night with Marie."

Larry Friese had the funniest fuck story. He saw, 'with his own eyes' a Gook guard fuck a duck. His detailed description of feathers flying, wings flapping and painful quacking brought the house down.

'Freeze' swears it's a true story.

Don Waltman was tough to top. He had grown up in Kellogg, Idaho, which is close to Wallace. Both are rough mining towns, and both have several 'houses of ill repute.' 'The Lux Rooms' is in Kellogg, the madame was (and maybe is) a woman called Dixie. Anyway—Don's favorite story was: "The Lux offered special student rates to anyone who could produce a current Kellogg or Wallace High School student body card."

Don added, "So I was told."

Mailings

Once in a while, one of our representatives fails to support our men. When this happens we make a 'response' mailing. We ask everybody we can think of to jump on his back.

This month Senator Henry Jackson of Washington State was the subject of one of our mailings.

July 19, 1970

Dear Relative of Missing or Captured Personnel:

Senator Jackson of Washington State refused to sign the letter from the U.S. Senate to the Premier of North Vietnam protesting the treatment of personnel in Southeast Asia. This letter also asked for the release of our prisoners.

Please write Senator Jackson telling him that in your opinion he has abandoned our military men. He is acting in a deplorable, uninformed manner. Demand an explanation from him. His address is:

Senate Office Building
Washington, D.C. 20510

Virginia Nasmyth

Mail

We've got a new benevolent turnkey whom we dubbed Hollywood. He's a handsome young boy, combs his hair in a duck-tail like Jimmy Dean, speaks a little jag of English. Things are starting to loosen up, and the mail's starting to flow. The guys in the other cells around us are getting quite a bit of mail. Every night they call in, "Hey, so and so got a letter; his wife spent his money on a new car."

Will Gideon and I haven't ever received mail; Ed and Charlie have gotten a few letters. This didn't concern us too much, we're busy making bets, pinpointing exactly when we'll be going home. Next month? Thirty days? Hell, they're just kissing our asses. Something is really going on. No doubt we'll be home by Christmas.

Will was taken up to the interrogation shack, and he came back smiling with his first letter.
"Who from, Will?"
"My wife, everybody's fine."
"Shit hot."
The guard told me to put on my long-sleeved shirt and long pants.
"Hot Damn!" (My turn.)

I walked into the shack; Spot was sitting there.
"Nahshit, shit down."
(Jesus, wonder if this stupid little fag will ever learn to say sit.)
Spot started asking me a bunch of questions about my family, and I could see the letter he was holding in his lap with an American stamp on it.
(You little turd, I see my name on it, why don't you give it to me?)
"Nahshit, why you lie to us?"

"Lie? Me?"

"Yes, you say you are not married."

"I'm not."

Ah, but you lie, you have wife and two children."

(These stupid monkeys, they'd fuck up a wet dream.)

"I don't know where you got your information, but it's not true, I'm not married and I don't have any kids."

"Return to your cell, think of your lie, think clearly. We talk again."

I went back to my cell without getting my letter. Kinda crummy. I told everybody what had happened. We conned up a little story between us. The next guy who goes up for a letter, when he comes back he's going to pass the word around that he saw a letter addressed to me.

A couple of days later, Ed Martin was called up for a letter. A few minutes after he came back, I got hold of a guard and told him I wanted to speak to an English-speaking officer. Rabbit came down to the cell and I told him that my roommate, Ed Martin, had just seen a letter for me, with my name on it, when he was getting his own letter.

"Why won't the camp authority give it to me? Many times you have said any time mail comes we will receive it. Now a letter has come and you won't let me see it."

Rabbit hemmed and hawed, "Only if you tell the truth will you receive a letter."

"Well, hell, I am telling the truth. I know the questions the other officer was asking me, he thinks I'm married. Listen, I have two sisters. Their last names are Nasmyth, same as mine. That doesn't mean we're married. I just have two sisters."

"I will check, if any mail comes, you will get it."

The next day they called me up. Without a word they handed me my letter. It was my first letter, a letter from my sister, Gebo. It was obviously a letter in which she assumed I had received previous letters. It just covered a little period of time. It didn't make sense to me. She signed her name Patricia Nasmyth Berger. When I left, she was Patricia Crawford. Now who the hell is Berger? It had two pictures of little kids, Larry and Carol, said, "We love you, Uncle Spike." Kind of nice. I read it while Spot sat there watching, looked at the two pictures, handed it all back to him, then went back to my cell.

The Fourth

I've yet to consciously take note of Spike's notorious shoot-down anniversary, September 4. Around the first of September, 1970, occupied with thoughts of Spike having to face another year tick by, I started to dread the coming of the fourth. As the second and third roll by, things begin to get cloudy, my head fills up. Another year has passed. We can begin to tread water all over again. By September sixth or seventh, I suddenly realize that I've missed the fourth again.

I always feel guilty about not thinking about Spike on the fourth, so when it happens, when it's all over, I call Mother. "I feel crummy when I don't think about Spike on the fourth, Mom. Remind me next year, will you?"

Each year she responds by saying, "Why?"

Mock POW Camp

November is already here, and November is tough. Spike's thirtieth birthday is coming up and he is still in Hanoi. If he is there on the fourteenth of November, he will have celebrated five birthdays in a cell. Man, there goes his beautiful youth. God, this is a hard time at home. I hope it's not too rough on him there.

We've been racking our brains for something to do this year. We are not going to let another significant day slip by without raising hell.

We are trying to get everybody working for our prisoners. When people not directly involved get caught up in this mess, we get all fired up. When we are fired up, our enthusiasm spreads and we reach more people. We're becoming more creative and wilder in our campaign strategy.

Rick and I think it's time for something creative in San Diego. We do a lot of work there and we've got a great relationship with the San Diego press.

We've been talking about this idea for months, so we brought it up at a bull session at Mom's.

We want to put up a mock POW camp. Where to put it? That's easy. Every day when I drive down Interstate Eight, our 'Hanoi Release John Nasmyth' billboard screams at me. There is a manmade hill, vacant and level on top, just twenty-five yards east of the billboard. And it is very visible from the freeway.

By the way, Jack Schrade's office keeps tabs on the traffic on Interstate Eight. Seventy thousand cars pass by this site every day.

So we sprang our idea on the family. Of course, Mother was all for it: "Let's do it." Dad started jotting down the practical things he'd need to make the mechanics of the thing work: plans for the cell and an electric generator so it can be lighted at night. We wouldn't want to miss the night traffic. Rick was in charge of getting permission, permits, etc. I did the fact sheets and press releases.

Now, an empty prison cell was no good. We needed somebody to sit in it over the long weekend. It would be Spike's birthday, so the occupant should do something special. He should fast. I'd have done it, but that would probably look ridiculous. Of course, Rick volunteered, but the story would have more significance for the press if Spike's brother did it.

It made sense, having Pete fasting in a cell here in the U.S. while his brother rots away in Hanoi. I must say Pete wasn't too thrilled, but the wheels were turning, plans were made, press releases were mailed, and finally he said, "Okay, I'll do it."

After brainstorming a little longer, we decided to have a bamboo cage too. That's what the prisoners in South Vietnam are held in. Again all of us were willing to sit and fast in the cage, but having a brother there made for a better story. And that's what we were after, news coverage.

When you think about hard-working POW families, the Rehmann family immediately comes to mind. So we gave David Rehmann's family a call. David has been a POW almost as long as Spike. David's younger brother Don jumped at the chance of hitting the media with their story. He agreed to occupy the cage.

We had less than two weeks to bring this thing to fruition.

Dad, the master architect, designed the cell with help from all of us. We decided upon two sides ten feet by ten feet, a metal roof and a plank bed. Dad and Pete put it together. Mom, Pete, and the kids painted it. The grown-ups were having a rough time making the paint look old, so they turned the job over to Pete's two boys, Little Pete and Jeff. They found the formula: the kids walked through the paint, threw dirt on the walls and smeared them with sticks. It really looked authentic.

Rick and I went back to San Diego to take care of arrangements at our end. We figured Pete and Don should wear POW pajamas. The Rehmann family had a picture of Dave in maroon and grey pajamas.

We had also seen pictures of other POWs in solid grey garb. I spent a day buying unbleached muslin and sewing up two pair of men's pajamas, very rough, size extra-large. When I finished I took them up to the local laundromat and dyed them charcoal grey. It worked; they looked great, all blotchy and old-looking. Then Tracy Barns, my gorgeous six-foot-tall next-door neighbor, and I laid Don's pajamas out on the sidewalk. With a package of maroon dye, a little water and a paint brush we striped Don's pajamas (as well as the sidewalk). They looked terrific. We finished them off with a drawstring around the waist.

Meanwhile Rick saw Terry Brown, the owner of much of Mission Valley, and got permission to put up our prison camp on his property.

Next day we went to Pacific Outdoor Advertising and talked them into putting up a 'Hanoi Release the Prisoners' billboard next to our mock camp. These professional billboards are huge, great eye-catchers.

Back in L.A. Mom had the task of coming up with a cage. One of the local Boy Scout troops had been calling Mother, offering to do anything to help. Mom gave them a ring: "We need a bamboo cage in three days." The troopmaster and boys came over the next afternoon to get started. Mom drew a picture of what we needed. She told them where to find bamboo, about a mile away along the Rio Hondo River. They left a little bewildered-looking, but returned three days later with a great-looking, and well constructed bamboo cage, six feet by three feet by four feet.

Having read reports on prisoners in the South, we know that some of them wear leg irons. Dad designed a set and an engineer where he worked made them for us.

Thursday the cell and cage were ready to go. Rick and I drove halfway to L.A., to the Colony Kitchen Restaurant where we met Mom. She was bringing the cage in the back of a Ranchero, an open truck, and it was really giving her trouble, threatening to fly out. She lost a couple of pieces of bamboo but had some spares.

Mom, Rick and I stood overlooking the freeway in the Colony Kitchen's parking lot watching for Pete. It was raining. He was bringing the cell down to our site in an old flatbed truck. We waited twenty-five minutes or so, nervous as cats watching for him. We were just about to pile in the car and go look for Pete when we saw this peculiar-looking jail cell crawling along in the slow lane. He didn't stop, he just drove on by us as we hollered and screamed and cheered his progress.

Dad arrived before dark with carload of electrical equipment, tools, and an electric generator. Dad, Pete, and Rick then erected the cell for the first time. As Rick said, "It was no small thing." They worked all evening setting it up and hooking up the electrical system. By 10 p.m. or so it was ready.

Everybody crashed at my house in San Diego, then we were back at the site before 6 a.m. Pete and Don got into their POW pajamas and put the finishing touches on the cell. They nailed the roof on, set up the bed, and secured the cage.

A big change came over the brothers when they pulled on their baggy grey POW pajamas. They quit smiling and cracking jokes. Don crawled into his cage, we strapped on the leg irons. Pete sat down on his plank bed, head in hands and just stayed there. We left them alone.

The Rehmann clan and about a dozen other families came down for our press conference. At 10 a.m. the TV cameras from San Diego and Los Angeles arrived. The newspaper people were there as well as a couple of radio stations. They interviewed everybody, focusing on the brothers.

Pete, dressed in our homemade POW pajamas, fasts for Spike's 30th birthday.

Pete and Don spent an uncomfortable night in their cell and cage. One thing we hadn't anticipated was the number of passers-by who stopped and climbed up the fifteen-foot muddy slope to the 'prison camp' to talk to them. Several hundred people stopped by the first day.

We immediately set up a table with petitions for people to sign, free bumper stickers, and POW information books.

It was a very moving experience for our family, especially Mother, to see her son in the grey pajamas his brother must be wearing.

We were all milling around the site Saturday morning, Spike's birthday, rehashing the press coverage we had already seen, asking Pete and Don about their night, wishing there was more we could do, when a patrolman waded through the mud and climbed up the hill toward us. (Uh oh, here comes trouble. We probably should have gotten a permit.)

The patrolman brought us a message to phone a neighbor in South San Gabriel, something about the mail.

Mom and I immediately drove to a gas station to use the phone. She called the neighbor who had picked up our mail that afternoon, since Mom never leaves the mailbox unattended. Mom got Wallace on the phone and asked, "What's up?"

Wallace replied, "I've got an envelope here postmarked Hanoi."

I was listening too. "Really! Bring it down."

Mom said, "No, open it. See if it's really from Spike."

Wallace opened the envelope. "Virginia, there are three letters here from Spike."

Amid our squeals he went on, "There are two for John and Virginia and one for little Virginia."

Mom said, "Read them."

"Do you want me to read them?"

"Yes, read them."

And Wallace proceeded to read every word of the addresses, return addresses, and finally the messages in our letters from Spike. Once, slowly, just for us to hear and then several more times while we copied them down, every word.

God, how we want him home. These letters are like getting a little piece of him. And look, he wrote one to me! Oh, I'm so happy and proud and feel so much love for him. I just wish I could hug him and tell him what a wonderful big brother he is, even in prison camp.

NGÀY VIẾT (Dated) 24 June 1970

Dear Mom Dad and Family. A late happy Mothers Day Mom, Happy Fathers Day Dad and Happy Birthday Mom. I got your last package, It was perfect. I would like some real good tasting tooth-paste. I do a lot of exercise and I'm in good condition. Follow this letter format exactly. Send pictures of all in family with letters. Love Spike

NGÀY VIẾT (Dated) 27 July 1970

Dear Mom, Dad and Family. Your last package was fine. I really like the chocolate and nuts. How about some cashew nuts, p-nut butter and blackberry jam? I sure would like to hit the beach with Virginia this summer. Better yet I'd like to pick up a good looking beach bunny. I'm in good health, just waiting for that day. Love Spike

NGÀY VIẾT (Dated) _10 August 1970_

Dear Virginia. How's my favorite little sister? I bet by now that you're really a knock-out. I spend a lot of time talking about you, and my room-mates are all hot to see you. Send me pictures of you showing the new fashions, from mini skirts to swim suits. I'm looking forward to hearing from you and the rest of the family. Have a ball, remember, you only live once.

Love Spike

CHI CHÚ (N.B.):

1. Phải viết rõ và chỉ được viết trên những dòng kẻ sẵn (Write legibly and only on the lines).

2. Gia đình gửi đến cũng phải theo đúng mẫu, khuôn khổ và quy định này (Notes from families should also conform to this proforma).

He says he has roommates. What a relief. What a goddamn relief. My God, he has somebody to talk to after all.

Later, in the afternoon, Mrs. Rehmann called with good news for Don. The Rehmanns received a letter from Dave today, too. His writing is strong and he sounds good.

Nothing could have made Spike's thirtieth birthday more special for us. Our mock POW camp seemed like such a success now. Even while Pete and Don were sitting in their cell and cage, we were talking about what to do next—planning, planning, planning.

The brothers spent another night incarcerated in their self-imposed prison camp.

During the weekend over eight hundred people stopped by to get information, offer their support, and sign letters and petitions. Even a San Diego hook and ladder fire truck pulled up to the site. The firemen scrambled up the hill to sign petitions and letters to Hanoi.

We have decided to deliver our 'letters to Hanoi' to the North Vietnamese in Paris on Christmas Day. We'll work out the details later.

That afternoon a reporter from one of San Diego's two news stations caught me at home while I was feeding my cat. He said he had heard that we got a letter from Spike today. I said, "Yes, we got three letters from Spike today. Not only that, one of them was for me. Isn't that wonderful, to get letters from him on his birthday?"

The reporter said, "Do you expect me to believe that it's just mere coincidence that you received a letter today? You didn't really get a letter today."

"You're kidding," I retorted, "You think we'd lie about something as important as Spike's letters? Of course they came today. My Mother is on her way to Los Angeles to pick them up right now." I was starting to shake.

The reporter replied, "Well, I don't believe you, I think this is some stunt you're pulling."

"Well, you son-of-a-bitch . . . ." I'm afraid that for the first time I completely lost my cool with the press. I got a little wild on the phone, started crying and slammed down the receiver.

Rick was listening to the whole thing. When he finally got me to calm down, I told him who this guy was. Rick calmly called him up and told him what had happened. As the discussion continued, Rick also proceeded to lose his cool and tell the reporter what a stupid 'S.O.B.' he was.

Rick always makes me feel better.

Meanwhile, Mom was on her way home to get Spike's letters and feed the dog and cats. When she pulled into the driveway, the telephone was ringing. Opening the back door in a hurry to answer the phone, she could see Spike's letters on the kitchen table.

She walked into the house, answered the phone, and it was George Putnam's secretary, Sal, who said, "George Putman calling Virginia Nasmyth."

Then in his resonant voice, he said, as he always does, "George Putnam speaking. I want that cage in my studio by 9 p.m. tonight."

They had a little chat. George asked, "Do you think you could get me a pair of POW pajamas, too?"

Mother answered, "You'll have it all at 9 o'clock tonight."

Mom gathered up her purse and Spike's letters and headed for her car to make the return trip to San Diego for the cage. She hadn't even had a chance to read the letters.

As she was going out the door, Wallace drove into the driveway in his Ranchero. She told him about George's call and they hopped into his car, drove to San Diego as fast as they could.

It took just under two hours to get there. They really flew, arriving just before 7 o'clock. It was pitch dark. Pete, Don, Rick, Dad and I were dismantling the cell in the dark.

We were surprised to see Mom back so soon. We swarmed her for the letters. Then Mom told us that George Putnam needed the cage in two hours. And she said, "Don, I gotta have your pajamas." He said, "Sure, take them," and he slipped them off. So they were a little smelly, so what.

We threw the cage into the back of Wallace's truck and quickly tied it down.

Meanwhile, back at his studio, George was dictating his 'I am a POW' soliloquy to Sal. She typed out the sincere, moving words George would use on the evening news.

Mom and Wallace took off for George's studio, Channel 5 on Sunset Boulevard in Hollywood. They had to stop for a tank of gas even before they got on the freeway.

When they pulled up in front of the studio, George met them. George recalled:

"When they drove onto the lot I caught my first sight of that cage. It was eerie. I could imagine myself being put right into that tiger cage with those long-suffering guys. I suddenly felt that I was really a part of their suffering.

"After we unloaded the cage, we had a hell of a time getting it into the studio. But we disassembled it and got it through the door.

"Then I got into the cage. While hunched over in it I asked Virginia if it was possible for me to use it for the actual broadcast. I said, 'Do you think I should get in it while we're on the air? Would it be ludicrous, ridiculous, or somehow irrelevant if I were to do my broadcast from the cage?'

"Virginia looked me right in the eye and said, 'No Way!'

"Then she handed me the striped pajamas. So I slipped them on. This, I felt, drew me one step closer to our boys.

"That night, doing the broadcast from within the cramped space of the cage, it vividly depicted the conditions in which those fellows are kept.

"It was all I could do to get through the broadcast. When it was over, I realized that one of the highlights of my life was going on the air while in that cage."

The Kit

Our birthday celebration for Spike was a brutal look at POW life. It was a unique campaign, two men in cells just like those their brothers have been rotting in for the past four years. Our spectacle graphically demonstrated the living conditions of Spike, Dave and their buddies, arousing a tremendous response from the media and general public throughout the country. We asked everyone to write Hanoi.

POW families we've never even heard of responded to our latest publicity. Requests came in for information, billboards and the POW pajamas they saw on TV.

We had lots of material to send anyone who was interested. Earlier in the year we put together a POW publicity kit. Its main point was: personalize the campaign. Plans for the POW cell, bamboo cage, directions on how to make the grey striped pajamas, personalized billboards, how to write press releases, and most important, how to get press coverage were among the paraphernalia available through our brochure.

PERSONALIZE THE CAMPAIGN

My brother, John Nasmyth, has been a Prisoner of War since 1966. We heard nothing for 3½ years. September '69 we embarked on a campaign to secure John's release and inform the public of the POW situation. We have had tremendous success in displaying billboards which read: HANOI RELEASE JOHN NASMYTH. By success, I mean that in November 1969 the North Vietnamese officially listed John as a POW. That December we received a letter from John; since then three letters have followed. About 300 of the following billboards have gone up in 1970:

HANOI RELEASE THE PRISONERS
HANOI RELEASE MY HUSBAND
HANOI RELEASE MY SON
HANOI RELEASE MY BROTHER
HANOI RELEASE MY FATHER

The following items are also available to you to help personalize the campaign. Envelope stickers reading any of the above messages or HANOI RELEASE your man's name: 500 for $1.00. Get HANOI RELEASE THE PRISONERS and have your friends use them.

Bumper stickers reading:
HANOI RELEASE your man's name
HANOI RELEASE THE PRISONERS
HANOI RELEASE MY FATHER
HANOI RELEASE MY SON
HANOI RELEASE MY BROTHER
HANOI RELEASE MY HUSBAND

PLEASE SEND ANY SPARE NEWS CLIPPINGS YOU HAVE. ONCE A WEEK WE SEND THESE TO VARIOUS OF THE 200 NORTH VIETNAMESE EMBASSIES AROUND THE WORLD.

The following items are available:

CAGE—Plans are available for constructing this 6' by 3' by 4' bamboo cage. It was designed by Maj. Rowe, an ex-POW who lived in a similar cage for 5½ years. This cage is typical of what the Pathet Lao and Viet Cong use to hold American POWs. (Include 25¢ with order for postage.)

CELL—Plans are available for this 10' by 10' two walled cell, metal roof and plank bed. The cell was designed by ex-prisoners of war held in similar cells in Hanoi. (Include 25¢ with order for postage.)

PHOTO SPEECH KIT—Eight 8" by 10" black and white glossy prints are available for $2.00 or 25¢ each. An explanation of each picture is included.

HANOI: RELEASE THE PRISONERS—Bumper Stickers available at 5¢ each. For a great quantity the price drops a cent.

POWs NEVER HAVE A NICE DAY —Bumper Stickers available at 5¢ each. For a great quantity the price drops a cent.

GREY POW PAJAMAS—Available for $8.00, indicate size. We use these pajamas for visual aid in speaking and campaigning for the prisoners.

STRIPED POW PAJAMAS—Available for $9.00, indicate size. Striped pajamas copied after POW David Rehmann's prison garb as seen in *Life Magazine* October 1967.

POW BRACELET—Order blanks are available through us. Or send $2.50 for a nickel-plated bracelet, or $3.00 for a copper-plated bracelet. Names which the bracelets bear are randomly selected unless you request a specific name. Each bracelet bears the name of one POW or MIA and the date he was lost. Upon accepting a POW bracelet one vows to wear it until the man is returned home.

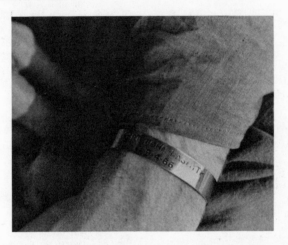

POW NOTE PAPER—Which folds up into a post card. 100 sheets for $1.00. When folded, one side bears the black and white picture of the POW in a Cell, the other side is blank for the address.

POW-MIA documentary available to your area TV stations. "The Stolen Years" is a one-hour show featuring five returnees from North and South Vietnam POW camps. Available only on videotape.

IF YOU WOULD LIKE A BILLBOARD IN YOUR AREA, HERE'S WHAT TO DO

1. Contact your local outdoor advertising company. Explain your cause. Ask for a donation of standard 24- or 30-sheet billboard space.

2. Order your billboard, give two weeks for delivery.

3. Arrange for a time to have the paper glued up on the billboard.

FOR PUBLICITY:

Send a news release to all radio stations, TV networks, and newspapers in your area. Send it three or four days before your billboard goes up. Call them once or twice to make sure they're going to show up. Hand deliver your news releases to local papers and talk to the editor explaining what you're doing and why. Ask for his help.

4. Try to have your billboard unveiled before 2 p.m. on a weekday. This makes it possible for the press to be there and get it in the evening news.

5. Make up a fact sheet and send it along with your news release. Have fact sheets available for the press at the unveiling of your billboard. Have available pictures of your man, bumper stickers and literature about the POWs.

6. Invite all your friends and the nearby next of kin. Be at the billboard unveiling and tell your personal story. Personalize the campaign.

7. Keep in mind something to tell the public to do through the media. I suggest asking the public to write the President of North Vietnam and the International Red Cross in Geneva, Switzerland.

8. Your news release should be short, to the point, and include the time and place of the unveiling, who's going to be there and possibly a fact or two about the missing man.

9. Your fact sheet should have time, place, years missing and any personal facts that make your story more interesting to the public.

10. Be sure to invite your mayor, senator or town organizations.

11. If you would like to build your own 15 × 20 foot billboard, write to us for the plans.

PERSONALIZE THE CAMPAIGN,
HELP THE PUBLIC FOCUS
ON THE SUFFERING INDIVIDUALS

Better Conditions

Toward the end of the summer of 1970, the conditions at the Zoo were really getting pretty good. They started letting us outside. Occasionally different cells were let out together. The guards were backing off. We'd go outside to pick up our food. We might run into other Americans who were coming out of their cells or just coming back from picking up their food. We'd say hello to them. Nobody was getting too excited about it. Nobody was getting hit. We thought things were really gonna go.

Then late at night about the middle of September, there was a big commotion. A lot of guys, blindfolded, left camp in trucks in the dark. The next day we had to gather up all our stuff, except what was hidden in the bricks. Our whole cell was moved over to another building. For the first time we could see out. They had built a courtyard out back, and it looked like we were going to be able to get outside together.

I was only in that cell for one day. Next morning, the guards opened up, and took me and the other four guys out. We all went in different directions. I headed back to the Barn. I walked up to this 'new' cell. There were three guys standing there. The guard motioned, 'go in' and it's the same fucking cell I lived in for three years, back with John Brown, John Blevins, A.J. Myers and Jim Pirie. Right back in the same room, but now it's different. They've also knocked the bricks out of the back window. All we could see from the window was a wall.

So I moved into this cell with a guy I'd never heard of named Ed Martin. I didn't even know he was a prisoner. There was also Will Gideon whom I knew was a prisoner, he was Tom Browning's first roommate, and a guy named Chuck Baldock, crazy as a loon.

Right away we tapped on the wall to the guys next door. We found out from these guys, who had just moved in, that the Vietnamese had told them we would be outside together tomorrow. We spent the night talking about why in the hell was the treatment getting so much better and they were gonna let us get out and talk to each other. Of course, we were speculating, the war was just about over. Home by Christmas!

And the next day did it. They started out by bringing us breakfast, half a loaf of bread for breakfast. So we were getting breakfast plus two regular meals. Then they opened up all the cells and let all twelve of us out together. It was three cells with four guys in each one. Now the court-yard is for twelve people. We can talk among ourselves, but we can't communicate with the other cell blocks. There are walls all around specifically built to prevent it. But, of course, we manage to communicate with the other cell blocks anyway.

Everybody in the new group is easy to get along with. The four of us have never been together, we're from four different places. We've got nothing but a million things to talk about. Ed Martin's a commander in the Navy, which is like a lieutenant colonel in the Air Force, so he's our high ranker. Will Gideon is a major so he's second. I'm next and Charlie Baldock is the junior. Even though Ed Martin is a pretty high-ranking officer, he's really a fine man. I admire him. He's one of the best officers I've ever known, and we get along great.

Pumpkin Soup

We are learning about the media. We have consistently been able to get decent coverage. We are telling the same story to the American people each week—just the statistics are changing. It's like an episodic drama. Each week we look at the story from a different angle.

One week ago, Pete and Don were fasting in our homemade prison camp. It was newsworthy because for the first time the living conditions of our men in Hanoi were brought home to the American people. Average citizens have no idea what it is like for our men. Up until now, they'd only heard about the living conditions, and now they have witnessed them. But, our good people forget; so we've got to keep confronting them with the plight of our guys in Hanoi again and again.

So we decided to put on another demonstration and serve pumpkin soup and pig fat for Thanksgiving dinner.

Thanksgiving was a crummy time anyway. It hasn't been much fun for the past couple of years sitting around eating a delicious turkey dinner without Spike.

Rick and I were driving up to L.A. and we got to talking about how we could spend Thanksgiving and decided it was a good idea. One thing led to another. We sent invitations off to the other POW-MIA families in the area. We got a permit to have a public gathering in Pershing Square in downtown Los Angeles. I hammered out the press releases and got them into the mail.

We talked about having pumpkin soup and pig fat, but we didn't know how to make it. Mom contacted Joe Carpenter in Arizona. Joe had been a POW in Hanoi for six months, and his release was one of Hanoi's goodwill gestures. He gave Mom his soup recipe: you boil chunks of pumpkin in water with a few chunks of pork fat, little or no seasoning, and a few onion greens. That's it. He instructed us: "If you cook it up and it looks awful and tastes worse, you've followed the recipe correctly."

November 25, Mom and I went to the grocery store and bought a pumpkin, the fat off a pork roast, and some green onions.

We were actually very careful and serious while preparing this stuff. We spent the entire evening making about five gallons of lousy smelling soup.

Early Thanksgiving morning, Mom, Dad, Pete, Rick, and I set out for Pershing Square with the same Thanksgiving dinner Spike probably had the night before.

At Pershing Square we were joined by the families of thirty-nine other prisoners and missing men, a pretty gloomy-looking bunch. Everybody brought his own bowl and spoon.

We set up the bamboo cage and a couple of card tables with our black cauldron full of pumpkin soup on top. Joe McCain and Don Rehmann (brothers of POWs) sat in the cage, pajamaed and manacled. It was a stark-looking spread.

When you've got someone missing or held in Hanoi, Thanksgiving is so depressing. Today was no exception.

Eating the trash our guys are subjected to brought us all way down. It was a sad way to spend the day, kids of missing guys milling around, the press shooting the whole scene.

But our bad-tasting meal got the national press coverage we've been after. The American people were forced to remember their prisoners. And thousands of them were moved enough to let us know they wanted to help. We asked them to write Hanoi.

In San Diego, Concern for POWs has made 'Write Hanoi' its special project this year. They plan to send a truck convoy across the United States to stop in dozens of key places to pick up mail for Hanoi. It will all be shipped to France, picked up by more trucks, and dumped into the laps of the North Vietnamese with all the pomp and circumstance possible; a super idea for the conservative organizations to have come up with.

Bull Session

When Rick and I have been mulling over an idea for a time, or Mom and I have come up with some great scheme over the phone or sometimes simply for lack of new ideas, we feel the need for a 'bull session.' Rick and I have been driving up from San Diego once or twice a week during the hectic times to see how Mom is doing and to get some enthusiasm worked up. The way it usually works out is, Mom buys a couple of steaks or makes her 'garbage meal,' an endearing term for her delicious everything-in-the-kitchen dish. Pete shows up. We break out a bottle of whiskey and some beer and start talking about getting Spike out.

A prerequisite for a bull session is getting all four of us together. Rick, Mom and I can have a session, but the bull doesn't start to fly till Pete gets there. Pete's enthusiasm is contagious. There is only one unwritten rule, that is, no idea is too stupid or too wild to talk about.

By the time our eyelids are at half mast, the ideas start to sound pretty damn good.

First, we always take care of what Spike might be getting away with over there. The last bull session, Pete was sure Spike might be getting a piece of ass. We got so worked up about it, that night, we rushed out and bought Spike a box of rubbers for his next package. Our rationale: if anyone could get some action, Spike could.

Then we try out ideas on each other. From such sessions were born the 'Hanoi Release John Nasmyth' billboard, our trip around the world, our visit with Governor Reagan, the mock-POW camp and the Thanksgiving meal.

During many of these sessions we'd come up with an idea, develop it and work out the details nonstop. For instance, when we talked about the original billboard, after deciding yes, we would have a billboard, just getting the message written took hours.

First we came up with, 'Please Hanoi, Release John Nasmyth.' Should we use please or not use please? After much heated discussion, Mom said, "Hell no, we're not going to ask them for anything, we're going to tell them, demand it!" Shall we say Hanoi or North Vietnam? What about his name? Should it be John Nasmyth or Spike Nasmyth? This was probably the most talked about and the most difficult decision we made in the whole campign. None of us think of Spike as John, never have. But, there was some kind of fear in the backs of our minds that 'Spike,' might be construed as a code or something, it might get him into trouble. I don't know why we thought this, but it probably stems from our understanding of the Military Code of Conduct, the old name, rank, and serial number stuff.

When we decided on the message, then we had to decide on the color scheme . . . all red? all black? What color for the background? We decided upon a red 'Hanoi' and black 'Release John Nasmyth.' Now how do we letter a billboard? We didn't know how. But we got help. Jon Dahlstrum, an old schoolmate of Spike's, was a commercial artist, so we asked him to do the lettering.

Then we had to figure out how to build a billboard, how to erect it, how to make it permanent, how big to make it? Where should we put this thing? We decided on a location very close to home and hit up our neighbors for their permission. During this session I was taking notes like mad.

We wanted the press to cover this, so we had a lot of brainstorming to do. How do we do it? We talked about press releases, what day, time of day, and how far ahead to tell the press. Did we want a crowd of people there? No, just the family. What should we ask the press and people to do to show their support? It took days to come up with this answer.

Lastly, and boy, this was a 'biggy.' Who in the family should be the spokesman? Who would be the most appealing? We went round and round on each one of us, pros and cons, and finally we came up with me. I would be the spokesman for the family.

It would be getting late, all of us drained from our serious discussions and planning. Then we would decide to get the war over quick, to bomb 'em, bomb Hanoi. We thought that was a great idea, but are American bombers accurate enough to miss bombing the prison camps? How about dumping sleeping gas on Hanoi and walking in there and carrying the prisoners out? I'm sure we could do if it we wanted to.

Our 'bull sessions' always ended with the infamous commando raid. We thought Mike Rowe, the biggest, meanest guy on Spike's high school football team should lead it. He was a D.I. during his hitch in the army.

Pete, the Green boys, old high school friends, and some of the local cops, all friends of Spike, would all somehow get themselves to 'Nam. Led by Mike, they'd storm right up the middle of North Vietnam, descending upon the prison camps to rescue Spike. They'd be so damn glad to see them.

Ah, the commando raid is so tantalizing.

Bombs

In the middle of the night, November 21, 1970, pitch black, I'm awake, aware that everybody else is awake, listening. I thought I heard some kind of rumbling. Shit, I did. Everybody did. We're all up, tense, still quiet, listening.

The regular bombing of North Vietnam stopped back in November of '68. There hasn't been much noise up here since then.

Now we can hear it. Jesus, there is all kinds of stuff going off. We can see the SAMs and the ack-ack going up, then hear the air raid siren.

Everybody's guessing.

"The bombing's started again."

"Commando raid."

"Bullshit."

"Whadaya mean bullshit, you think they're gonna let us rot here?"

There are Gooks running around everywhere. Machine guns everyplace. Our guards are given bullets for the first time in a long time. Some of them can't remember how to load their guns.

The Gooks are running up and down the halls, checking doors, yelling, screaming. Something has scared the shit out of them.

(God damn, maybe it is Commandos.)

What are we gonna do if it is Commandos? If they come here? Some figure the Gooks'll kill us before the Commandos get here. What are your odds? Commandos come, got a fifty-fifty chance of making it. We've been here six years now. That's better than a 100% chance of being here forever, right? Might as well be dead forever as be a prisoner forever. Right! The concensus is bring on the Commandos, giving us a fifty-fifty shot at making it. No one wants a 100% chance of rotting in a Commie jail forever.

It's real late. We're waiting. Then the noise stops suddenly. Nobody comes. We don't hear another sound from the direction of Hanoi.

At dawn the Gooks are still running around—they're digging foxholes right outside our cell.

You've heard of a Chinese fire drill, well, a Gook fire drill is even more exciting. They've got machine guns set up all over the prison yard and they're digging the foxholes deep, real deep. All the cell windows are covered, nobody can look out. And foxholes, I can't believe all the friggin' foxholes. First time I've seen the little bastards work up a sweat. And they're digging fast. They are still afraid the helicopters are gonna come, great big U.S. choppers loaded with great big U.S. Green Berets.

(Oh Jesus, what a perfect way to leave this dump. Maybe there'll be enough room so I can take that fuckin Clyde along. I bet that crazy bastard McSwain* is going ape.)

---

*George spent hours planning Commando rescue raids. Later, when I read the Son Tay Plan, it was precisely how George would have done it.

Son Tay

I was pounding away on my typewriter one November morning, I was always pounding away on my typewriter, when my neighbor Trudy came flying over. "Virginia, have you heard the news? The Americans have just made a Commando raid on a prison camp in North Vietnam."

"You're kidding, are you sure?"

"Yes, turn on the news."

(I never have the radio on when something important happens.)

Trudy left me to call Mother. Mom has radios playing softly in both her kitchen and her bedroom, tuned to L.A.'s all-news station, KFWB, twenty-four hours a day.

Mom knew the story. Yes, there had been a POW rescue attempt. "Oh, my God." They were calling it the Son Tay Raid. A rescue attempt! Americans landed at a North Vietnamese prison camp, but nobody was there.

"No prisoners in the prison camp, you gotta be kidding."

Dad called me, I called Gebo, she talked to Mom . . . we all called each other and talked about the implications of the raid. When we got to thinking about it, we were pretty disgusted that American intelligence was so inept they raided an empty camp.

On the other hand, it was a pretty wild thing to do. The POWs over there are sure to hear about the rescue attempt and that should lift their morale. Now maybe they know that the country cares about them. At least this country is finally doing something about the POWs, and we're delighted.

After a few days passed, we realized that the best thing about the Son Tay Raid was how it stirred up this country. Everybody has been talking about POWs. The men involved in the raid came back heroes. They were so emotional on TV, you could tell how badly they wanted to bring our guys home again.

The media was all wound up, too. They actually sought us out this month. For the first time *Time* magazine contacted us. Their reporter spent an entire day with me talking about what we've been doing, taking notes and some pictures. It was exciting to be a part of their coverage of POW family activists. All those readers got to see a photo of our billboard for Spike, in the December 7, 1970 issue.

December is here and I am convinced that Spike will be home by Christmas. The climate is right. Things are really changing for him. He actually told us in his letter to me that he has roommates. His handwriting looks better and the tone of his 'birthday letters' sounds so hopeful. We've been working at a feverish pitch this year. You can't pick up a newspaper or a magazine without a POW story staring you in the face. The stuff we've got planned for December will knock'em dead.

The North Vietnamese just plain look bad. In order for them to ingratiate themselves with the rest of the world, I expect they will pull a humanitarian prisoner release. And, why not Spike? At least if they got rid of him they would get us off their backs.

We've decided that in order to keep the pressure up, one of us should go back to Paris. Dad is going this time. And, not just as a father. He will be the envoy of the children of the missing men and prisoners. The first week in December we put the idea to the families here in Southern California. They liked it and we are working on the project now.

On the seventeenth of December I typed up the press releases for Dad's trip, ran them down to the printers, addressed the envelopes and got them into the mail.

It will feel good to have a Nasmyth pounding away at the North Vietnamese this Christmas. Maybe they will finally get our message.

PRESS RELEASE

December 22, 1970 at 12:00 noon, at the L.A. International Airport, John Nasmyth, Sr., father of American Prisoner of War Capt. John 'Spike' Nasmyth; Mr. Tracy Cadenhead, a concerned citizen; and Mrs. Laura Johnson, French-born, a concerned citizen, will board TWA's noon nonstop polar flight to Paris.

The Los Angeles POW-MIA families will see Nasmyth, Cadenhead and Johnson off.

The two businessmen and their businesswoman French-English interpreter are taking with them several thousand letters from the

-212-

children of POWs and MIAs. The letters, directed to the North Vietnamese, urge the President of North Vietnam to release the prisoners for Christmas. Some of the letters were written by interested school children in Southern California.

Nasmyth has wired ahead for appointments with the North Vietnamese Delegation General at 2 Rue Le Verrier, Paris, France and Xuan Thuy at 8 Ave. General LeClerc, Choisy Le Roi, Paris, France.

The Tustin Branch Office of Concern for Prisoners of War Inc. is financing part of this trip. This is the first of many scheduled trips throughout the world which this office will sponsor on behalf of our Missing Men and Prisoners held in Laos, Cambodia, North Vietnam, South Vietnam and China. We will not give up until each and every man is accounted for and home.

THIS IS POW CAPT. JOHN 'SPIKE' NASMYTH'S FIFTH CHRISTMAS IN HANOI.

As Major Carpenter of Phoenix, Arizona, an ex-POW in North Vietnam says:
'It is urgent that we bring all our POWs home now. We can't wait until it's politically expedient—they won't last that long.'

Around Christmas the press is usually after us for information for a 'write-up' about POWs. As we have in the years past, we are trying to provide a fresh slant to make the stories attract attention.

The day before Christmas we arranged for a special church service for the POW-MIA families. When the idea came up in one of our bull sessions, it was only a matter of a day's work to get it rolling.

We contacted Reverend Oliver Warner, a Methodist minister who wanted to help. He offered his church. Then we called some of the very active family members: Janice Lyon, Connie Hestle, the Rehmanns and MIA Larry Stevens' family. They contacted a military choir, clergymen Father Buja and Rabbi Douglas, and organized the service, each family taking part.

We sent out invitations to the several hundred families in the Southland. Over a hundred wanted to attend.

On the twentieth, we went through typing the news releases, printing them up and getting them into the mail. Then we followed up with a personal phone call to the key press people. Everybody showed up. The religious service was beautiful, and the families taking part made it especially touching. No one stayed dry-eyed while the four-service medley was being sung.

I didn't make it to the church, though. We were finishing up the stuff

Pete needs to take on the truck convoy to Paris, when Pete, his temper short, got super pissed off at me. I got to crying and couldn't stop.

It has been so exhausting. Now we just had a few hours left before Christmas.

We went back to the house, which was a wreck. The kitchen table was covered with news releases, bumper stickers, the typewriter; crumpled pieces of typing paper lay strewn about, fabric for POW pajamas piled in one corner, the sewing machine on top. Two radios hummed away with the news, the color TV was tuned to the news. Black and white photos, clippings pasted to the fronts of china closets, boxes of stationery, brochures, clippings, mail to be gone through, letters to be answered . . . there wasn't a single thing that spoke of Christmas in the house. And Christmas is such a special time for our family.

Then I realized that we didn't have a Christmas tree. Mother said, "Forget it, I'm hitting the sack." But I wanted a tree. So, Rick and I took off and bought a dried-out little pine tree at the first lot we could find.

About the time we got back with the tree, I realized I didn't have a present for this guy I'm in love with. I hopped into the car, arriving at J.C. Penney's just before the store closed. I ran in and grabbed two striped T-shirts, raced home and put them under the tree in the store's brown bag. Someone had found the huge box Gebo sent. We opened it and put a beautifully wrapped present for everyone under the tree.

We hauled the box of Christmas ornaments down from Mother's closet, but that's as far as we got. Watched the late news, saw our stories on TV. Exhausted and very, very disappointed, went to sleep.

'Freeze'

Christmas 1970: they passed out packages that we couldn't believe. I don't know if I got a special Christmas package from home or what, but I got a ton. It's the first package that looks like it's from my family, the junk looks like Nasymth junk, a green scarf—green's my favorite color.

This time everybody's getting something; if there wasn't a package for a guy the Gooks took portions of others and made him one.

I mean we got more damn junk than you can believe. We've got two tubes of American toothpaste, two tooth brushes, seventeen bars of chocolate, candy, tobacco, powdered milk, powdered this, powdered that, a pound of coffee. I mean we've got so much junk we can hardly sleep, stuff is stuck all over the place. We've got to sleep with it under our nets so the bugs and rats don't get to it.

It's gonna be a party for the next couple of months.

Christmas day comes, the Gooks tried to stage a propaganda show. Ed Martin said, "We will not participate!!" That was it, no one in our cell block did.

The next morning the Gooks open the door and tell Charlie Baldock to roll up his gear, another switch. Minutes later they open the gate to the prison yard and in walks a terribly mutilated, wounded man on one crutch, a bald head, gaping wounds on his thigh, his leg, and his back. He's limping but carrying his own stuff, a tough son of a bitch.

Close behind is a man with a stiff leg, wearing glasses and cursing the guard. Beside him is a prisoner who's obviously been here too long. The guy's a loony. His eyes are wild, he looks spaced-out. He looks like he ought to be riding a motorcycle with the Hell's Angels. He's taken his prison uniform, tucked in the shirt real tight at the waist, he's wearing socks he picked up someplace, he's stuffed his pants down into his socks.

He's got all kinds of shit stuck down his pants legs. He looks like he just got off a chopper. He's got a funny little hat on, made out of a white rag. As he gets a little closer, we can see it's a handkerchief, tied at the corners, that's his hat, carefully placed over a real long angular face and crazy blue eyes. I look over at Will Gideon, who's a little loony too, and Ed.

"That poor fucker's been here too long."

"Hope they don't put him in our cell."

The badly wounded guy and 'stiff leg' limp past us to the next two cells, 'loony tunes' strolls into ours.

He looks at us, a grin on his face, bobbing his head up and down, eyes shut. In a hollow voice he laughs, "Ha ha ha ha ha ha ha ha ha ha ha ha." He just laughs.

"Wow!" What have we got here?"

The door slams shut. This is Larry Friese. Crazy as hell, maybe, but for sure, (as I was soon to find out) if not *the* smartest, one of the smartest men I've ever known.

"How's it going, I'm Ed Martin."

"Will Gideon."

"Spike Nasmyth."

"Ha ha ha I'm the Freeze, Gooks call me Fi. You fuckers sure are skinny. How long you lived in this neck of the woods?"

"Will and Spike four years, three for me."

"How 'bout you?"

"Ha ha, oh shit man, ha ha, I was in college when they got you dudes, I been here round a year—ha ha—guess I'm at least three years smarter than all of you—ha ha ha . . ."

"Did the Gooks try to get any propaganda out of you?"

"Yeah, you know these little monkeys, always trying but always messing up. Couple weeks ago they put a ping pong table outside our cell, wanted us to play while they took movies. You know, they wanted to show the world their 'humane and lenient policy towards captured American Air Pirates'—ha ha ha—we said 'kiss off.' They took the table away. Then the next day they led me to a room and told me to sit behind a table. In walked about twenty Gooks with movie cameras, lights and tape recorders. I was given a six-line letter from home and told to open it and read it while the cameras and recorders were operating. I wouldn't do it. The dirty little bastards with the tape recorder rapped me in the lips with the microphone. So I spat on the table, tore up the letter and called that Gook the dirtiest name I could think of that begins with the letter c, ends in -er, and refers to someone who engages in oral stimulation of the male sex organ—ha ha ha."

"What did they do to you?"

"Shit man, ten days solitary, that's all. I bet I'm the only American alive who's ever sat across a table from a whole mob of Commies and called one a cocksucker. And I only got ten days—ha ha ha—! Jeeesus, where'd you get all this shit? This joint looks more like a supermarket than a Commie cell!"

"Didn't you get a package?"

"Nah, they're pissed at me."

"Who are the two guys who came through the gate with you?"

"Dale Osborne and Gobel James, Gobel's got the stiff leg.

"How bad is Osborne?"*

"Bad, Gooks have really fucked him up, he should-a died fifty times, but he won't, too damn tough. Let him tell you the story, it will blow your mind."

Friese has only been with us a couple of hours when the door opens. It's Rabbit: "Stand against the wall, take all clothes off."

(Inspection—the little creeps.)

The four of us are standing there naked as jaybirds. The Gooks bring some boxes in and start throwing all our package goodies in them.

"Hey, Will, they're taking our stuff!"

"You can't do that, we just got it. That's mine, get your own!"

Will was furious, he loved food.

"We return package in some days."

"Ha ha ha—lying little monkeys—ha ha ha."

"Could we at least eat a candy bar while we're standing here?"

"No!! Keep silent!"

"Ha ha ha."

"Why you laugh?"

Then they proceed to look in our ears, mouths and up our assholes.

"Hey, Will, have you got a bomb stuck up your ass?"

"Wish I did."

"Ha ha ha."

"No laugh! Keep silent!"

After we had been thoroughly inspected and robbed of our packages, Rabbit told us to get dressed and line up in front of the cell.

They took everything, mosquito nets, mats, extra clothes, all we had were the clothes on our backs.

*Dale Osborne—Badly wounded when captured but some of his worst injuries came at the hands of the Vietnamese. His semi-conscious body was thrown into the back of a truck. The bed of the truck had several bolts sticking up, as his body bounced the bolts dug massive holes in his back. Twice they threw his body from the truck to let him die. Each time he managed to crawl until he found someone. I never heard him bitch.

All eleven from our cell block assembled. I got a chance to say hello to Gobel and Dale before Rabbit started yelling.

"Get in line! One behind other."

"Follow guard to truck, keep silent!"

We walked up to the front of the camp and crawled into the back of an army truck. There were ten or twelve trucks, looked like a big move. A guard jumped in and put a blindfold on each of us, standard procedure.

The truck ride from the Zoo to our destination took about forty-five minutes. The driver hit every bomb crater in town.

When the truck stopped we were still blindfolded. But most of us had adjusted our blindfolds so we could see pretty well.

"Get out, stand in line!"

"Put hand on man in front and follow!"

"Anybody know where we are?"

"Hell, yeah, look around."

(Holy shit, this is where I started out, 'The Hanoi Hilton!')

Off to the left I could see 'New Guy Village,' to the right 'Little Vegas.' In a few seconds we walked through a covered hall past 'Heartbreak Hotel.'

(Damn, I was hopin' I'd never see this dump again, hope these guys got the word about the treatment change.)

Like a bunch of blind men, a human chain, each man's hand on the next man's shoulder. We stumbled into a part of the Hilton that was new to all of us.

We stopped; a big iron door opened.

"Take off blindfolds, go in, keep silent!"

Our new home was huge, about sixty feet long, twenty feet wide, with sloped cement slabs on each side for beds, room for at least forty men. A huge pile on the floor in the middle of the room turned out to be our nets, mats and the extra clothes they took from us back at the Zoo.

The little creeps kept all the goodies.

Dad's Trip

Back before Christmas, on December 21, Dad left for Paris, his preparations for the trip having begun months before.

The fall of 1970 had been pretty ghastly for Dad, an era of complete confusion and frustration. Then sometime in November he was sitting in a little restaurant in Lynwood with a fellow by the name of Tracy Cadenhead. After a couple of martinis he told Tracy, "I've got to go to Europe." Tracy said, "Why don't you?" Dad asked Tracy, "Will you go with me?" He said, "Yeah, I will."

Later on that month in a meeting with the family, he offered to approach the North Vietnamese on Christmas Day. We'd have some real impact then. Everybody thought it was a good idea. After the meeting he called Laura Johnston on the phone. Born in Paris, she could act as his interpreter. The press got wind of it: 'POW Dad Asks Red Meet.' We got word around to all the families that a trip to Paris for Christmas was on.

Then the most pitiful thing of all happened: the wives of the missing men and POWs began to gather innocent little letters from their children to the President of North Vietnam and delivered them into Dad's care. He was to present them to the North Vietnamese in Paris.

Came the day he was to leave, Mom and I and many of the wives and children were at the airport to see him off. We handed him two great big sacks of mail holding over a thousand letters from POWs' children.

Dad, Tracy and Laura arrived in Paris with a minimum of luggage and maximum of mail sacks. There they were in a foreign country with a woman who spoke French, two gentlemen (Dad very much the Victorian gentleman) who didn't. Dad couldn't even ask where the bathroom was. Now what did they do? To get the ball rolling, they started calling the North Vietnamese Embassy. Laura was a little timid about it to begin with, but after the first flat turndown she got the hang of it. They found that even the logistics of placing a call was a pain. Each time they wanted to call the North Vietnamese Embassy, they all tramped downstairs and stood around the girl at the switchboard while she tried to get through to the embassy. Then Laura began the frustrating job of trying to make an appointment with the Vietnamese.

"We're busy."

"The person you wish to talk with is not here."

It all boiled down to the fact that no appointment was going to be granted.

Our mail carriers and envoys called back every two hours for days. Always the North Vietnamese answered with the same crisp, "Hello," and their rebuff, "We are all busy."

In the middle of the telephoning, Dad taxied to the American Embassy for a meeting with Ambassador Habib. He was very graciously received; the conversation was cordial and friendly. As he was leaving, Mr. Habib and his secretary promised them every bit of help they could give, which was absolutely none.

So there they were, Christmas Eve, feeling helpless, back in the hotel room getting turned down. If Christmas Eve was bad, Christmas morning was grim. They got up early, found it was very cold and snowing in Paris. Still in the hotel, they had not made any favorable contact with the North Vietnamese or anybody else. Just to cheer themselves up, they went out for walk. After a few drinks, Christmas Day didn't seem so bad. The unhappy trio headed for lunch in the Eiffel Tower. There the food was horrible, everything on the first level was closed, it was snowing and sleeting. During the lunch, Big John excused himself and had his first experience with a French 'pissoir' instead of a restroom. Back at the table Laura and Tracy were consumed with apoplectic laughter when he told them about it.

On their return to the hotel they began to discuss what to do with the children's letters, so innocently entrusted to them. Doubting that they would ever get inside the embassy and with time running out, they decided they had better deliver the kids' letters by mail, over a thousand of them.

That's when the room service people really went out of their minds. When the maid entered Dad's room that day they were all trimming letters, there were piles and piles of clipped letters and cut-off pieces strewn across the floor.

You see, children tend to scrawl a few lines right in the center of a large piece of paper. They were trimming these letters from the children in an attempt to meet the minimum postage weight. Dad sent Tracy downstairs to borrow a scale from the hotel to weigh them.

After they got over a thousand envelopes filled and licked, they rushed off to the post office to buy stamps. Then they stamped and addressed them, went out into the cold, snowy streets and filled every Paris mailbox they could find. They made trip after trip out of the hotel with the kids' mail. They sent every pitiful letter.

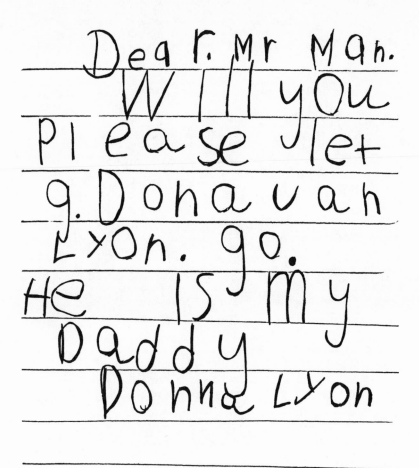

Dear. Mr Man.
Will you
Please let
g. Donavah
Lyon. go.
He is my
Daddy
Donna Lyon

Donna's father, Donavan Lyon, has been missing in action since March 22, 1968.

Xuan Thuy

Dear Sir,
    My name is Suzanne Lyon.
My father Donavan Lyon is Missing-
In-Action.
    I would realy like to
know if he is alive or not.
I am sure that if you were
a little boy and your father
was missing you would like to
know.
    My mother writes to dad,
I write to Dad, We send him
Christmas presants but we don't
even know if he gets them.
    I am 11 I haven't seen him
since I was 8.
    If you are punishing him because
he shot at people you are wrong.
That was his 2 day there, he was
being shown around. We know he
got out of the plane. His Co pilot
Col. Theodore Guy has been seen
in your camp.
                        Suzanne
                        Lyon

Dear Mr. Thuy, Don Lyon is Donnas'
daddy. IS he alive? Please
let him and all the
other men come home. _Carla_

Yes___
No___

NORth VIeTNaMese
please   let
UNCLE   SPIKE
COME   HOME
Jeff NaSmyth

Peter NaSmyth

During the day when they weren't calling the North Vietnamese or addressing letters, they worked on contacting every newspaper in Paris. They ended up with the senior reporter of *Le Monde,* the biggest newspaper in Paris. They gave a long interview to Jacques O. Conrey, in which he showed himself to be anti-American. They were left unimpressed with the Parisians' choice of a foreign correspondent, but were anxious to speak with him because he had just returned from spending several days in North Vietnam. Had he seen Spike? Of course that was too much to ask for. He had no feeling whatsoever for American prisoners of war. Dad's interview with Mr. Conrey made him sick to his stomach.

Dad was getting pretty low, felt like he was spinning his wheels. Having Tracy along helped out. He saw humor in every situation and Tracy provided some humor of his own. There was Tracy in his ridiculous striped nightshirt running around the hotel. First thing every morning Tracy and Dad would ask for a bucket of ice cubes. Well, that put room service into a turmoil. The French were having coffee and hot buns for breakfast; they were having screwdrivers. Of course room service was aware of it. This just threw them into a tizzy.

Finally the day after Christmas, Dad said to Tracy, "Look, we're not getting anyplace. Laura and I are going storm the bastions. We are going to assault the Hanoi Embassy." It was the morning of the day they were to leave. After a couple of brandies to get their courage up they hailed a taxi.

On the ride over Laura confided to Big John that she was a little apprehensive, "I am just so worried because we know what kind of people they are, they might drag me in the door."

They arrived at 2 Rue Le Verrier. Stepping out of the cab they noticed several gendarmes conspicuously situated around the Embassy looking off into the sky.

Dad knocked on the door . . . no answer. He pounded on the door. After a long wait, the door was slowly opened by a thin, slight, angular-faced man, peering out through an iron grill. Dad hesitated, then involuntarily gasped upon seeing face to face one of the hierarchy responsible for giving his son so much pain. Laura paled. Through Laura he said, "I want to see the man in charge." The Vietnamese said, "He is very busy." Laura interpreted, "We came a long way to talk to him. We have new ideas which we want to talk about. We want to discuss the prisoner situation in both North and South Vietnam." He asked, "Are you a delegation? If so, we are tired of delegations."

"We are not a delegation, we are concerned citizens who are here on a humanitarian mission." Dad could see just in talking to this miserable little guy, that he couldn't care less about our boys. "You are holding my son!"

The man's expression never changed from cold, piercing hatred. Dad and Laura offered him a bundle of letters from the children. "We're not interested," he said, "we don't want them." All this in French, of course. "And, we are not interested in talking any further or any more on the subject. Everybody is busy now. I am finished, the interview is over." He slammed the grille and sent them away. It was over so quickly. The whole time they were talking, there had been a man standing in the shadows listening.

Dad felt a little queasy having talked to these people.

Back at the hotel there was a call for John Nasmyth, Sr., from Mr. Habib's office in the American Embassy. Habib wanted to meet Dad at the embassy.

Dad, Laura and Tracy hurried over. They were met by a young fellow who led them through a succession of doors opened with combination locks. Suddenly they were in the environs of the CIA. Their host invited them, "Please look at some pictures. Can you identify who it was you talked to at the North Vietnamese Embassy?" They flipped through stacks of pictures of thin, little, angular-faced North Vietnamese who all seemed to look alike. After studying them they were able to identify who it was they had talked to, as well as the man who had been lurking in the background monitoring their talk.

The CIA gave no further explanation. When finished with the pictures, they left directly for the airport to catch their flight home.

The essence of the whole thing is just this: the more publicity we give to this whole cause, the more world opinion we muster, the better chance our men will be kept alive. It is a tremendous burden.

Back at home, listening to Dad tell about his trip, we knew what he had been through. What could we say? At least the Nasmyth family had represented itself in Paris at Christmas.

Talking about what we should do next, an uncomfortable problem we are experiencing right now came up. During this whole mess, most of the mail we've received from Hanoi (five short letters) has come through the Committee of Liaison. While Mother and I were on our trip around the world last year, we received our first communication from this group.

> Dear Mrs. Nasmyth,
> We have just received word from Hanoi that a letter
> from John H. Nasmyth has been mailed to you from North

Vietnam. His name has been included in a list of 80 servicemen just received . . .

    The Committee of Liaison was set up to facilitate com-
munication between the men who are held in North Vietnam and their families . . . .

This letter was signed by Cora Weiss and Dave Dellinger. We got to
talking about it and Dad let it all hang out: "If there is anybody in this
world I hate with a passion, it's Cora Weiss and Dave Dellinger. They
are the two most un-American people I've ever heard of. They are playing on the passions of the American public like a violin. They are Communists, they are anti-Americans. And yet, they control over ninety percent of the mail that has gone in or out of North Vietnam during this whole
horrible period.

    "Somehow the government caved in when these two parasites came
on the scene. This has been one of the darkest periods of American history,
when our government allowed these people to get a handle on the prisoners
and their families.

    "They are the ones who sent that rotten little actress to Hanoi. How
they got all this power, I don't know. It could never have happened in
anything but the Vietnam war. If it had happened during WW II, they
would have executed them, the bastards."

We have thought and talked a great deal about going through the Committee for our mail. We finally came to the conclusion that getting a letter to Spike is infinitely more important than fighting Weiss and her Committee. The most important thing we can do is let Spike know we care,
we're pulling for him. It was an easy decision because we really want to
communicate with Spike, but on the other hand, it has been a difficult
decision morally.

Comm Team

Eleven in one cell, biggest group I've been with yet: Ed Martin, Art Chauncy, Bob Sawhill, Will Gideon, Jim Hiteshew, Dale Osborne, Gobel James, Ron Byrne, Larry Friese, Don Odell and me. Byrne is senior.

"Hey, couple of you guys watch for Gooks, I'll call the next cell and see what's up."

Within a few minutes we knew that we were in cell number six of the Hilton. Almost all the POWs had been consolidated here right after the commando raid at Son Tay, more than 300 here in eight cells. Some of the cells were extremely crowded, and we could expect ours to fill up soon. Colonel Flynn was senior man in the camp. More tomorrow.

We spent the next couple of hours talking, guessing and speculating. Every few minutes a guard would bang on the door.

"Schleep! Schleep!"

My admiration for the courage of Dale Osborne increased as I heard bits and pieces of his ordeal, and a friendship started that night that proved lasting. My first impression of Gobel was right; he proved himself to be as smart as he was clever. A level head under these circumstances is a rarity. Another lasting friendship.

My first impression of Friese was wrong, all wrong. Well, not completely wrong; he is crazy, crazy like a fox, a slightly demented fox.

Next night the Gooks had a big shuffle. No one ever figured out why they moved us the way they did, it defied logic, and they outdid themselves that night. After three hours of exhaustive commotion they had everybody situated where they wanted them.

"These dumb bastards. I moved three times tonight, here I am right where I started."

"That's nothin, I was in six cells tonight."

"Stupid shits, thought I was Tom McNish, moved me to cell four, Tom was already there."

"Tom McNish! Jesus, he's about 6'4", what are you?"

"5'10" but our Gook names are close."

"Ha ha ha ha!"

"Who the hell is he?"

"I dunno, weird, huh?"

"Who's in charge here?"

"Hope it ain't him."

"No shit."

"Isn't that McNish over there?"

"Yeah, I saw him 'bout an hour ago in four."

"You already told me."

Cell six started to fill up, and we went from eleven to thirty-five.

Friese and I stood on the elevated slab and watched a lot of new and some old faces walk in—pure pandemonium.

"You know him?"

"Which one?"

"That guy that looks pissed off?"

"Well, I'll be damned."

"George! Hey, McSwain, get your ass over here, you crazy bastard, I thought they would have shot you by now."

"How's it hangin, Spike? Long time no see, where you been?"

"Ha ha ha."

"George, this is 'The Freeze.'"

"Whadaya say, Freeze?"

"Understand you're quite the arm wrestler, ha ha ha aaaaa."

"Pull up a piece of cement, George, the shitter's at the other end, doesn't smell so bad down here."

"Good to see you Spike, I've got some stories to tell you, you won't believe 'em."

"Like what?"

"Later."

From four to eleven to thirty-five cell mates in two days, there's so much going on I can't keep up. New faces, new stories, new theories, old stories spiced up a bit; time flew by.

There was Rod Knutson, he and I had tapped to each other for two years, and finally we met. He was the same in person as in code—tough.

I'd been told by a former cellmate that Red Berg was a real loser, a first class prick. I despised that former cellmate and was sure his description of Red would turn out a hundred percent wrong. And so it did. Red's my kind of people, a super optimist, funny as hell and a fine card player. Red and I discussed this former cell mate and resolved the question of "Who's the prick?"

Next couple of days it was organize, organize, "let's get organized." I think we organized a committee in charge of organization.

We split ourselves into four equal groups, one in charge of serving food, one in charge of emptying the two huge shit buckets and keeping the cell clean, one in charge of keeping an eye on the Gooks while we communicated (several hours each day) and the fourth was off. The groups rotated jobs each week.

Each cell block called itself a squadron, and the squadrons were broken into four flights. The high-ranking man was squadron commander, the next four top ranks were flight commanders, and it worked out pretty well.

There were several other positions, all voluntary:

Medical officer. We always tried to pick someone who could get along with the Gooks. This guy told them who was sick and tried to get some medicine out of them. It was important that he be able to get the message across without getting into a name calling contest. (McSwain would not be the right man.)

Education officer. His job was to seek out those who knew enough about a subject to present a class or at least a lecture, then set up a schedule. If he was good, everybody could stay as busy as he wanted.

Chaplain. He arranged some sort of religious service, depending on what the Gooks would allow; some were quickies, some long drawn-out.

Entertainment officer. He dug up the storytellers to relate movies and found the hams for skits.

Communications officer. In charge of the communications team who passed all info from the cell on our left to the cell on our right and made sure all the appropriate info was heard by all in our cell. This was no small task. The high rankers insisted that messages be passed verbatim and that every man got exactly what came from the boss's mouth. The communications load had always been time-comsuming, but now that we were all together it was staggering.

I was always on the communications team, for several reasons.

First, because quite often communicating had to be done over great distances, and my eyes were perfect.

Second, we used several types of hand codes that required good dexterity, and both of my hands worked fine.

Third, reading code requires a quick mind, we send it so fast. My brain still worked.

Fourth, often we communicated hanging from the top of a window or in some other contorted position. Also, if the danger signal was given, you had to move fast, real fast. I was skinny but in good shape.

Fifth, we usually communicated during siesta time (approximately 11 a.m. to 2 p.m.) and I never napped after my wounds healed.

Sixth, (the real reason), it was fun, it gave me something to do. I knew everything, all the gossip, who was doing what, who was mad at whom. Many of the messages were from one man to another with no one else supposed to hear a word of it. Of course, if the sender was in cell number seven and the receiver was in cell number four, the message had to go through the 'comm teams.' We were sworn to keep this type of message confidential and we did, but they couldn't order me to forget a message I'd just passed.

Pete's Trip

'Operation One Hundred Tons.' I don't know who coined the phrase, but that's how we dumped several million letters in the North Vietnameses' lap.

It was the brain child of Denise Evers, a twenty-year old girl from San Diego. The Concern for POWs group in San Diego sponsored it.

The 'Write Hanoi' campaign had been going on for months, with families and POW groups gathering many thousands of letters. We stockpiled them, waiting for the POW truck convoy to carry them to Paris.

Two wonderful men, tough road-hardened Teamsters, Skeeter Barns and Roscoe Slider, drove the big 'semi' plastered with POW billboards and bumper stickers. They carried our letters, our message, and, God, I hope the persuasion to get this mess over with.

They were flanked by a motley crew: three brothers of POWs and a dedicated girl. First there was quiet, polite Don Rehmann, dressed in red and grey striped pajamas for the entire trip (his brother, Dave, has been a POW since Spike's time). Then came crazy Joe McCain, son of an Admiral, brother of POW John McCain, also in red and grey pajamas. Then gungho Pete Nasmyth, dressed in grey, and Denise Evers, one of the Americans who picked up the ball for the POW-MIA families.

The brothers, dressed in my homemade POW pajamas, one pair each for the entire trip (and unwashable because of the dye) and Denise began their 6,000-mile trek. With them they carried our message: Hanoi Release the POWs. It was Christmas Eve, 1970.

They loaded piles of mail in L.A. and San Diego, then picked up the Phoenix mail in Gebo's front yard Christmas morning. On to Mrs. Applebee's house in Tucson for a pile of mail six feet by ten feet.

They made El Paso and Dallas the next day. Whoever planned the itinerary didn't plan time for sleep, so they didn't sleep.

Their POW pajamas were starting to look and smell like real POWs' pajamas.

The truck and men were treated like royalty in Mississippi, where they gave another press conference from their bamboo cage.

Every police car in Alabama had a POW-MIA bumber sticker, and in Alanta, Georgia, Governor Lester Maddox watched as Denise and the brothers unrolled their mile-long petition. So moved was the Governor that he asked Pete for the POW bracelet off his wrist and pressed it onto his own.

After logging only a couple of hours' sleep, they pushed on to Washington, D.C.

"God help this truck get through," Roscoe whispered as he saw the back of it in his mirror fishtailing on the ice. Pete swerved to miss an oncoming car and miraculously avoided the car's fate as it careened over an embankment.

On New Year's Eve they met Cathy Plowman, Jo Ann Vincent and Lt. Frishman atop their huge pile of mail in front of the Federal Post Office in Washington, D.C. Here they were to meet with the 'Dove' Senators, Fulbright and Kennedy, so the Senators could sign their mile-long petition.

Neither Senator showed up.

On the trek across the country, Pete noticed that the truck kept filling up with newspapers, old beer cans, pop bottles and garbage. Pete kept shoveling out the truck at gas stations. Sometimes the litter piled up in front of the windshield until he couldn't even see out.

Joe McCain's presence was everywhere. Not only did Joe gather clutter, Joe lost things. All across the nation, Joe strung out his belongings. He lost suitcases, his pants, his boots, several note books and airplane tickets. In D.C., ready to board the flight to Europe, Joe's ticket was lost.

For the first time, Joe, 145 pounds soaking wet, gathered his trash around him for the search. Pete, Don, Denise and the rest of the party were amazed. He had two suitcases (they were heavy), two big satchels of clothes on his back, a guitar, notebooks and pencils in his hands and a typewriter, but no ticket.

For the rest of the trip, they found themselves carrying Joe's luggage.

The entourage spent two weeks in Paris battling about how to deliver 100 tons of mail to the North Vietnamese. Joe opted for dump trucks. Just back right up and dump the mail on the North Vietnamese. But dump trucks were too wide for the narrow Paris streets.

They settled for stake trucks, hired several and headed out for 2 Rue Le Verrier. With the help of another POW group from Tennessee, they began throwing sacks of mail, piles of mail, literally tons of mail on the North Vietnameses' doorstep. No Vietnamese staff ventured out.

Next morning, they met the press in front of the Viet Cong's headquarters and ceremoniously began to unroll their mile-long petition amid shouts of protest from a heavy-set man at the Viet Cong's delegation fence. A bearded man joined his comrade shouting, waving his arms, demanding in French and English, "Arrest these people, arrest them, I demand you arrest them right now."

Our people just kept unrolling their petition. Seven bodyguards emerged from the embassy house and put themselves in the path of the petition, blocking the three brothers in their POW pajamas and Denise holding the petition. Joe was shouting, "We're not terrorists like you, we're here for our prisoners-of-war."

Arnold McCain from CBS News, in front of the TV cameras, was saying into his microphone, "We are not terrorists, we shall return . . ." when rurrah, rurrah, motorcycle cops stormed up in their helmets, boots and battle regalia. They positioned themselves along the petition.

The bodyguards stood mute; they didn't lift a finger. The heavy-set guy and bearded man shouted and shook the fence while Denise and the brothers carried out their press conference.

Next day as they left Paris, groups from Iowa, Tennessee, Missouri and three delegates from Brigham Young University stayed behind to carry on.

Resisting

Since most of us have only been POWs for four or five years, I guess the Heavies (the high-ranking prisoners) decided we needed a little guidance. Guidance as far as what you can and can't say when talking to an English-speaking Gook, how we are to conduct ourselves, answers to almost every question one can imagine:

If the Gooks say, "You're going home. These conditions must be filled—."

If you are released here's what you can and cannot say—and on, and on and on . . .

From day one, we as a group were never treated according to the Geneva Convention regarding treatment of prisoners of war. We bitched about it as much as treatment would allow. Now that most of us were together and the sadistic and brutal treatment had changed to mild harassment, we made plans to try to achieve complete recognition as POWs.* The communications network was flooded with ideas on how to go about it. Plans were decided on, then policies sent down the line. First, they must recognize our military chain of command. If a POW was told to do anything, he was to tell the guard to talk to the senior man in the cell.

The response was typical Gook, they assigned the most junior man in each cell as 'in charge.' Our sick guys would get no medicine unless this man asked for it. When our senior men gave orders and we followed, they were removed from the cell for punishment, mostly some time in solitary.

---

*We were called 'war criminals' until 1970; 1970-1972 called 'criminals' or 'air pirates' but treatment became bearable. The last month prior to release 'prisoners.' The North Vietnamese never observed the Geneva Convention on POWs.

Some of the tactics of the men in various cells caused me to raise my eyebrows in disbelief. (Of course, what do junior officers know? Get back to teaching Spanish and French and psychology and English and writing dictionaries.)*

The cell next to us decided to go on a hunger strike. Being on the 'comm team' I passed their reasoning from our cell to Dog Brennerman in cell number four, then on around the camp to the Heavies.

"The war will be over soon. The V will want us to look good when released. We think V will give in to some demands just to get us to eat. We will ask for food for the sick. Read back."

The 'read back' was a direction to repeat the message, to make sure it had been understood correctly.

Ken North, the cell six 'comm' officer, received the message from cell number seven, brought it down to the other end of the cell where I was receiving from Dog in number four.

"Get this off right now! '7' says it's hot."

I gave Dog Brennerman the hold signal indicating that what I had was 'hot.'

(The messages were read by the code receiver in a low voice and written on an enamel painted plate by his assistant as they were read. This required a plate, no problem, and a pencil. Pencils are a piece of cake. We stole them from the Gooks. Our thieves had a surplus. Ralph Gaither and Charlie Tyler could steal anything. One day Charlie passed a six-foot-long solid steel crowbar from cell number five to us. Ralph and I passed it on to John Dramesi and Jim Kasler in number seven. The assistant had to be able to write fast. Dog and I were that fast.)

He and I were never in the same cell, but we became good friends communicating in hand code. We stood on piles of folded blankets, he in number four and I in number six, about thirty feet away.

Sad news—Dog looked like he might cry any second. His 'happy' look was great, but Dog was best when it came to the more difficult facial contortions. His 'surprised' look was better than Charlie Chaplin's! No one has ever said, "Are You Shittin' Me!!!' better than Dog without saying it out loud.

When I started sending this 'hot' message, Dog began reading it to his writer, and the further into it I got the more incredulous the look on his face became. Dog could read hand code perfectly, but he gave me the 'repeat' signal after each sentence, as if to say "You're kidding." At the end Dog fell off his pile of blankets in a 'dead faint' act.

*We made dictionaries from the rough toilet paper that was issued. The Vietnamese destroyed them when found. I wrote from memory approximately twenty Spanish, fifteen French and fifty English dictionaries.

When we finished the rest of the 'business' Dog gave me a 'B.S.' meaning he wanted to gab with me if the guys clearing didn't care. I asked, they said, "Okay, couple of minutes."

"Are they serious about not eating?"

"I guess so."

"Jesus!"

"I can't believe it, some of the PW's in number seven are skinny as hell. Render Craighton looks like he's on his last leg."

"I heard from McCain that Render doesn't eat half his food anyway."

"Why?"

"Thinks we should all starve so when we get out we're real skinny. Then the whole world will know how shitty it was before treatment got better."

"Ron Taylor starved himself to death. Said the same thing."

"I eat all I can get, don't know when the V will cut food off again."

"Me too!"

"C.U.L." (See You Later.)

"What did you think of the 'hot' news, Freeze? Can you imagine refusing to eat, holy shit, that whole bunch of nuts is acting as crazy as I did a couple of years ago when I pulled off my starvation act."

"Ha ha ha."

The Gooks reacted to the mass hunger strike the same way I would have, they cut the water supply down to a cup per man per day and completely cut off cigarettes and bathing.

The 'Bug' told cell number seven, "When you want food tell the guard, he will tell cook."

"Hey George, how long do you think number seven will stay on their strike?"

"The smokers will put a stop to it, they didn't count on losing their smokes."

Some amazing and unbelievable reactions followed. A percentage of POWs wanted to join in and make the strike unanimous. Some of the non-smokers suggested the smokers pass half their daily ration over to number seven.

"Bullshit!!" I would gladly share my cigs, food and water as most of us have in the past when we were resisting, but this is different, what the fuck are those clowns resisting? All they have to do is say the word and they'll get their water and butts back.

The strikers decided that another course of action would be more appropriate to 'force' the V to accept our status as POWs.

After much discussion through the 'comm net' the Heavies sent down another order, and I mean they sent down some dumb fucking orders. "We are going to show the Gooks that we are united, but, never let them know we are united." The command told us just how we were to unite and demand our rights as prisoners of war. "There will be an immediate letter writing moratorium. No prisoner shall write a letter home to the United States until we are granted our rights as prisoners."

Larry Friese and I were sitting on the bunk talking when they made the announcement. "If that's not the dumbest fucking idea I ever heard of!"

They went on. "Now for our thinking behind all this . . ." (I say our, but I don't want to include me. I didn't think bat shit of a letter-writing moratorium, Friese didn't think much of it, Jim Warner didn't go along with the Heavies either.)

"The theory behind the moratorium is complex to say the least, but—it is felt by those in the know that the V are making propaganda out of the letters we write home. (By this time almost all prisoners wrote a six-line letter once a month.) If all outgoing mail stops at once, the outside world will ask why? The V will be accused of not allowing us to write. It will be very embarrassing to the government of North Vietnam, hence they will make concessions to us to get us back writing."

The Gook reaction was mixed: they offered us the opportunity to write monthly, at the same time they cut off our mail and packages from home. Giving up mail and packages didn't kill anybody, but we did miss the chocolate, powdered milk, Kool-Aid, real American pipe tobacco and the other goodies our families sent.

Giving up packages was more than just an annoyance for some of us. Jim Warner had put himself through college driving an ambulance. He had read every medical book he could get his hands on, remembering every word. He was the closest thing there was to a doctor in North Vietnam.

Lots of POWs had broken teeth, either they had been knocked out or had been broken off by rocks in the food. I had both the above problems plus two impacted lower wisdom teeth.

When I complained of toothaches 'Doc Warner' prescribed tobacco. I was willing to try anything. Following his example I put a pinch of 'Sir Walter Raleigh' between my lips and gums. Instant relief! Tobacco has a deadening effect much like aspirin. From that moment on I had a mouthful, that is until our packages were cut off.

It bugged the Gooks that we refused to write. One summer morning five months into the letter moratorium I was called up to the Interrogation Shack. Sitting there looking pleased with himself was 'The Bug,' with his right eye rolling uncontrollably, giving him a Cyclops look. "I have tortured all men in this camp," he bragged.

(I wonder what this murdering son of a bitch wants?)

"Nahshit, how are you?"

"Terrible. I need a doctor. I have needed a doctor for five years. My teeth are in bad shape, my mouth is infected. If you would follow the Geneva Convention rules on treatment of prisoners and let Red Cross doctors come to the camp, we would not have to suffer so much."

"Shut you mouth! Shut you mouth! You are not prisoner, you are criminal."

Whenever any of us talked to the English-speaking officers we had a list of things to bitch about.

"Nahshit, do you want to write letter?"

"Yes, but you won't allow me to tell the truth in my letter. I want to tell my family to send me medicine because you won't give it to me."

"Shut you mouth! Shut you mouth!"

When asked if we wished to write home during the moratorium, we were to say yes, then write something they wouldn't allow to go out.

"Nahshit, what else you want?"

Shit, we all wanted out, but I looked him in the eye thinking of this stupid moratorium we're all a part of: "I have been here five years and you have given me only two letters from my family. I would like letters from home. My friend Red Berg has been here six years, you give him no mail. We all want mail and packages."

"Nahshit, listen, listen clearly, I explain to you why you not get letters and packages. You not send letter to your family for six months, is this true?"

"Yes."

"I think you get no letters because your family forgets your address."

(Jesus, how do these dumb monkeys fight a war?)

I laughed out loud. A few years earlier my laughing would have had me back in the ropes.

"Return to your cell."

"Attention, attention! Bug just told me why we're not getting mail or packages—our families have forgotten our addresses!"

"Ha ha ha."

The bigger our groups got, the braver we got. The less obvious control they had over us, the more obnoxious, stupid things we did.

Resist, resist, every cell got into the act. It didn't take long before somebody realized the Gooks were making officers do manual labor.

(Only five years!) We have to clean up our own quarters and make coal balls. You take the kind of coal that's real powdery, mix it with water and pat it into little balls. When it dries it becomes a piece of charcoal. Prisoners always made them. Somebody remembered reading the Geneva Convention: 'You cannot make an officer do manual labor.' So the guys in the cell adjacent to the coal pit said they would no longer make coal balls. The Gooks responded, "Alright, we won't cook anymore." That's an obvious loser. The coal ball resistance lasted about a day.

The senior ranking officer of our cell, Ron Byrne, had a different attitude, "Just don't piss 'em off, just play along. We're gonna get out of this crummy fucking prison, maybe next week, maybe next year, but let's not get killed doing it. We're not gonna get out because of our efforts. Somebody's gonna get us out. So, let's stay alive and stay in one piece."

We proceeded to do just that. Then one day the Gooks did something that really pissed us off. It didn't really piss me off, but it pissed off the committee in charge of 'why we should be pissed off.' So the resisters once again came up with a plan. Unfortunately for my cell, the committee got to Byrne, and he succumbed to their pressure.

"By order of the cell commander, our cell is to go on a 'Hate Campaign.'

Somebody asked, "How do you go on a hate campaign?"

The Commander had the ground rules all figured out: "You look mean at the guards. You refuse to do anything they say, and you don't go outside to wash. You look at 'em and you say things under you breath, and, you get together in little groups and you murmur." This was the plan. (I don't know, maybe they decided we'd all stink so bad we'd rot the country out of existence.)

Everybody sat around murmuring like they were gonna kill Gooks. Anybody could kill them—they're little tiny guys, but they have the guns and the food and the keys.

Whenever a guard looked in, he was met by the most horrible stares the haters could conjure up. With 'kill Gook' faces, of course the Gooks kept us locked in the cell. The longer we stayed locked up the worse we smelled and the more pissed off we became. We spent several days just sitting there, smelling, looking mean, murmuring and hating.

That night the cell door banged open, fifteen guards stormed in, not our regular guards, Gestapo-types, black helmets and real machine guns. Their machine guns were pointed at us. An officer stepped forward, began reading a list of names, and every man on the hate committee was on the list. These men were instructed to 'roll up' and prepare to move.

After the last hater filed out, the door slammed. They were gone.

A few days later we got the word that the guys in the 'Hate Campaign' were taken out to an isolated camp called Camp Huey. They put each one in solitary confinement. End of 'Hate Campaign.'

A few more days passed, then word came down that the guys out at Huey had started writing letters. None of us were writing. We got this message when a few men out at Huey became really sick and were brought back here. Apparently the Gooks had spread the word at Huey that *we* were writing letters. So the guys out there actually started writing. Then they brought a couple of sick guys back to get the word to us. (Clever devils.)

Word came down from the head man, "If you want to write, write; if you don't want to write, don't write." It petered off to become a zero-effect thing.

It boils down to this: Americans do dumber things in large groups than they ever have before. A certain segment formed an official resistance committee. The war was almost over, the guards obviously couldn't do shit to us, you could tell a guard to go get fucked, he couldn't belt you unless he got permission from somebody higher up. Time to resist. Time to unite.

The resistance committee decided we should demand our rights as prisoners of war, even though we had demanded them before but never got 'em. Back then, you didn't demand them very hard because they kept hitting you in the face with shoes, kicking you in the gut. So now that the Gooks weren't being so mean, we demand our rights, right? Red Cross packages, Red Cross doctors, a letter home a month, a letter from home a month . . .

Futile as it sounds, we did make some progress.

We had all sorts of groups, resistance, communications, overt, covert, educational, etc., etc. My favorite group was referred to as 'The Garbage Men.' This elite group had four charter members, Will Gideon, Ed Davis, Jim Warner and me. We met twice each day, at chow time. Our objective: to cut down on wasted food.

"Announcement, announcement! Anybody who has any grub left over, don't throw it away, bring it to the front of the cell. That's all and thank you."

There's no way to describe on a piece of paper some of the shit they fed us. And there's no way to describe some the shit Will Gideon would eat.

As the treatment got better, we were always hollering for meat: "We need meat, we are a meat-eating society."

Finally the Gooks said, "We will give you meat."

They gave us pork fat. There is no comparison between an American pig and a Vietnamese pig. An American pig is 80 percent meat, a Vietnamese pig is 92 percent fat. They took great chunks of pork fat, cut it into cubes and boiled it. It came out boiled blobs of fat covered with little tiny fat bubbles, some with a bit of fatty meat running through, and a hair sticking out here or there. They'd give us a big pot filled deep with these cold boiled fat cubes. Each man's portion is two or three squares of fat and a little bit of grease. Will Gideon could drink it. God, drink grease! Some guys couldn't even take a spoon of it. It gave them instant barfs. Our cell mates would bring us all this stuff they couldn't eat, set it in front of us, 'The Pigs' they called us. We split the fat and grease up, spread the grease on bread, let it harden and there you have it, a sandwich, a grease sandwich. We had a terrible reputation. Just indescribable shit they fed us. To hell with our pride. We were hungry all the time, so we ate it.

"Who called us pigs?"

"Hyatt."

"Leo? He's got the nerve. He took a dump this morning, smelled so bad I thought I was gonna puke."

"Warner, you are a pig! How am I supposed to eat this crap while you're talking about Leo's rotten butt?"

"Where'd you get all your manners, Fast Eddie, at the boat school?"

"Speakin' of pigs—hey, Sully, you ate everything, nothin' left for us."

"You guys must be nuts."

"This stuff's good, what you think, Will?"

"Nothin' like boiled cabbage."

"You ever get enough to eat, Will?"

"Spike, my boy, when I get out of here I'm always going to carry a piece of cherry pie in my pocket.'

MARCH 29, 1971

A court-martial jury convicted Lt. William L. Calley, Jr., of the premeditated murder of twenty-two South Vietnamese men, women and children at My Lai.

Letters

With the 'letter moratorium' at an end, we started getting letters and pictures from home again. The Gooks let us keep the photos in our cells but for some reason not the letters.

Since we couldn't keep the letters, most of the men who got one would read it and in the five minutes allowed try to memorize it, then when time was up, dash back to the cell and rewrite it exactly on the black floor. Bits of orange tile from the roof made good chalk.

Now the fun began. Everybody went over and over each word, phrase, sentence and paragraph looking for the hidden meaning or the clue to the code we were sure was there.

"I've got it, it's the date, March 27th. Just take every second and seventh word, that's it!"

"How's it work out?"

"Kids—couldn't—tree—long—of———"

"That's not it."

Some letters had obvious messages which got by the Vietnamese due to their poor English.

"The gold leaves have turned to silver," simply meant someone had been promoted from major to lieutenant colonel.

"There's a new eagle in our tree" tells the letter recipient he's now a full colonel.

One wife used the first letter in each word as her code.

"Please always remember I still think about loving kisses sweetheart. So eager remain I over ur safety."

Extract the first letter and you have—"Paris talks serious."

My only coded letter came from my sister Virginia, semi-coded.

"Dear Spike, how's my favorite man? Finally moved the rose garden to the front of the house. We are all healthy. Mom works as hard as always. Would you like any medicine or clothing in your next package? We sent the food for Christmas. I miss you very much. Am 21 now and want to go out drinking with you. My trips to Europe have been in pursuit of my favorite man. Glad you got our letter. I got one from you. My Christmas love. Virginia"

'How's my favorite man?' and trips to Europe 'in pursuit of my favorite man' along with a few other hints ('Paris talks serious') told us more about the negotiations in Paris than the Vietnamese ever did.

Some of the photos we received had little messages telling us something of the outside world. A photo of a wife in front of the Eiffel Tower, a mother standing next to the Swiss Red Cross headquarters confirmed the family's involvement in the 'movement.'

With some ingenuity, we came up with a crude magnifying glass and discovered what was written on bumper stickers that were in the background of several photos: POWs NEVER HAVE A NICE DAY, HANOI RELEASE THE PRISONERS, etc.

These innuendos were enough to let us know that quite a commotion had been raised over our predicament, but the extent of that commotion would not be realized until our release.

The Gooks passed out mail, photos and packages in typical Gook fashion, with no visible rhyme or reason. Since the beginning, a handful had received mail on an 'almost' regular basis. These weren't favorites of the Gooks, but enough of a cross-section to keep us confused. A few never got a thing, package or letter. Some received lots of letters, photos and packages, while the majority got an average of one letter for each six months incarcerated.

One almost sure way to get a letter was if it contained bad news. Christmas Day of 1971, Robbie Risner was shown 'the humane and lenient policy' once again. His leg irons were taken off long enough so he could go read a letter from his wife telling of his mother's death.

Apparently a few wives had a clearer understanding of our captors' thinking processes than we ever did. They opened each letter with grave news.

"Uncle Ted died. We miss you . . ." Of course there was no 'Uncle Ted' or 'Aunt Sue' or 'Brother Bill,' but these women got the most letters through to their men. The phony bad news mail kept all of us smiling. 'The Bug' smirked gleefully as he handed out sad news, the receiver chuckled silently knowing at least someone in his family had outsmarted the Gooks.

Impatience

Two more letters arrived this week from Spike, making us feel like the world is back together again.

NGÀY VIẾT (Dated) *18 Sept 1970*

Dear Mom, Dad and Family. How's everyone? I'm fine, nothing wrong with me that a good woman and a bottle of booze couldn't fix. I really liked your last packages. Keep sending lots of cocoa, Butter Brickle, coolaid with sugar (rasberry) chocolate etc. How about a bunch of little containers of cheeze spreads, also de-hydrated milk. Hope to see you all soon Love Spike

CHI CHÚ (N.B.):

1. Phải viết rõ và chỉ được viết trên những dòng kẻ sẵn (*Write legibly and only on the lines*).

2. Gia đình gửi đến cũng phải theo đúng mẫu, khuôn khổ và quy định này (*Notes from families should also conform to this proforma*).

NGÀY VIẾT (Dated) 12 Oct 1970

Dear Mom Dad and Virginia and Family. Recieved letter from Dad, Gebo and Virginia so far I'm thrilled to Know that everyone is fine. Got photo of Larry and Carolondy. Third trip to Europe sounds great, but I wonder why its serious, mabey a man involved? Send a big can of Turtles next package. Packages are fine I'm in good health and spirits. Love and miss you all. Love Spike

Although we've all been pretty down since last Christmas, these new letters snapped us out of it.

Mom was interviewed by the press about her spirits and she grinned and said, "Crying or moping isn't going to get us anywhere. Besides, Spike wouldn't like it."

Regarding the remarks of some of our diplomats that "prisoner-of-war mothers should keep to their knitting . . ." Mom's reply was, "They should have a son who is a prisoner-of-war."

The newspapers like Mom. They are beginning to pick up on her pioneer spirit and straight talk. Her attitude about campaigning on an international front: "We've got to nag 'em to death . . . if we want to get our boys back."

Some of the representatives haven't got the message yet. We're just incensed at our leaders for screwing around with the lives of our guys. Strangers, too, share these feelings. Often someone will send a copy of one of their letters to Congress on to us, to boost our morale. My favorite letter to date is:

June 30, 1971

Mr. Fulbright:
    We would like to recommend that the U.S. Government trade two
Senators for every POW returned to us.
    We realize this is not a fair trade, because the POWs are worth

much more than that.

Here's hoping you will be the first one traded.

Sincerely,

Frank and Mary Lou Morehead

Over 1,300 of our guys are either missing or POWs and we are still having a hell of a time getting our U.S. Representatives to take the situation seriously. America is sick of watching our officials skirt the issue. And the families' frustrations are at the breaking point. I can hardly restrain myself when one of our so called 'leaders' makes remarks damaging to our guys. I'll never forget when Senator Vance Hartke, while addressing an audience of school children, fielded a question from the audience:

A student inquired: "Senator Hartke, what do you think of the POW situation?"

And Hartke replied, "Well, how did the POWs get there anyway, except by fighting a war we don't believe in . . ."

That from a Senator of the United States! It hit the wires, by evening it was all over the papers.

We fell on him like a swarm of angry bees. All of us sent him telegrams demanding apologies, insisting that he shut up. We sent out hundreds of our famous letters citing his outrageous comments and asking families and friends and interested citizens on all our mailing lists to write, call and telegram Hartke too. Governor Edgar D. Whitcomb of Indiana responded by sending us a beautiful letter assuring us the people of Indiana did not agree with Hartke.

You see, we can't have the North Vietnamese believing that we in the U.S aren't absolutely, one hundred percent, behind our men. I sent the most outraged letter I've ever composed to Hartke over this. I'm afraid I suggested (in great detail) that I might like to help Mr. Hartke take his remarks and cram 'em.

We've had it with our damned leaders not standing up for our men.

All of our speaking, writing, appointments with mayors, organizations, leaders and interviews with the press have become an endless blur. What is it going to take to get Nixon and Congress off their duff? We're working our tails off. When we started this campaign we thought we'd only have to 'inform' our leaders about the POWs and MIAs, that they'd take the ball from there, get stirred into patriotic action . . . Not so! They can't do something just because 'it's right,' they must wait around until, 'the time is right.' Can't have our precious leaders sticking their necks out supporting their own POWs, the men they sent to war, oh no!

That's why Dad and Mr. Munoz, whose son David is MIA, are speaking on college campuses. Boy, Mr. Munoz's story is a tear jerker. He is a wonderful man and he loves his son. His story is typical of the many, many MIA families.

Talking to students at California State College, Los Angeles, Mr. Munoz talked about David:

"David arrived 'in-country' on April 25, 1969. He turned 21 on May 1. On May 13, he was officially reported as MIA.

"He and a Japanese boy were on watch with machine guns. When his company pulled out and regrouped, they discovered both of them were missing. When they returned to the area, all that was found was a bloody 82nd patch and a deck of cards. Our family has had no word since then.

"I have one stake in this war, my boy. Like most relatives, all I'm concerned about is information on my son, and not politics. We have written to the governments of the U.S., USSR, North Vietnam, South Vietnam, Sweden, and all other countries we've been told to write. But for the past two years we've had no answers.

"It is all a humanitarian effort!"

Mother, Pat Mearns (whose husband is MIA), Ken Massot (an ex-G.I. and leader in our fight for our POWs) and I met with Mayor Sam Yorty Friday morning to help kick off 'POW Week in L.A.' This along with the speeches and interviews we're doing, is our latest effort to get our government moving.

Finally we can feel it. The country is behind us. Our POWs have become the pride of the people. The momentum of the POW campaign has carried the responsibility of actually campaigning right out of our hands. Sure, we're working as hard as ever, but things are igniting all around us. Since Pete's trip with the mail we no longer feel that one of the Nasmyths has to be pounding on doors in Europe or Asia. There are Americans proudly doing it for us, and for the others who wait and hope.

Besides being invited to make speeches, sometimes twice in one day, and helping anybody who asks for it we are also the audience. We are watching the cry to free American POWs grow louder and more powerful every day.

In March we sent two girls off on a three-week trip to some of the places we've determined are promising. The new Tustin POW office funded part of their trip. We hope this is the beginning of an organized stream of families from the West Coast going abroad with their stories.

We'd like to send somebody out of the country once a month and to Washington, D.C., every two weeks.

I'm slated to represent the California families in D.C. the first of April.

The Jocks

"Hey George, what you doin' tonight?"

"Going to the movies."

"What's showin'?"

At least once a week it was movie time. One of the hams would relate in great detail a movie he had seen sometime in the past. There was only one rule: if you had also seen the movie and the teller got off the track, keep your mouth shut. Who cared how bad *Lawrence of Arabia* was screwed up as long as it was a good story.

Jim Warner was the undisputed Academy-Award-winning movie raconteur. His best weren't repeats from Hollywood but originals from the depths of his weird, sardonic, macabre, lascivious, adroit, droll and outrageously unique mind.

'Sunshine Jackson' is the funniest story I've ever heard. Jim conjured it up one afternoon when he wasn't busy teaching philosophy, history, French, Spanish, or giving a lecture on first aid or discussing Brian Woods'* poker skills.

Warner's stories were surpassed only by his ability to tell them. His timing, emphasis and fierce blue eyes said as much as the words. He drew crowds talking about his mom and dad or the time he babysat a boa constrictor.

"How'd you like 'Sunshine Jackson,' Fast Eddie?"

"Let me tell you, Spike, that Warner ought to be on the stage. I damn near wet my pants laughing."

"Where you going?"

"Down to lust over that new picture of Leo's wife."

"Yeah, she's a fox."

*Brian Woods—Worst poker player in the world, luckily he also had a super sense of humor.

"Leo, my boy, me and Fast Eddie have almost forgotten what real women look like. Can we borrow your wife again?"

"You two are going to wear the damn picture out."

"Spike, you're a two-timer, I heard you ask Hinckley the same thing. Besides we're all going to die here."

"I want to take both of them the sad news."

Leo Hyatt, also known as 'The Black Cloud of Hanoi,' felt that the whole world was squatting over him, taking a dump. You might say Leo saw the dark side of everything. When we got more food, he knew the reason.

"They're building up our strength so we can take more torture."

Some people hate Leo passionately. To me he's a most unforgettable character, one of my favorite people. One of Leo's greatest regrets is that his combat flying was in an unarmed photo reconnaissance plane. He's always been furious about that.

"I never got to kill any of the little creeps; if I'd just had a bomb or two I would have evened the score. After I punched out I hope that damn plane crashed into a mess of 'em. Shit, with my luck it probably landed undamaged in a rice paddy; they'll turn the metal into knives and cut my throat with one of 'em."

Leo's left arm was badly dislocated soon after his capture. Since medicine in North Vietnam has only advanced to the stone age, Leo's arm was never relocated. He hurt bad, he was always in pain. Five years of constant pain didn't help Leo's already hostile personality, and his morning tirades were legendary.

Everybody's a little loony now. We have our own rules. You don't get up at five a.m. and do your exercises, you wait till six when the Gooks ring the gong. Then everybody has to get up. Then you do your exercises. Guys sneak out at two minutes before six and do pushups. Next morning another guy sneaks up three minutes to six. Then a week later it's seven minutes to six. Pretty soon they're up at five.

Tom McNish is already up this morning. It's way before six. He's a great 'sweat-er.' He starts sweating and doing pushups, grunting, making awful noises.

"Dumb shit." I wanted to hit the fucker with a nail, but I knew somebody else would sooner or later, so I didn't have to. I was crazy enough so I didn't want it to show that his pre-gong exercise regimen bothered me.

"Hey, Freeze, what are those loonies trying to prove?"

"Which ones?"

"The jocks."

"They're staying ahead of us."

"Why me, God? Why me?"

Friese bumps me, "Watch this, watch Leo."

Leo's getting up and Leo is in the end of his cycle. He has a cycle kind of like a woman. This part of the month is his most exciting. We could just hear him sit up and grunt, "F-U-C-K." Not an unusual morning for Leo. He grabbed his net and yanked it, making a terrible ripping sound as it pulled out from under his mat. He threw it down, got up and said with authority, "Mother-fucker." (Leo's in a bad mood.) He stomps off down toward the shitter cursing all the way, in a deep gurgling, raspy voice.

There's this little tiny door they've built for the shitter, I don't even know why. There is no privacy. Leo kicks open the stupid door, slams it so hard it flies off the hinges, just splinters the goddam thing. He takes two steps up, squats over the rusty fifty-gallon bucket, then he strains. The muscles in his neck stand way out. His face is scarlet, he's still raving. About forty-five mosquitoes are biting him on his bare feet, because the mosquitoes don't haul ass till it gets really light. Leo doesn't even notice. He just stares at these bastards doing their push-ups and jogging. They never even look at him.

Leo snarls, "This is for all you early bird bastards, for the rest of my life I will think of you freaks every time I take a shit!"

About the time everybody decided Leo Hyatt was gonna have a heart attack, Red McDaniels, one of the intelligent POWs, went to Ron, our C.O. and said, "Tell these fuckers to get back in bed and not get up until the gong goes off."

I mean what are they saving? Twenty minutes! For what? I talked to Tom McNish about it one time, the dumb fucker.

"You dumb shit, you get up at twenty minutes till gong time, what ever the hell time that is. Why?"

Tom's reply, "Well, I like to get done with my exercises."

I say, "So you can what?"

He says, "So I can relax."

Increduously, I ask, "Before you what?"

Genius

In 1969 'The Hells Angels'* offered to send a detachment of their members to Vietnam: "We are true red-blooded Americans, we know how to fight, we won't fuck around, we'll kill all the little creeps and get the war over with, etc. etc."

Larry Friese, (The Freeze) may have been an undercover 'Hells Angels' agent; if not, he looked the part. I gave him the green silk scarf from my last package, he made it into a cap to replace his tattered white one. The Freeze looked ready to ride.

Looks can be deceiving. Friese owns one of the most intricate minds I've ever encountered. How his brain revealed itself only made it seem more complex.

Three or four holders of engineering degrees of one sort or another were working on a problem of gigantic proportions: how to send a rocket to the moon, then get it back, a really complicated problem which took up about twenty square feet of floor space. With no books, all the formulas and diagrams scratched out on the floor had to come from the engineers' memories.

The moon men pleaded with us not to walk on this project until it was completed.**

"Pi R squared = mass minus gravity ± infinity ×
temperature ÷ the speed of sound—the speed of light +
three martinis = a piece of ass bla, bla, bla . . ."

---

*They really did make the offer. It was not accepted. (It should have been.)

**With pieces of chalk, the black floor as a blackboard, anyone walking over the project would be the eraser.

Something was missing. They got this poor astronaut to the moon but couldn't get him back. Bedlam reigned. 'Hot' messages flashed all over the camp: "Who remembers such and such formula? We are desperate!"

No answer. Frantic, our scientists are blowing their minds.

'The Freeze' and I have been playing a stupid dice game called 'Acie-Deucie' which he always wins.

"Ha, ha ha aaa, that was easier than last time."

"Fuck you!"

"AAAAAAaaaaaa"

Still chuckling and gloating over his victory, 'The Freeze' stands up, stretches, and looks down toward the engineers, probably thinking to himself, "Those dumb shits still on that same problem?"

'Freeze' took a couple of laps around the cell in his motorcycle outfit, hands behind his back as though strolling in the park. Each time he passed the 'problem' he'd glance it over and chuckle, "Ha aaa ha aaa . . ."

On his third lap he stops at mid-problem. He erases this monstrous formula with his bare foot. The look of death comes over the faces of about fifteen of these engineers. Ignoring the moon men's shrieks, 'The Freeze' leans down with a piece of chalk and fills in the spaces he just erased with new hieroglyphs.

"You son-of-a-bitch, what the hell are you doin?"

"Ha ha ha aaaaaaa."

'The Freeze' strolled off.

"Jesus Christ, all this shit is right."

"Look! come here, look! Now we can get 'em back, God damn, we got it, this is great, I knew we'd get it . . ."

"AAAAAAaaaa."

"Holy shit."

They hated the fucker for it. He knew the answer all along.

"Hi ya, Leo."

"Hi, Friese, what's new?"

"Is the Naval Academy really that fucked-up a place to go to school?"

"Bullshit, it's the best goddam school in the country!!"

"Yeah, I thought it was good, but Jerry Singleton just told me it was a piece of shit compared to the Air Force Academy."

"Why that dumb fucker . . ."

"Hi ya, Jerry."

"Hi, Friese, what's up?"

"Not much, say is that Air Force Academy really as lousy a school as Leo and Ralph say?"

"They don't know what they're talking about, especially Ralph, he's just jealous, they never let him in."

"Ralph, baby, how's it goin?"

"Good, real good Friese, how 'bout you?"

"Okay. Say, Ralph, are you really as illiterate and ignorant as Jerry and Leo say?"

"What did those two tin soldiers say? I probably forgot more last week than those two ever learned. They know zero except how to kiss ass."

'The Freeze' has just incited the most fantastic prison fight ever heard. Three grown men screaming at the top of their lungs, shaking fists, ready to do mortal combat.

Leaning against the wall laughing and chuckling is Hanoi's own 'Angel.'

"Ha Ha AAAA aaaa . . ."

Every week we have a duplicate bridge tournament; most of the guys who know how to play participate. 'The Freeze' and Jim Warner have never learned the game, so they don't compete.

Red Wilson loves to chide Friese about his lack of knowledge regarding the great game of bridge, 'cuz that's about the only thing he doesn't know about.

One day Friese and Warner asked me to show them the bidding system I use, 'The Big Club.' After several minutes of intensive instruction, Warner made a grandiose announcement to all in cell number six.

"Attention, attention, if I could have your undivided attention for a few seconds, even though that is longer than the average attention span in this uncouth place."

"Get to the point, Warner!"

"Friese and I have in the last five minutes learned all there is to know about this trivial game of bridge. We will enter the competition this coming Sunday and we shall win. That is all."

"Oh, yeah. You won't win one point!"

"You'll eat those words, Warner."

"Put some money where your mouth is, Warner."

"God, I can't wait to destroy you. You think you're so smart."

"Ha Ha Ha Ha aaaa."

Much to the annoyance of almost everyone, Friese and Warner won their bridge tournament debut.

As the gods would have it, the deciding hand was between the teams of Friese-Warner and Bob Lilly-Red Wilson. Red made a defensive bid to stop Friese-Warner from reaching an easy slam contract.

"That's about the dumbest bid I ever heard, Red. I thought you had better sense."

"Shove it, Friese, what are you gonna do about it?"

"I double."

Instead of playing and making slam, which would have earned Friese-Warner 500 points, they defended against Lilly-Wilson at an impossibly high level. The Lilly-Wilson team went down six doubled which gave Friese-Warner over 1,000 points for the hand, and enough to come in first overall.

"Ha Ha Ha Ha aaaaaaaaa . . ."

"NO RED, DON'T! DON'T DO IT!"

In a complete rage, Red threw the deck of cards out the window, out between the bars, never to be seen again.

"Ha Ha Ha aaaaa . . ."

The Film

Hot damn! Was Mother excited when she received a letter from the Air Force this week. She read the letter and kept the information to herself.

The message said that an Air Force installation out by Los Angeles International Airport had a film of American prisoners of war taken in North Vietnam. They would be showing it in a few days and she was invited to come and view it. Invited to come and view it! Hell, she couldn't wait.

Wednesday morning early, she drove out to the Air Force Base. There were about a hundred POW families, POW people milling around; Dorothy Brazelton, Gladys, the Rehmanns, Margaret, Lorraine, Patty, Carol, everybody was there.

They had all been together hundreds of times working on behalf of the POWs, but this was the first time for a film. They were sitting in a room set up just like a movie theater: men, women, kids, you know, families.

Colonel Gratch gave a short preparation speech.

"I have a short film here, I'd like you to watch. I hope some of you can identify some of these men."

A wave of anticipation moved through the room. The families didn't know what to expect, everybody was just cool.

So he showed it. Everybody sat there still as a mouse. They sat there and watched the film very quietly. Not a single person made a comment, the film just raced by.

After he had shown it once, he said everyone was welcome to join him for coffee and cookies. (He knew what he was doing, the sly ole fox.) He led his audience out for a few refreshments. Afterwards he would show it again. Meanwhile, they were just a bunch of unconnected people milling around in a building. There were a couple of card tables set up with refreshments over at the other end of the room. Mom, a cup of coffee in her hand, milled around with everyone else making inconsequential small talk. Everyone's mind was still on that murky film.

Then he had them sit down and he showed the film again.

The film was half finished and still silence. A few moments later Elaine Pyle's voice rang out: "Hey, that's Darrell!" Somebody else said, "There's my son." Shirley Pitchford picked out her John and Kathryn Rehmann recognized Dave; Corita Chambers recognized her son, Dennis.

Then the film got to the part with the back of the neck and it hit Mom. She stood up, "That's Spike!" Then she started seeing him everywhere, because he was the one who was serving the cookies.

The film was over. Nobody cried, but then everybody who had recognized somebody, and there were a lot of them, got all fired up. And the ones who didn't recognize anyone in the film just sat there very, very quiet, still waiting. They knew it then and there, their man wasn't in the film, but they kept looking. They asked to see the film three or four more times. People called out, "Stop it there! " "Back up." "Can you hold that frame?" Colonel Gratch worked to find each frame they wanted to see.

Mom didn't know what to say. Some of the families were so happy and relieved. There was no cheering or back-slapping, though, because of the families who couldn't find their guys in the film. Some of our friends were in incredibly low spirits.

The film was being shown all over the nation. It was going to Phoenix in two days.

Mom phoned Gebo and told her, "You must go see this film." She gave her no hints as to what to look for. She wanted to see if Gebo could independently identify Spike. Gebo saw it at 9 a.m. at her local Air Force Base. Then she immediately called me in San Diego.

"What!? You've got a film with Spike in it? Can you keep it for a couple of hours? I'll be right there."

I called Mom, got money from her for a flight and caught the next plane to Phoenix. I arrived about three hours after Gebo had called. Gebo had the Air Force hold the film over and they rescreened it for me.

Gebo told me Spike was definitely in the film but would give me no clues. She wanted me to independently identify him, just as she and Mother had.

The film started. I was straining forward in my chair to see him. Just couldn't wait. After fifteen seconds I was afraid he'd gone by without my recognizing him. Gebo just said, "Keep watching." The lighting in the film suddenly changed and there was the back of Spike's head and neck right in front of me. "There's Spike, there's Spike!" He turned with a silly look on his face. He was standing upright, holding a tray of cookies. We watched him take a few steps (walking normally, no limps) stop, and bend while two prisoners took a cookie each. As they reached for their cookies there was a brief covert exchange, Spike talking out of the side of his mouth. (We could only imagine what they were saying.) It was such an unnatural exchange, everyone so staged, so careful.

While we watched this brief scene, I wondered if these POWs had ever been together before, or had they just let them out of solitary confinement for the filming? Could this be the first time they had come together? Speculating on what kind of information was being passed between Spike and the other prisoners, we found it thrilling to see them getting away with something. We watched as Spike began to turn full face toward us, then it was over.

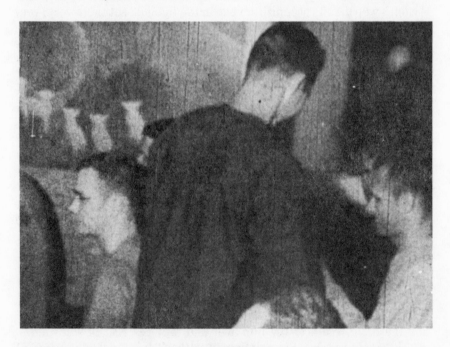

Back of Spike's neck, one still frame from the U.S. Air Force film of the POWs.

"Oh my God, show it again!"

They showed it again and again. Now Gebo and I were talking during the film.

"He looks great; look, no burns and he's holding the tray."

"Both hands look okay and best of all, he's walking."

After finishing with the film, and it was hard to stop looking at it, we went to Gebo's home and the phone calls started.

Gebo has two phones. We called Mom. Now that we had recognized Spike in the film, she let go with a flood of emotion. Boy, were we excited. We talked and talked, especially about how good he looked.

Then we called Dad and Pete, and I called everybody I could think of.

Back in L.A., when the meeting with Colonel Gratch had broken up, Mom had extracted a promise from him to get a copy of the film. I don't think he was supposed to make a copy, but a couple of weeks later she received a good, clear reel of the film from start to finish and a black and white print of every frame.

She immediately told everybody she knew that she had the film and the prints. The local folk descended upon the house like a herd of buffalo. There hadn't been time to study the film out at the Base, but you could really study the stills. They used the stills and brought magnifying glasses and black and white photographs of their men from home for comparison. Mom gave away stills to the families whose guys were in them. It was only a couple of hundred frames, as the film ran about a minute.

Carol Hanson came over once or twice to look at the pictures. Patty Hardy came over every couple of weeks for a while, trying to dig Jack out of the fuzzy guys in the background.

Pretty soon the news people came out for interviews and asked Mother if she had seen the new POW film from Vietnam. She said, "Sure, I've got a copy of it." They asked to see it.

She brought out the film and the stills. "You want to use it?" They did.

Several different times, different news outfits asked Mom if she had seen the POW Christmas program. Each time she said, "Yes, I have, I have a copy of it. You can borrow it, but I have to have it back."

They promised everything, chopped it up to suit themselves and returned the scraps. The last time it came back, it was an empty can.

Rats

There were a couple of unsung heros in this outfit. Ralph 'Gator' Gaither, besides being one of the most obnoxious, opinionated SOB's who ever walked, was one of them.

He was such a religious fanatic I used to call him the 'Preacher.' The son of a bitch gave real sermons on Sunday. And I mean you thought you were listening to a hellfire Baptist with a Charlton Heston voice. Gator could quote the Bible better than the Pope and he did and did and did.

Ralph, a big, muscular, stubborn mother fucker, made you want to hit him. If you knew him ten minutes though, you wouldn't want to hit him because it would break your arm, so you'd want to hit him with a bat, or better, a lead pipe.

However, this man was a master with his hands. He could make anything. His skill contributed to the mental well-being of every member of cell number six.

The last man captured before President Johnson stopped the bombing in '68 was Mark Ruhling, who moved into number six sometime in '71. Now, the first night he came into our cell he slept next to me and Larry Friese, me next to the shitter because the smell didn't seem to bother me. They always put the guys who ate all the junk down there because we farted a lot. So this guy comes into the cell. About midnight Friese gives me the elbow. He whispers, "Rats, rats, get the stick." We have a big board we use to kill rats with, we've killed lots of them. I get this damn club, Friese grabs his club. Friese tugs on Ed Davis, who's a rat killer, and a couple of other rat killers. We sneak down by the shitter. We block the door. No rat can get out, we've got him blocked. We look in there, there's no rat, but we can hear the son-of-a-bitch. We track him down.

Friese says, "He's down by what's-his-name's head."

Here we are, four men, sneaking around this guy's mosquito net, stalking toward his head. We've all got these big fucking sticks, we're gonna kill this stinking rat. Rats here are as big as cats. We can hear it, we're tracking right in on it. I figure the rat's chewing on this new guy's ear or something. Quietly we raise his net so we won't scare the rat off. Now we're all huddled around this poor guy, our clubs raised. No rat! We can see his jaw going round and round. Shit! He's grinding his teeth. It's like nothing you've ever heard, a high, piercing, squeaking noise, and it sounds exactly like a rat.

Now men at the other end of the cell sixty feet away are getting up, they hear the 'rat' too.

Leo Hyatt is in the last bed because they always put him as far away from everybody as possible. He walks down toward us, he's pissed. "Fucking Gooks, fucking Gook rats. Even the rats are keeping me awake. What's the matter with the fucking rat patrol?"

There are about twenty of us looking down at this guy's jaw, going back and forth, back and forth. Man, this guy's gonna drive us crazy. Half the cell's already listening to this shrill noise made by his grinding teeth.

We wake him up, he looks around at all of us. "Oh shit, I'm sorry, I've got this problem."

Mark Ruhling sits up and tells us of his teeth-grinding habit, which has been with him all his life. When he got married his wife insisted he do something about it. He had a mouthpiece, like a boxer wears, made which he always wore in bed so his wife could sleep.

"Well, pal, you can either stop sleeping or stop grinding your teeth. You're driving us nuts. We've been living in this rat infested hole . . ."

Ralph Gaither was standing around listening to Ruhling's story. 'Gator' can make anything. I swear he can make something out of nothing. Some of the stuff he made was important, like drills. When we needed to drill a hole through a wall from one cell to the next for communication purposes Gator made the drill. He made drills from pieces of wire better than you can buy at the hardware store. His drills buzzed, they were that fast, took only twenty minutes to get through three feet of cement.

"Hey, Ralph, I want to drill through two bricks, what should I use?"

"Use a Gaither #4."

The next morning, without saying a word 'Gator' takes some wet bread dough, walks over to Mark and sticks it into his mouth. Then he takes his 'cast' and a piece of plastic, somebody's red-handled toothbrush and goes to work.

Gaither was like a hermit. The son of a bitch went down to the end of the cell with one of our punks (twisted paper smouldering to light cigarettes) and this toothbrush, sat with his back to everybody, didn't say a word.

That evening right before we went to bed, Ralph walks over to Mark, takes this red bent piece of plastic, sticks it into his mouth. One fitting, popped it in.

"I can't believe it. This is better than the two hundred and fifty dollar one the doctor made back home!"*

There are lots of ways to keep people from going even crazier after you've been in a prison for five or six years.

You might be a master craftsman capable of making tools from nothing or changing a piece of plastic into a mouthpiece, or perhaps you're a champion poker chip maker.

Dick Bolstad was and I'm sure still is the master poker chip and dice maker in POW history. His chips were perfect, perfectly round, perfectly decorated, perfectly colored and hard as a rock. Sandy Koufax could throw a Bolstad chip against a steel wall and it would bounce back unmarred.

Dick's chips were beautiful things, some were the color of brick dust, a pretty shade of red-orange, others colored with coal came out flat black. When Dick could convince Zorba the Gook that he was suffering from foot fungus and score a little foot medicine, he made dark purple chips.

Making poker chips in a prison cell from bread dough mixed with various coloring agents created more problems than one might think. When the semi-finished chips were laid on the window sill to dry, there was a fairly good chance that the rats would carry them off or just take a bite or two. Bolstad found some secret ingredient to mix in with his chips which kept the rats away. This discovery kept his chips tops in quality.

With Dick's high-quality chips and the low-quality Gook playing cards, a mighty poker game was inevitable. It started as a sporadic thing, then as the disease took hold, poker became a ritual.

When the 'heavies' heard of our big games they of course sent guidance down to us of less judgment:

"Poker can be played only if these rules are strictly
followed:
1. 25¢ limit with three raises.

---

*Rumor has it Mark still wears his plastic mouthpiece.

2. If any man loses $1,000.00 he can no longer participate.

Of course, we had no money, so a running score had to be kept of each man's winnings or losses. That was the job of the 'Poker Czar.' I was Czar of cell number six.

At the end of each game the total amount won had to match the total lost to the penny. After balancing it out I would then adjust each man's total on the master list. It showed every player's total winnings, or in more than half the cases, his losses. The plan was that after release I would collect from the losers and pay the winners (which I did). Every loser paid and every winner was paid.

Since the Gooks wouldn't let us have pencils or paper, the master poker tally was illegal and would have been confiscated had they found it. For this reason I kept the record on a piece of cigarette paper which could be wadded up and stuck in my ear in case of INSPECTION.

I took a great deal of care with the master tally, my concern was justifiable, because my total winnings came to $3,740.25.

Expendable

There is a sort of division among the POW families. Hell, it's more like a bunch of old hens scratching and pecking at each other. It became more and more apparent as I prepared for my upcoming trip to Washington, D.C. The POW families are torn: the Nasmyths, Rehmanns, Salzarulos and some others believe that persistent, hard action in the U.S. and all over the world is what's going to get the POWs out. No tip-toeing around with formalities for us.

Many of the other families are for discreet letter-writing, polite chats with government officials, and allowing the National League to carry the ball in Washington, D.C.

Some of these people are timid; in my mind some of them are just plain wrong.

We've got POW organizations all over the country now. Most of them are very good, but some have begun playing the power game. Rather than have the National League continue to discuss the POW situation through 'proper channels', we want to see individuals from California (the mavericks, so to speak) carry the word back and apply some of that uncomfortable public pressure.

In April, when my turn came up, I flew back to D.C. with my childhood friend, Mary Flournoy. She came as a traveling companion, the voice of a concerned citizen and as my source of strength. I need that because, frankly, bringing the POW story back to Washington after five years, still seeking some concrete action by our leaders, has left me a little shaky.

We got off our plane, settled in a hotel within walking distance of the Capitol and set out for our first meeting. We had an appointment with Captain Ellis, aide to General Chappy James, at the Pentagon.

I was a small 22-year-old woman, my friend Mary was just 20, blonde and about five-foot-three—not a particularly formidable looking pair of individuals. But when we walked into the following four offices with mouths set, pad and pencils in hand, you should have seen them squirm. The faster we wrote, the less they said and the more uneasy they became.

At each of our interviews I presented myself as having personal views as well as carrying the opinions of many POW families with whom I am in contact. I explained our setup: a POW family member travels with our funds and blessings in an effort to inform, pressure, communicate and show how great the public support is for our POWs, and that we shall not stop until all our men are home and accounted for. My manner was very tired, intense, emotional, determined and pleading, all of which I felt in turn.

Wandering around the Pentagon to find our way to our first appointment with Captain Ellis, we ran into Bob Dornan. Bob's been a flamboyant POW supporter, both as a broadcaster and elected official, tireless in his efforts for a couple of years now. Bob has an appointment in the White House tomorrow, but we couldn't get an appointment with the White House. He couldn't get one with the Pentagon. So we invited Bob to go with us and we'll join him tomorrow.

First stop, Captain Ellis. After we were all seated around his very small office, I started off at the top of my list of questions.

"Captain Ellis, what is the United States' official policy on North Vietnam's demand for a withdrawal date?"

Captain Ellis' reply: "The North Vietnamese have not officially said they would release U.S. POWs according to the Geneva Convention. They have officially only stated that they, as North Vietnamese, would begin to discuss the POWs when the U.S. set the date."

Bob Dornan suggested that President Nixon demand time on national television to discuss POWs. Ellis made no comment.

I asked why Chappy James' luncheon speeches were four-fifths patriotic and only one-fifth POW.

Ellis: "Why not?"

Me: "But bringing American POWs home should be a point of national pride."

No response.

Then I asked, "Is there one man in charge of POWs, one man responsible, one man who can really tell us what is going on?"

Captain Ellis referred us to the President's POW Committee. Then I suggested that Nixon offer to meet with the North Vietnamese anywhere to negotiate for our POWs.

Ellis said, "That's what Paris is all about."

I asked Ellis, "Do you feel attuned to the POW families? Many of us are impatient, sick of it, ashamed of the U.S. government."

Captain Ellis shifted in his chair a little, didn't say anything.

From me again, "What is happening, what is our Government doing for our POWs?"

Ellis was ready for this one. "That's what Paris is all about. The lack of results there isn't our fault. We're at their mercy." (Can you feature that, the U.S. at anybody's mercy?) "We are open for ideas. We must think of more than exclusively the problem of the POWs." (Now it's a 'problem,' how convenient.) "Does he, the President, want to start World War Three to free the POWs? Do you have any ideas about what we should do?"

I answered him. "Hey, it's not fair to ask POW families for ideas. You're the leaders, you're the experts."

Ellis was really rolling now. "The POW families should write letters, inform the public."

Boy, what bullshit. I thought it, but I didn't say it. Didn't he know we had just completed Operation One Hundred Tons, the biggest letter writing campaign in history?

Exasperated, I asked, "Does our country feel responsible for these men?"

Captain Ellis, "Yes, who else would?"

There's nothing like being treated like a moron. As we were getting up to leave, Ellis threw in the giant appeaser, "The United States is working through third parties . . ." (i.e. foreign intrigue, the CIA, Spooks . . .) and that was that.

Next morning Mary and I set out for our appointment with Mr. Daniel Henkin, Department of Defense. We followed the same routine. She and I were seated taking notes while Mr. Henkin responded as we reeled off our questions. For Mr. Henkin we started at the top of the list, just as we had with Mr. Ellis. "What is the United States' official policy on the North Vietnamese demand for a withdrawal date?"

Henkin came back with, "Officially the North Vietnamese have stated only that upon receiving a withdrawal date from the President, they, the North Vietnamese, will 'begin to discuss the prisoner of war situation!' Contrary to what it sounds like in the press, this is what they have offered in Paris. Giving a withdrawal date is strategically a bad move. The U.S. will not move into the hands of the enemy."

We went through some of the same questions with Henkin that we used with Ellis yesterday. We weren't really getting anywhere, so we switched to talking about the sensitive subject of Cora Weiss and the Committee of Liaison, the North Vietnamese choice for our mail carriers. I asked if the Government was going to move on this. Weiss and her Committee have a terrible hold on the families. It definitely goes against our grain to use her to get mail into and out of Hanoi, but we feel we must.

We are afraid as individuals to tell her to take a flying leap, but we sure would like the government to step in and close her down. How did the Committee get to be our only link with Hanoi? It's another blunder on our government's part, letting a bunch of traitors harass and intimidate the families. So we asked, "Will the government do something about Cora Weiss? Our family and some other families feel we are subtly being harassed."

Henkin said, "No. Many of the POW families fear that if the Committee of Liaison's mail channel is cut off, no new mail route will open up. The Government will not offend those families nor take any chances with the little mail which is coming in." This he said, "is due to the majority of the families' opinions. However, apparently a few men and families are receiving mail through other channels."

Here it is again. A classic case of the Government not coming out strong about anything regarding our prisoners of war. We can't stand the thought of shutting off our communications with Spike. But, for-crying-out-loud, we should never have been put into this position. Uncle Sam should have shut Cora down the day she opened up.

We told Mr. Henkin that we felt it was time we had one man in charge of all aspects of the POW issue. We want one man who has all the information all the time. Henkin referred to the 'White House POW Committee.' He gave us the names: "Colonel James Hughes heads it up and then there's General James, and Frank Sieverts. This committee meets once a week. Colonel Hughes reports directly to President Nixon."

We suggested that Vice President Agnew take on the POW project. It was tossed around as a good idea.

"Why doesn't Nixon offer to meet anywhere in the world to specifically talk POWs?" He mentioned Paris again.

We told Henkin of the families' dissatisfaction with what, if anything, the Government is doing. "What *is* the Government doing?"

"The President is doing everything within his power to repatriate our men. Third parties are involved . . . You know what that means . . ."

God, I hate that phrase, that false-hope-raising phrase.

We went on: "Why doesn't the government make our POWs a point of national pride? Economic pressures could be put on the North Vietnamese allies. We ought to be acting like a country that wants our 1,600 men home." It was all kicked around as an idea with 'potential.' Another false-hope-raising phrase.

Our interview wound up when something was said like, "Don't worry, we'll never abandon our men." I came back with, "You know we are ashamed of our government. We feel our men *have* been abandoned.Wouldn't you call eight years as a POW in some hell-hole abandoned?"

Last on our list for Henkin, we discussed Spike's request for Thermo-clast (medicated) toothpaste. We thought this was an example of the physical deterioration he must be going through.

With each person we visited, we left off an example of the latest letter-writing campaign we have under way. This one offers support for Nixon in getting the POWs out. We also left a picture of Spike before he left for Vietnam and a picture of Spike now, a POW in Hanoi.

Our next meeting was with a giant black man, General Chappy James, the first black four-star General. He wouldn't even let us sit down until we promised to call him Uncle Chappy. He acted as a friend, and we considered him a good one.

General James' attitude was, (and you darn well better believe it while in his presence anyway): "We are doing everything we can. My job in the Pentagon is to muster public support for the POWs, among other things." He did have a rigorous speaking schedule.

We asked: "What is our government doing for the POWs which is definite, something we can put our finger on?"

We heard about the weekly White House conference again, that our complaints, concerns and ideas or suggestions were being brought up then. On a possible withdrawal date, we were told flatly: "It will not be given. North Vietnam will not budge."

We went through our whole list of questions, kicked them around and only jumped on one new point. That is: "Prior to our visit it was strongly suggested to Secretary of State Rogers, by the families, that on his present international tour he talk about the POWs. This has yet to happen. He hasn't said a word. Rogers, a figurehead of sorts, could be expected to at least mention them." (When I look at Rogers I wonder if he is even aware of the POW problem, but we didn't go into that.)

Uncle Chappy was warm, consoling and fun to talk to. Although when we were finished with our meeting and out of the office, we realized we had been party to his 'mustering support for our POWs,' among other things. It felt great, but we hadn't accomplished anything of substance.

Our frustrations have been building over the past few months spent trying to think of something new to do for Spike and his buddies. It has taken two or three years to show the government some very elementary points:

Being *for* the POWs is not antiwar.

The POWs can unite the country.

The POWs are the first issue in the war which cuts across political party lines.

Both 'Doves' and 'Hawks' alike can rally behind our POWs.

So, we came to Washington excited and hopeful, wanting to believe in the government's interest, and we delivered our message: "Hey you guys, we're glad you're going to take the ball." Only to have them throw it right back to us.

I didn't keep notes on our last interview, but I'll never, never forget that day.

We accompanied Bob Dornan on his appointment to the White House. We were Bob's tag-alongs as he held the appointment with the head of Nixon's POW Committee, Colonel James R. Hughes. Bob, Mary, and I were picked up by a limousine and driven to the White House. It was a bit awesome being escorted onto the White House grounds, such a powerful, serene-looking place, if only to see Nixon's chief of military affairs, Colonel Hughes. After being shown to his office we all sat around his large, very tidy desk. The office was decked out in patriotic paraphernalia, as you might expect in a military man's office, an American flag in the corner. I love seeing our flag.

Bob Dornan came on strong, bringing up the issues we had previously discussed at the Pentagon.

Colonel Hughes, not one for idle chatter, yet not particularly comforting either, rattled off what I call the perfunctory 'get 'em off my back' answers.

We could all see we were getting nowhere, when I hit him with: "Colonel Hughes, we, the families, don't think it's fair for you, the experts, the leaders of this country, to ask us what we think should be done. We've just been told to start a letter-writing campaign to inform the country about the POWs. The country knows about the POWs now. They want them back. We're sick of it, and we're becoming ashamed of the U.S. government. What does it take to get this government to get our men back?"

The Colonel looked piqued. He looked right at me, right into my eyes. He spoke at me in a brisk, 'I'm going to tell you some facts of life' manner. He said, "Young lady, these are professional military men we're talking about. They knew what they were getting into when they flew over North Vietnam. If it comes right down to it, they are expendable."

I felt very hot and very numb. I know I turned red. That's all I remember of the meeting. That horrible, unmentionable possibility came right out of the mouth of a man sitting in an office in the White House, one of the men on the President's select POW Committee.

Later, back at our hotel with Mary, I tried to take stock of what was happening. Here we had been sitting in the White House, facing one of the President's advisors on POWs. We had delivered our message of disgruntlement from the POW families to the State Department, the DOD, the Pentagon, and now, Colonel Hughes. Prior to meeting Hughes, everyone else had told us we ought to start a letter-writing campaign. How ludicrous of them to suggest such a campaign. To 'inform the people,' when it had already been done successfully with our blood, sweat and tears over the past three years (without the help or blessings of our government). The 'Write Hanoi' campaign had peaked last December with the truck convoy to Paris.

So now we were able to look at our leaders with new insight. It finally dawned on me that we were being used, that they didn't give a damn how long the POW mess might drag on, that they were only going to milk it for all it was worth.

You see, the nation's outcry for our POWs is a united cry. The POWs have become a point of national pride. The more stirred up the country becomes and the prouder we become of our POWs, the better it is for the government's goal, a united people.

Colonel Hughes' remarks amplified my feelings that the families and our men were being used. To me this message said, "Go ahead and publicize your story, write letters denouncing the North Vietnamese, unite the country for our men. It's alright as long as it benefits the government, our President. But don't hassle us, baby. They are expendable, you know. We've got the power. As long as you're working for us, okay. If it gets sticky, well, we could dump them."

I thought about it and thought about it, searched Mary's eyes for some answers, but we didn't talk about it any more.

Crushing despair is the only way to describe how I felt then—useless, ineffective and used.

Mary flew straight to California. I went down and spent a couple of days with Rick in Florida, where he was in Aviation Officer Candidate School. I reported on what had happened. Still feeling miserable about the POWs, I returned to California.

I told Mom about most of what had gone on, that we got the familiar runaround in D.C., but I didn't tell her exactly what Colonel Hughes had said. It was too awful. And I didn't report back to the families at our next meeting. I should have felt guilty about it, but I had just plain run out of energy.

Making a speech to a women's club luncheon a week or so after my trip to Washington, I burst into tears. They had been so eager to hear what I had to say. My crying made everyone so uncomfortable I knew I shouldn't go on making speeches anymore. I didn't initiate anything the rest of the spring.

Toothache

Two or three years before I was captured, a dentist had told me that in a few years my wisdom teeth would start to come in. "They'll have to come out. But no use worrying about removing the teeth until they start to bother you."

My wisdom teeth started coming in soon after my arrival in Hanoi, just like the dentist had said; only one problem—the dentist wasn't around.

Since mid '67 or for the last five years, my bottom wisdom teeth had been giving me trouble, nothing serious, just a constant throbbing pain.

I was enjoying my bowl of rice one evening when I squished the gum that's over one wisdom tooth with a rock that looked exactly like a grain of rice. It was a most common thing to happen.

"AAAAA!!"

Man, it hurt, then it got infected, puffed up like a tennis ball in my mouth. In a couple of days I couldn't open my mouth, I couldn't even move it. (Christ, I have lockjaw.)

The only thing I could eat was the liquid from our daily green soup. Luckily there were enough men in the cell to keep me going on liquid. I lost a little weight.*

"You on a diet, Spike?"

"Eh eh eh eh eh."

"Hey, Doc Warner, what did he say?"

"Who?"

"Spike."

"He said, 'Eh eh eh eh eh.'"

"What's that mean?"

---

*When you weigh 110 pounds and then you go on a liquid diet and lose ten more, there's not much left.

"It means, 'May your wife give you a dose of the clap when you get home.'"

This went on for a few days, and no improvement.

Doc Warner told the cell thieves to get a razor blade. 'Gator' (Ralph Gaither) said he had several stashed already, and when he heard why it was needed he produced a nice shiny one.

Breaking the blade in half changed it to a scalpel, then a wedge of wood was jammed between my teeth to hold my mouth open. When Doc lanced the swollen gum, the pus went flying out.

"Jesus, look at all that goo, must be at least a cupful."

"Man, it stinks."

"Feel better, Spike?"

"Uh huh."

The swelling came right back, then another operation, then more swelling. Each time the period of semi-comfort grew shorter: ten days, four days, two days, then no relief at all.

"Spike, we gotta get that tooth pulled so you can eat; I'm gonna send for Zorba."

When Zorba the Gook and an interpreter showed up a few days later, he and Doc Warner had quite a chat.

"You must pull this man's bottom wisdom tooth or he may die."

Zorba looked in my mouth, studied the situation, scratched his jaw, then said via the interpreter:

"If we pull this man's bottom tooth he will die. It is still under the skin and our dentist is not very good at cutting."

"Oh Jesus, holy shit!"

The Doc and Zorba squatted down Gook-style and continued their conversation, drawing diagrams in the dirt with their fingers.

After five minutes of talking and drawing, Doc Warner turned toward me with a satisfied look on his face. "Zorba says the dentist can pull the upper wisdom tooth because it's fully exposed."

I couldn't believe my ears. "What?!! There's nothing wrong with the upper one, it's been there four years; holy shit, Doc, are you nuts, too!!!"

"Wait a minute, Spike, Zorba may be right. Come over here and look at this drawing Zorba scratched in the dirt."

I went over and squatted with Doc, Zorba, the interpreter and several guards who were all talking and pointing at one diagram or another.

"Now, look, Spike, if we pull the top tooth then you'll have room to close your mouth, and besides, it's better than nothing."

So it was all agreed, I was going to let these savages pull a perfectly good tooth, so I'd be able to eat again, maybe.

"Oh, by the way, Spike, there's still one problem, the tooth can't be pulled as long as there's still infection and swelling."

"How do I get rid of the swelling and infection?"

Doc and Zorba jabbered about this latest problem. "Zorba says that you shouldn't eat anything solid for a couple of weeks and you have to put something between your teeth when sleeping so your upper tooth can't irritate the swollen gum any more."

(God, deliver me from Gook medicine.)

So I don't eat. I drink liquid and sleep with a piece of wood wedged between my teeth so my jaw doesn't close and smack the thing.

Sure enough, after ten days of doing nothing but drinking anything I can get hold of, the infection seems to go away. Warner calls in Zorba the Gook.

Zorba comes into the cell. He signals for me to come with him down to the office. They're gonna pull my tooth tonight.

I follow Zorba down to the medic's shack. It's funny because they take Jim Warner with me. We're walking down toward the shack, I'm feeling weak as a kitten anyway from not eating for so long when I hear more footsteps. I look over my shoulder and there's Tom McNish, the biggest son-of-a-bitch in the cell. Warner, of course, is as big as a house. I feel a shudder run down my spine. "Oh, brother." Now I'm getting the picture of what's gonna go down.

There are about eight guards standing around a straight-backed wooden chair, a bare light bulb hanging over it. Without a pause they sit me down in the chair and Zorba says, "Ba a la la . . ." They're on me like a pack of rodents. Every one of 'em has a death grip on me. I break out in a cold sweat.

Now this little broad about five-foot-high and about as wide comes out of the shadows in the corner with a giant pair of crooked pliers. She says, "blalalalalala." They open my mouth and the lights go out. I mean the goddam town went black. They have power failures all the time. They just keep holding me.

A minute later a guy walks in with a little bitty lantern. He holds it up to my face, then 'sexy' grabs the back of my neck and sticks those huge pliers in my mouth. She tells the guy holding the lantern to move it so she can see better, she squints in making sure she has hold of the right tooth, then she yanks.

It feels like my head's coming off. I don't know what's worse, the yanking, the gagging from the pliers or everybody holding on to me. I'm drenched with sweat. She yanks again. Seven or eight yanks, then she starts twisting and yanking till she gets that 'mother' out.

Ohhh, it felt good when she stopped. I didn't yell, not that I'm so tough, but how can you scream with your mouth full of pliers and fingers? The pain was almost welcome, hopefully the beginning of the end. Hell, how could it hurt anymore? I mean my mouth has been aching so long, I had begun to wish somebody would come along with an ax and cut the side of my face off. It's not a matter of a little pain, like the poke of a knife. I mean the son of a bitch has been hurting for a year and a half, maybe two and a half. I just knew it was gonna feel better later.

Within ten days I was eating everything in sight.
Hail Zorba, Hail the Doc, Hail that fat Gook chick with the pliers.

Egress Recap

Rick and I were married in June in the open-beam, natural redwood living room of my parents' home. It was beautiful, the whole family gathered together for a happy event for once.

The ceremony took place in front of our massive rock fireplace, in the presence of Mom, Dad, Gebo, Pete, a small gathering of friends, and under the gaze of the four Nasmyth children's portraits, Spike's included.

After the ceremony, during the celebration, Rick and I cut a giant piece of our pink-flowered wedding cake and put it away in Mom's freezer for Spike.

Rick's first assignment with the Navy was to Denver, Colorado. He had seen a change in me after my dismal trip to Washington, D.C., so he wasn't too sure how I was handling all this.

When Sandy Salzarulo (Spike's back-seater's wife) and I started planning to turn her state upside-down, Rick said 'NO!' We were going to take a few months off, a few months for us. So we did. In our first little chocolate-brown house with no heat and no furniture except our bed, we were blissfully happy. We had my old black cat, Petit, and we skied every weekend.

The rest of the family slowed down too. Gebo was busy with a new husband and her two small children. Then, right after the wedding, and quite unexpectedly, Marty's two adolescent children chose to move in with their dad and new stepmother.

If Gebo thought she was busy with a new marriage, she was really busy now. Her new stepdaughter, Barbara, fifteen years old, had been stricken with polio at age five. Barbara, confined to a wheelchair, had been enormously over-protected by her natural mother and couldn't function as a self-sufficient adult.

Gebo's heart went out to Barbara and she set out to teach her everything. It started with swimming. Gebo's kids, Larry and Carol, were great swimmers. Gebo introduced Barbara to the pool, and it was an immediate success.

Barbara adored her new mom. Next Gebo started to show Barbara how to do some housekeeping and cooking. Barbara was thrilled. A few months passed and Gebo and Marty set up a hand-controlled sewing machine for Barbara. Again, success.

About the time Barbara got going on all fronts, Marty's son Joe began adjusting to his new family. Gebo and Marty also had a new baby daughter, Kathleen. Gebo was blissfully happy now, although she needed a 36-hour day just to tend to her new extended family.

Pete, a bachelor now, had made it through that awful period of depression he found himself in right after his divorce. He still seemed pretty shook up, hurting, when he picked up his boys every other weekend. But they did man-stuff together, hiking, fishing, wrestling, which seemed to help. He had a new job, too. I think Pete was born to sell real estate. He tackled that with his usual enthusiasm—like a Mack truck—and he was on his way to success.

I don't think Dad was too thrilled with apartment life. He visibly mourned for the old homestead. After all, he was one of the men who built it. But it had to be that way. He was picking up the pieces of his new single life. Quite strange at first, I'm sure, after 33 years with Mom. But Dad had a new circle of friends, he began entertaining and decorated his apartment beautifully with treasures from the Old West which he had gathered over the years. I liked seeing Dad now, we could get along much better.

Mom was the one who let me know up-front that she was doing all right.

She had only been back in the old house for three or four days before our trip around the world, barely time enough to get her shirt-tail in.

The trip felt good, and it seemed as if we'd accomplished something. So she felt good about what was going on for Spike.

Mom went to work selling real estate and she liked it. So she had a neat job, plenty of money, a boyfriend, we had heard from Spike several times; hell, she was starting to live again. Living, but she was still out front every morning to meet the mailman, watching for mail.

A few months passed. The news became exciting again. Dan Pitzer, a POW held by the Viet Cong, had been released. Dan was coming to Colorado to hold a new type of briefing.

Of course we were there for the briefing. Back right smack-dab in the middle of the campaign.

But, God, it was exciting. We were titillated. Dan was well-rounded, healthy, a down-to-earth guy, and he had been there and come back. Dan was talking to us about 'Egress Recap' (how to repatriate a returned POW).

That got us going. "My God, they're talking about POWs coming home." (What do they know? Something must be up.)

I was so gullible and eager, I believed everything everybody said. Not so with Dad. After his first 'Egress Recap' briefing, Dad coined the name 'Egress Recrap.'

The 'Egress Recap' meetings dragged on and on, month after month. At one point the military presented us with their plan for picking up our men on a large ship and steaming them back to the United States over a period of weeks or even two or three months, to allow them to adjust to re-entry into society.

One look at any of the men who had already been released and you knew that was ridiculous, not needed at all. Besides, it was all premature. There was no release in sight.

Pretty soon we realized nothing was up. It was just another stall tactic on the part of the military to keep the families off their back.

After this 'Egress Recap' got going, I did some serious research on what happened when POWs from Vietnam, Korea and Japan had come home. I talked to men who had been through it. I asked them, "How was it to be a POW and come home?" I had figured out in my own mind that what they needed was a good welcome home; it was obvious. But an ex-Korean POW clinched it. When he came home the military and his family had warned everybody, his friends, neighbors, the press and the whole country, that he was a 'sicky,' that he was worn out and in shock from having been a POW, that they should leave him alone. When he came home they did leave him alone. He told me that no one welcomed him, no one came to see him, no one patted him on the back. He thought he was going to go insane, being isolated like that. He still regrets that nobody said, 'Welcome Home, Hero.' In his isolation, he became ashamed.

That, along with our family's common sense, added up to: what the hell do you do with a hero? You welcome him home!

The military was telling us, be prepared for anti-social behavior, be prepared for impotency, he might not like the children or be a stranger in his own home.

When we realized to what extent the military had these ridiculous ideas in mind, I took my research notes and wrote a lengthy paper on what we should do for the POWs' homecoming and why we should do it. This I forwarded to the Air Force, Pentagon and State Department.

Fifth Christmas

Christmas, 1971: the first Christmas I recall not having the expectation Spike would make it home to celebrate with us.

The family came together at Gebo's house in Phoenix. We felt pretty cynical that Christmas because Nixon had been in office three years and nothing had happened. Of course, the election was coming up in November. It looked to us like Nixon planned to bring the POWs home right before we went to the polls, to ensure his reelection. This thought just couldn't help but piss us off. Making them stay there any time at all, even one extra day, would be unbelievable, just gross. Although it finally looked like Nixon was planning on bringing the POWs home, we were not trusting him any more.

A pretty morose bunch of people were sitting around Gebo's kitchen table when Mom arrived and set before us two postcards and a letter from Spike. The ink was hardly dry! They had left Hanoi just three days earlier, on December 20, with the infamous Committee of Liaison.

Boy, how we needed to hear from him. We just needed the contact. It was starting to get to us. To work so hard, wait so long, to want so badly to have Spike home with us and then to settle for six-line letters.

We thought about Spike like we always do, talked about him, hashed over his letters, and as we have every other time the family got together, we took pictures for Spike. Most difficult of all, we wrote our January letter to Spike on the six-line form.

Merry Christmas and
Happy New Year to
both of you.
    Hope to meet you
soon Rick, take care
of that girl, she's one
of the finest.
              Love Spike

XUNHASABA : HANOI, R.D. VIETNAM

F. 79

Virginia and Rick
c/o J.H. Nasmyth
1238 N. Delta St.
S. San Gabriel, Calif. U.S.A.

Orchidée Violacée
Lan chu đinh

Photo : XUNHASABA

Dear Virginia and Rick
I hope this is the
first of many happy
holidays for the two
of you.
    Looking forward
to meeting you Rick
          Spike

XUNHASABA : HANOI, R.D. VIETNAM

F. 86

Virginia Loy Nasmyth
1238 North Delta St.
So San Gabriel
California US A

Fleurs De Pamplemousse
Hoa bu'ở'i

Photo : XUNHASABA

November 13, 1971

Dear Mom Dad and Family. Merry Christmas and Happy New Year. Seems as though the family gets bigger each year, now Virginia has Rick and Gerro should have another addition by now. At your Christmas party remember to have a shot for Uncle Spike. Virginia, I hardly think your first kid would like the name Little Spike; what if its a girl? Sure hope this is the last Christmas that I miss. Be sure and take lots of photos and keep them comming. From now on send one letter per month only, with four pictures in each letter. Put things in photos you think I'd like to see, like Mom and Dad sitting in a new car, or someone wearing new fashions, and for morale, how about a cool picture of a fine chick in a bikini. There must be someone around who whould like to have a boyfriend living abroad. I'm in good health as usual, so don't worry about me. I see from recent photos that my nieces and nephews are growing like weeds. Larry and Carol, help your mom and keep her out of trouble, Pete and Jeff, looke like your dad takes you on lots of trips. Some day I'll take all of you to Disneyland or wherever you want to go. Virginia, youre really a fine looking head, and Mom and Dad seem to be getting younger. Say hello to all for me, and keep drinking that champagne. I'll be seeing you one of these days. Love Spike

Worms

For months, I have had a terrible case of pin worms, the little ones that just itch. I mean I'm going nuts. I'd tell the Gooks and they would say, "Well, everybody has pin worms. If you can show us some big ones then maybe we'll do something."

Now remember, these were the 'good-guy' days. Nothing really bad was happening unless you said 'Fuck Ho' (Ho Chi Minh). But, hell, I didn't say that. What good was it gonna do me to say, 'Fuck Ho.' One guy did, an oddball named Hal Donner. He was crazy. He hadn't resisted a few years earlier, when things were bad, so, trying to show how tough he was he said, 'Fuck Ho' at the top of his voice three times. They whipped him with a belt. I guess it made him feel a lot better, but it didn't make him any less crazy. I mean really, after all these years, to yell 'Fuck Ho' three times in front of five guards when everybody is sitting around eating canned Russian fish, guards are handing loaves of bread into the cell, handing out letters and packages from home, what does that show? Had he done it earlier, I'd have really thought he was crazy. They'd have beat him to death.

So, I've got this terrible case of worms. Dick Bolstad has a terrible case of worms. And Ed Davis has always had a terrible case of worms. We have a little pow-wow and decide to talk to the Gooks. Doc Warner gets Zorba the Gook to come down to our cell. He asks Zorba, "How can we get some worm medicine? These worms are eating all of our food and making us skinny, probably gonna kill us." Zorba's logical Gook reaction, "Present a worm. If it's a big worm, we'll give you medicine. If it's a little worm, no medicine. Everybody has little worms." He went so far as to bring a scoop of Gook shit to the cell so we could see for ourselves that it was buzzing with little worms.

So, Ed Davis, who has this ample supply of big worms, says, "Well, hell, I'll be happy to help you out."

For the next few weeks, everytime Ed took a shit, he'd shit on an upside-down lid. We'd stir through it. Whoever found a big worm would grab it, go show it to Zorba the Gook and maybe get some worm medicine. The worm medicine turned everything purple, your urine, everything. Ed had a bit of a problem though. He never could completely control his bowels. In other words, he'd get a worm about half out and that's as far as it would go. So, we had to grab it, and pull it out. Dick Bolstad was so greedy, he got hold of a nice eight-incher, yanked it so hard he tore it in half. So, he gave Zorba the half worm and got half a dosage of worm medicine. Didn't do us any good.

I'd grab hold of these worms and hold onto them. The worm would resist, after a while it gets tired, sort of lets go and slides out. I got a worm out of Ed's ass a foot long one day. Took it out, showed it to Zorba the Gook and he gave me diarrhea medicine. They had run out of worm medicine.

MAY 8, 1972

The mining of Haiphong and North Viet-nam's other ports was ordered by President Nixon.

Ups and Downs

Here we are in 1972, April or May, I've been a prisoner almost six years, Ed Alvarez has been a prisoner eight years. The Gooks are feeding us milk from Russia, canned fish from Hungary, a lot of good shit from a lot of foreign countries. At night the guards come along and bang on the cell doors, giving us extra bread if anybody wants it. I mean, fattening us up. It's obvious, the war is almost over. Home by Christmas!

We're hearing lots of things on the news every day, things they never let us hear before. The news is good, we hear a little about 'The Paris Peace Talks.' The Gooks are smiling, but the food is the real key. Why fatten us up if they're not about to let us go?

Everybody is really hyped up, even Leo Hyatt smiles once in a while. A million different theories as to when we get out, bets and pools, the person who picks the closest day wins. We are up, way up!

Now they tell us that Xuan Thuy, Pham Van Dong and some other really heavy Gooks are at the Paris talks. I'm so excited I can't sleep.

A bunch of us are sitting around talking like school kids.

"What you gonna do first?"

"Wonder what the broads look like?"

"Hope they still make Coors."

"Wonder if I'm still married?"

"I hope I'm not."

Boom! Boom!

"What the hell was that?"

"Sounded like a couple of bombs."

"Oh bullshit, Americans haven't dropped a bomb up here for over three years."

"Some Gook bomb defuser just went to the happy hunting grounds."

Boom! Boom! Boom! KaBoom!

"Jesus, those are bombs, is this fuckin' war starting again? Maybe Leo was right."

Right outside the prison wall a SAM missile takes off.

WOOOOSH!

"Holy shit, that was a SAM!"

"That's right, and they don't shoot SAMs at nothing, they shoot SAMs at airplanes."

The next goddam day bombs are going off all over the fucking place, and SAMs and airplanes. We see a couple of American airplanes coming in bombing, fighters, the little guys.

I was really down. "HOLY FUCK." We were almost out of here. Six years and God damn, they're bombing the fucking joint again. They're just going puff. A little dinky bomb here and a little dinky bomb there. Not doing any fucking damage. We bombed this dump for how long? Nine years, little bing here, bing there. What the hell, the Gooks don't give a shit. Kill a Gook here, a Gook there, doesn't do a thing. Obviously it hasn't done any good because here we are, right?!

The men were really down, God I was down. Everybody was down except the real haters. George McKnight, George McSwain.

"Kill 'em, kill the fucking Gooks."

"What the hell happened to the Paris Peace Talks?"

"Maybe Nixon said 'Fuck Ho.'"

So here we are, just a sprinkling of bombing going on. An airplane would come zinging by, a bomb would go off and a lot of Gook guns would go off. Next day they wouldn't let us out, thought they were gonna bomb us. Couple of days later they let us out to take a bath and a fire bird, a little jet, no pilot, just an automatic flying plane, goes by taking pictures. (There are pictures of us out there taking our little bath giving the 'bird' to this goddam fire bird.)

"Something must have happened in Paris."

"No shit."

The Gooks stop talking about the Peace Talks and the radio starts saying they are condemning the Americans, the same shit they said in '66, the same speeches!

"We condemn the American imperialists, the Nixon White House gang of lackeys, bla bla bla." Bullshit. They just changed Johnson's name to Nixon. The same bullshit, the same spiel, they never change their speeches . . .

"The heroic Vietnamese people have a glorious four-thousand-year history of valiant struggle. We will stand shoulder to shoulder until the last Yankee imperialist is driven from our land. The perfidious, bellicose and obdurate clique of White House warmongers will soon see that the light at the end of the tunnel is only another dawn and another day of defeat."

We're being brainwashed. This isn't really happening. Think clearly, your brain is fucked up. We started doing things like referring to the South Vietnamese army, our allies, as the Puppet army.

"The Puppet army, who do you suppose they are?" Friese asks.

"Wait a minute, Puppet army? That's what the Commies have been calling these guys for seven years. They're not the Puppet army, they're the RVN, our allies."

We started to get dicked over, their language slipping into our vocabulary, we were getting a little more and more brainwashed.

"What do you think is going on, Red?"

"Well, you know the Gooks and us are talkin' in Paris."

"Yeah."

"Well, we're at the table talking peace and we're just that close to a settlement."

"Yeah."

"Well, now Nixon is givin' them a shot in the ass to get 'em over the hill. You watch."

"Hope you're right."

"I am, just wait and see."

"I will."

Worried

What can I say! We've been down, we've been glum, we're mad at Nixon, disgusted with the National League, we'd like to shoot our congressmen, hang Cora Weiss, but then we got two letters from Spike today! His timing is uncanny. The minute Mom found the letters in the mail she called everyone in the family. All of us living in California, that's everybody except Gebo, we all headed home. Then the jubilation and celebration began.

We sat around the table, read our letters, opened a bottle of wine, toasted our courageous brother, and then we began to study these newest arrivals. Somebody pointed out these letters weren't quite as cheerful as they have been in the past.

NGÀY VIẾT (Dated) *11 January 1972*

Dear Mom Dad and Family. Hows everybody? Well, another year has started, mabey this will be the one. Send a one pound can of good pipe tobacco in each package. Looking foward to pictures of the big wedding so I can take a look at my new brother in law. Be sure your letters are very simple so I can get them. Love Spike

Dear Pete. Hows everything with you Pops. Happy birthday and all that. How about doing something with my furniture. You, Virginia, or whoever can use it, its not doing me any good. We've got a couple of o.k. looking brothers in law. Your boys look great, hope I'll make their college graduation. Look after all and get some for me. Spike

Up until now, Spike has always been very optimistic in his letters, at least we thought so. He's been cheering us up throughout this whole ordeal. But this time, when we got down to reading the letters we all had the same reaction. He sounded anxious, even depressed. We read them a few times more. Oh shit, he sounded so depressed, we all got worried. These letters are the first hint of a change in tone from Spike, a change in the way he is handling things.

We started hashing over ideas, figuring out other things that might be behind these letters.

We're pretty shook up, upset about how he sounds. The thing that throws me is when he says to Pete, "Your boys look great. Hope I'll make it to their college graduation." God, that's horrible, Pete's kids are only five and six years old!

Pete got his first letter this time. In it Spike asked us to do something with his furniture. Well, if there's one thing Spike cares about it's his belongings. That really got us. Thinking that he is beginning to give up, saying, "Go ahead and do something with my furniture, I'll never use it."

I just couldn't use his furniture, ever.

We kept on talking about it late into the evening, until we realized that we could do something with these letters after all, just like we have done with everything else that has come out of Hanoi.

So, next morning we called the press. We told them about the letters and then (pre-arranged at our family meeting) we stressed the anxiety and depression we found in them. Now, the press has always come out to the house when we got a letter from Spike and they have always written a story. We've had quite a few letters lately and not too much new to say about them. As in the past, there was just enough different about our story this time for the press to sink their teeth into it.

We let out our feelings to the media this time. When they were taking notes for this story about Spike's anxiety and despair, we also let them know that we've had it with President Nixon, that we expect him to pull something out of his hat before the election. We asked everybody we knew to write Nixon and tell him, "We want the POWs brought home now!"

They printed the story with big headlines and pictures and made a big deal out of it, giving Spike and the other POWs some more publicity. We got good press: "LETTERS HINT OF ANXIETY AND DEPRESSION."

Dogpatch

"Hey Leo, this is May the 13th, anything gonna happen?"
"They'll probably take us all out and shoot our brains out."

You can feel a bomb fifty miles away. It rumbles. Like an Indian can listen to a railroad track and hear a train a hundred miles away, if you're used to bombing, like we're used to it, you can hear it for miles.

Ed Davis is like a cat. We're all asleep. Out of the blue he hisses, real soft, "bombs." And two minutes later the rest of us hear them. He's part Indian.

We're all up, listening to the low rumbling going on out in the countryside. We're all quiet, sitting there, listening, wondering what the hell's going on, maybe remembering some of our own bombing missions five and six years ago.

Activity out in the prison yard breaks the spell. Trucks, men, boots . . . then the Gooks come in, a bunch of Gestapo types, machine guns, Black Jack and the boys. An officer starts reading off names from a list. They picked me, Red Berg, George McKnight, George McSwain, Friese, the 'Heavies,' but not all of them. To the man, they pick exactly half the POWs (204). Instead of kissing our asses like they've been doing, they start treating us like shit. We're blindfolded, handcuffed together and led out to waiting trucks. They throw down blocks of wood. We stumble up into the trucks. Every now and then off to the east we can hear bombs rumbling.

We're all secured in the truck. George McSwain, first in, is handcuffed to the roof. We haul ass.

Holy fuck! Instead of going from the Hanoi Hilton to the Zoo, which takes thirty minutes, we drive all the goddam night long. We drive under some trees and the trucks park, who knows where. It's a hundred and ninety freaking degrees in this lousy truck and they won't let us out. Nobody has to pee, we're all dehydrated. They pass little jugs of water into the trucks.

Nightfall, the trucks take off again.

"Do you think the driver is hitting the holes on purpose or all the roads this bad?"

"On purpose, he's a Gook, ain't he?"

"Anybody got a cuff-pick?"

"You still in those cuffs, Jesus, when did you get here?"

"Kiss my ass, I've got big wrists."

"And a thick skull."

"Ah, shut up."

Even the most stoic are put to the test of temper control by the bouncing and the heat. All I can make out of the others are their eyes peeking through crusts of dirt.

"Guess where we're going?"

"How the hell would you know?"

"I just saw a road sign."

"Where?"

"China is sixty kilometers from here."

"China!!"

"Holy balls!"

Everybody's heard stories about POWs in China who've been there seventy years! Poor bastards had been captured at age twenty and died at ninety.

Talk about a 'fuck it, let's escape' attitude, we've all been here forever. No new prisoners, all old guys and it looks like the war has just started. I think we would have done something stupid if it hadn't been for Red Berg. We've been sitting there in this steaming truck all day, hot, filthy, hurting and Red says, "You know something, they're at the peace table and the Gooks are that close. Now Nixon's gonna shoot 'em in the ass, get 'em over the hill. You watch!"

"Yeah, but where the fuck are we going, Red?"

"Maybe he's trying to save our lives, getting us out of Hanoi."

"Yeah, sure."

About midnight our third night out, the convoy arrived at our new home, a couple of miles from the Chinese border and smack in the middle of a rain forest. The trucks stop and each of us is led off to his assigned cell. The Gooks are halfway organized. I'm led to a cell block made up of eight solitary confinement cells. They're tiny, about four by seven feet.

The window is high and small, but it doesn't matter how big or where it is, the damn thing is covered with black tar paper. It's dark, pitch black.

This place is different. The floor is wet, not running water but wet. I ran my hand across the wall, it was murky. The ceiling seemed to seep. My bed was damp. It's so dark you either hang your mosquito net up by feel or fuck it.

The Gooks went to a lot of trouble to keep us from communicating. While they were going to all this trouble, we were busy communicating anyway.

After three days in our new home, we had named the fourteen cell blocks, voted on a name for the camp and knew who was in every cell. 'Dogpatch' won over 'The Rockpile' in a close vote.

While the Gooks were busy making sure we were in complete isolation, we spent hours via one code or another sending messages from cell block to cell block.

"Jesus, listen to this. You know why they named one of the cell blocks 'Cobra.'

"The night we moved in Will Gideon almost sat down on a seven-foot cobra."

"Holy shit."

"Here's the story. When Will entered his cell he sensed something, no noise, he just felt something was there. He threw his bundle on the bed and called for a guard. When the guard held a lantern it illuminated a poised and coiled cobra on the bed. Had he fumbled around putting up his mosquito net, he probably would have been killed."

"Holy shit."

The Vigil

Unfortunately, today (September 4, 1972) marks the beginning of Spike's seventh year in Hanoi. We never thought it would go on like this. Not for seven years. The awful thing about this is that now ten years is becoming a reality. Ten years is half of my lifetime. When I think about it in that context, I just can't imagine how he can stand it.

God, we've grown bitter over this administration's failure to bring home Spike and his buddies. We are trying to keep up the vigil, but false hope upon false hope is causing terrible disillusionment.

Since it's Spike's anniversary, the newspaper people came out to the house in South San Gabriel. We knew we were in trouble as far as campaigning today when a reporter talked to us, Mike McDonnell of the *Tribune,* because for the very first time ever, we cried. Mike asked questions and you could tell he was putting his heart into the story, and Mom and I sat at the kitchen table and cried through the whole thing. Not a great day for the Nasmyths.

We've been feeling extra rotten about things because a couple of weeks ago, for the first time I know of, one of the boxes of food and medicine we sent to Spike was rejected by Hanoi. There was no reason for their rejection. It just said 'Refused' on the address label when it came back to us. When Mom found the box in the mail, she kept it to herself. But when I found it in Spike's room on top of his crate of personal effects, I can't tell you how I felt. Man, I just about went through the ceiling. I went flying into the kitchen where Mom was doing something at the kitchen table . . . "What does this mean?"

Mom, in her style of understatement, just said, "Oh, the bastards sent it back."

I said, "My God, what does it mean? Are they trying to tell us he's dead?" It hurt her terribly when I said that. Then I realized how it hurt me to say it. We were so scared and everybody got tears in their eyes. Mom hung in there. She said, "Nah, I don't really think so, this isn't the first time it's happened. Several of those first boxes came back."

This is the first I'd heard of it. Mom had kept to herself the fact that some of these precious boxes we have been mailing to Spike for six years had come back.

Two weeks later we got a cold explanation through the press, from Cora Weiss, of the Committee of Liaison. She said 700 packages were returned this time: "Rather than sort through the hundreds of boxes for whom there is no recipient," Mrs. Weiss explains, "the North Vietnamese simply rejected the whole lot."

This is so vulgar and disgusting. With so many men missing in action, quite a few are alive. The North Vietnamese just want letters and packages going to 251 men, or whatever it is, whose names are on the official list. They don't want anything from the MIA families. I hope the MIA families *never* stop mailing packages to North Vietnam.

Courtesy of Paul Conrad.

Conrad's cartoon in the Los Angeles Times *really hit home.*

Mildew

It was always dark. The Gooks gave us one kerosene lantern for light. The eight of us spent a lot of time in one cell sitting around the lantern bullshitting.

The dark, wet, spider-infested cell was a little depressing. Fortunately I was with a good bunch who didn't let our lousy conditions get them down.

After a few weeks they made some improvements. During the day we'd play cards and once in a while they let us out front into a courtyard. It was an area surrounded by a brick wall, twenty feet by ten feet, covered by a canopy of trees.

We washed our duds, walked around a little bit, but we never got dry. You could hang a fucking handkerchief out for a hundred years and the thing would never get dry. Mildew started growing behind my ears, but that's all right. Everybody has mildew here.

In their funny way the Gooks were trying to be nice to us here at 'Dogpatch,' nevertheless, the 'Hanoi Hilton' was a real 'Hilton' compared to this shithole.

The food wasn't bad for a lousy Commie Gook maximum security jail as far out in the boondocks as possible and still in North Vietnam: lots of rice and bread, boiled greens, different greens from the north part of Vietnam and China. We were blessed with a few new dishes. Even I couldn't eat all of my 'gut' soup and my reputation as a garbage can had been well-earned. And once in a while we got meat: boiled water buffalo, which I'm sure was from an animal killed by a truck. It was so tough you couldn't swallow it, just chew it for the flavor. You could chew a chunk of meat for an hour, but if you haven't tasted a piece of beef for six years and you get one and chew on it, it tastes great.

Bunny Tally never ran out of stories. When he was a second lieutenant at McCoy Air Force Base in Florida he was assigned to the position of assistant supply officer. Once directed to order several thousand pencils for the base, Bunny hit a few wrong numbers on the computers. To his horror he received several thousand telephone poles, an entire trainload, instead of the pencils.

Bob Jones taught me how to play cribbage. During the day when there was enough light we played. After 5,000 games we came out within one or two games of each other.

One day we got into a hell of an argument over a hand, we were really pissed off.

"Well fuck it, if you're gonna be an asshole I'm through."

"Suits me, who needs it?"

A few hours later Bob came to me.

"This is pretty stupid you know, are we gonna be so small that a dumb argument ruins the only enjoyable pastime we've got? Jesus, Spike, you and I aren't like some of these other babies."

"Thanks, Bob, I hope I would have been man enough to say that if you hadn't first. God, what's happening to our heads?"

The game continued with the intensity of the World Series, after all, the stakes were high, an ice cream cone per game when we got home.

We were a little down in Hanoi. Now we're up here and there are no sounds. We used to judge the war by the sounds. We could hear the airplanes and bombs going off. Now we can hear nothing. Now we've got to rely on everything these little assholes say. What do you believe? You never believe them. Now you can't even believe your ears, because there is absolutely nothing to hear.

San Diego

Back in May, Rick and I moved to San Diego, where he started law school and I started looking for a job. I finally landed one as secretary for Concern for POWs, Inc., in downtown San Diego. This was my first inside job with a POW organization other than our own. Boy, did I have a lot to learn about the goings-on in one of these big non-profit, humanitarian organizations.

I was in the middle of everything. They assigned me as receptionist, telephone girl, secretary. I got all the incoming calls, among other things. Within two days I realized that the people running the office, although well-intentioned, didn't know a hell of a lot about POWs. I started informing the press and anybody that called about the current POW news and everything I knew. Whenever they wanted to do a story on POWs, because I knew just about everybody involved, I put them directly in touch with POW and MIA families anywhere. I compiled a list of families who would be receptive to the press should they be called upon. I asked families if they would allow the press to come to their homes, or answer inquiries on the phone, then put this information down on file cards.

When the press called and said, "We have information about the Paris Peace Talks, or Hanoi, etc., is there anybody who will make a statement?" Now I could say, "Yes, we have the 22-year-old child of a 5-year POW or a wife who has become active . . . and they are more than willing to talk to the press."

This way, immediately it got the press to quit talking to Concern, who didn't have anything to say. It got them directly to the families who had a lot to say.

So many people involved in these offices were caught up in running the offices. They kind of missed the boat about what they were supposed to be doing. Some of these people, particularly my boss at the time, were overwhelmingly ineffectual.

Rick wanted me to stay out of campaigning, just be his wife for a while, but this job put me smack-dab back in the middle. I knew the statistics, what was going on, every minute of every day. But, you know, it felt good. We had had a rest in Denver and I was ready to get back into things. I just couldn't take sitting around and not have something going on to help Spike.

Then on September 18, three POWs were released to their families and to a representative of the Committee of Liaison, to Cora Weiss in Hanoi. God, we were excited about it. We watched every moment of news on the TV, read every article waiting for Elias, Gartley and Charles to get home. We wanted to hear the names they brought out, whether they had seen Spike, or anyone else we cared about . . . what kind of shape they were in.

We were glad they were out, sad that it wasn't Spike, and very anxious too, for a first-hand talk with each of them.

The publicity surrounding their release was more disgusting than we thought it might be. The press played on everything. They blew up remarks made by Elias' mother. But, we've grown to expect that kind of stuff. You just shrug it off, at least the POWs were in the news.

Some kind of phony controversy was conjured up, and that's the fault of the press again. They quoted Cora Weiss as saying the POWs went from the imprisonment of Hanoi to the imprisonment of the U.S. government. For crying out loud, of course, they were hospitalized as soon as they got out. They had to be checked out physically. And of course the military didn't say why they wanted to talk to them, they had to be debriefed. Anybody with an ounce of brains knew that.

There was no real controversy, but to make waves, the press published this utter garbage.

For a couple of weeks the three new returnees were all over the news. We had three more men to take off our list of the men we have to get out of that place.

As soon as they were out, the military stepped up its program of making a horse's ass out of itself by publicizing more and more ridiculous stuff they were gonna pull with their 'Egress Recap.'

We were at one debriefing where the fellow in charge told the families not to be surprised if, when their man got home, he hunched down on the floor to eat because that's what he was used to. Every time they came out with some ridiculous stunt, we wrote and sent telegrams insisting that they not do it.

Politics

I have come to the terrible realization that if President Nixon is reelected I won't see Spike for another four years. God, what a thought. We've been sitting back just watching the election creep up. Now it's about here and it looks like Nixon is going to slide in again without getting the POWs out. Four years ago, when Nixon ran against Humphrey I cried all night while I watched the returns. I was so scared Nixon might lose. I really thought he was the only man who could get Spike out.

Now we've talked about it and we're not going to be able to live with ourselves if we don't do something.

McGovern's going to lose, that's for sure, but we've got to make some kind of move. Rick and I figured it was time to put the pressure on Nixon, and the best way to do that was to come out for McGovern. So we did. And we did it on October 9, 1972, exactly four years to the day President Nixon promised me and the American people that he would bring the POWs home in four years.

I didn't want to be in this kind of campaigning any more. It made me all hyped up and sweaty. Rick and I spent hours preparing for this press conference. He was asking me all the conceivable questions the press might throw at me. Since we're going political for the first time, I didn't figure the press would be too friendly.

For the purpose of coming out for McGovern, we took our San Diego 'Hanoi Release John Nasmyth' billboard over to the McGovern for President headquarters in Mission Valley, San Diego, and added a new message. Now our billboard read:

HANOI RELEASE JOHN NASMYTH

Vote for McGovern, John Would

That was hard, saying Spike would when we hadn't asked him. But what the hell, we had to do something.

We got on the phone with Pete and Gebo, and they agreed. They were coming out for McGovern, too. Called Mom; she's giving Nixon two more weeks. Then she might swing. That's a surprise—my own Mother even thinking of voting for a Democrat. She's a GOP all the way and a staunch Nixon supporter from the past. That sort of accentuated the gravity of the situation for me. I didn't dare tell Dad. He found out, though, when the L.A. *Times* called and told him what his baby daughter had done. I'm glad I wasn't up there. I hope Mom and Dad and Spike understand my reasoning. We've just got to do something.

We never considered making any additions to our billboard in South San Gabriel. We plan to have Spike tear that one down and burn it when he gets home. We'll leave it just the way it is. It's a symbol to the family.

A few days after the press conference, on October 12, McGovern's headquarters called and asked me to introduce McGovern to the San Diego Democratic Rally. Of course, I said I would. I called Mom, she said she'd come to the rally but not get up on the stage with me. Gebo said she'd be there and stand beside me.

Gebo arrived the evening before. Man, we were hyped. I'd never made a speech in front of 10,000 people before.

Rick went to bed and we sat up till 2 a.m. pounding out an appropriate speech for the McGovern rally.

Next morning we arrived at the Democratic headquarters early to make copies for them and the media. Next we went out to Balboa Park, where we were escorted up on the bandstand and seated right next to the podium in front of an enormous crowd. They filled the entire park. We could see Mom seated right down in front.

When McGovern came onto the stage, surrounded by Secret Service men, the crowd cheered. He was seated. After a few perfunctory words, the host introduced me. When I stood up in front of the crowd, they applauded. It was like getting hit in the chest, it took my breath away. Gebo came up and stood to my right. Before I could begin, I had to wait for a noisy aircraft to finish its ascent. It seemed like it took forever. I hoped I still had my voice. I did, it worked like a champ.

Our brother, Capt. John H. Nasmyth, has begun his 7th year as a prisoner of war in Hanoi. Our entire family put its faith in Richard Nixon on October 9, 1968, over four years ago, when he said, "Let me make one thing clear. Those who have had a chance for four years

and could not produce peace should not be given another chance."
President Nixon has failed. President Nixon has failed to end the war
in Vietnam. President Nixon has abandoned my brother Spike and
hundreds of other prisoners of war to another four years of captivity.
Last Monday we re-erected the 'Hanoi Release John Nasmyth' sign
here in San Diego. Our sign still reads 'Hanoi Release John Nasmyth'
but now we have added 'Vote For McGovern—John Would.' Think
of my brother and his buddies after years rotting in prison camps,
thinking, "If George McGovern is elected we'll be free in '73." But
if Nixon is reelected, their slogan must be 'Four More Years,' four
more years in prison camp. You've got two choices in this election.
You can chose Richard Nixon and doom my brother to prison camp
for another four years, or vote for George McGovern and bring John
Nasmyth and his fellow POWs home in 90 days. For Spike and his
buddies, vote for George McGovern so they will be 'Free in '73.'

Virginia Nasmyth Loy
Pat Nasmyth Berger
Sisters of John H. Nasmyth

During my speech there were two standing ovations. It really mov
me.

Following me, McGovern came on and made a long, rambling speech.
He seemed kind, sincere and I'm afraid, ineffective.

After his address, a moved and spontaneous Olga Charles, the young
active wife of Norris Charles, who had just been released from Hanoi,
rushed through the crowd, up to the microphone and threw in her support for McGovern.

It was all very exciting. After that speech there seemed nothing left
to do but wait for the election.

Peace is at Hand

He said it! "Peace is at hand." Henry Kissinger said, "Peace is at hand!"

I'll tell you, with the pressure inside me, I feel like I'm going to burst. Talked to Mom, the rest of the family's feeling the same way. We're boiling over. We want to cheer. There's sparkle back in everybody's eyes. But, as one, we seem to have put on a calm facade to the world. I don't know why but I know it's true with me. But for the eyes, you wouldn't know things have changed.

I've got to admit, Christmas is starting to look pretty good.

Breathless, anxious, hopeful but still protecting my fragile inner tumultuous self, I arrived at work and began my secretarial duties.

The phone calls were heavy that morning because of the news. Everybody wanted to believe this was the end.

A reporter from the San Diego *Evening Tribune* came in right in the middle of things. He asked me about how we're handling the waiting. What are we thinking, feeling? I tried to put it into words.

They were interviewing several other families in the area this morning. Pretty soon a photographer showed up. He took shots while I was going about the business of the office and talking with the reporter, all very low-key.

They left me and did the same with other people in the office.

That evening when I walked out of Concern, I took the same old brown elevator down to the ground floor. On the way out the door, I practically tripped over a stack of the evening papers placed inside our building by a vendor. There was something familiar about the folded picture on the front page. I picked up one of the papers for a closer look. The front page was fully two-thirds covered with a triple exposure of the 'Missing Man' poster and me. Wow! This work of art was captioned, 'The Agony of Hope—The War, Captivity and the Emotions of Those Left Behind'—a triple-exposure composite photo.

'The Agony of Hope,' how appropriate. How well the photographer, Jerry Rife, and the reporter captured the mood of our plight.

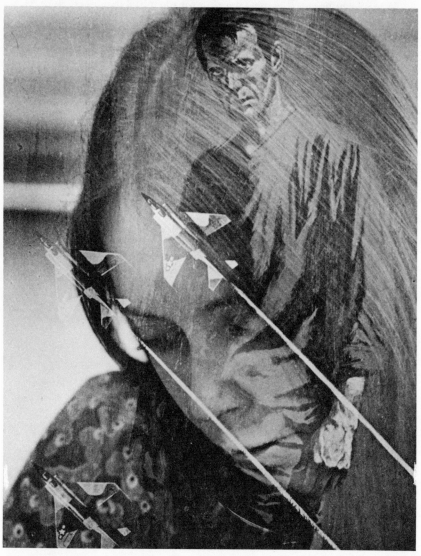

Montage from the San Diego Evening Tribune, *combining my photo with the 'missing man' flight formation and a POW composite drawing.*

I was so moved that they put the missing man photo over me. It was deeply touching.

Disbelieving all the evening papers would carry the triple exposure, I stopped at the first vending machine along the ride home; but sure enough, they were all alike. I bought a stack to take home to Rick.

When I got home, Rick was waiting for me with his own stack of *Evening Tribunes*.

Next morning Jerry Rife, the photographer, called to see if I had seen the front page. He said when he got the idea and went to his editor, they just kept making the photo larger, until they had created the biggest front page picture the San Diego *Evening Tribune* has ever run.

Some of the men in the press, they really get it.

Rumors

The rumors about the peace talks in Paris start flying again, the food gets better and the Gooks start smiling.

"Home by Christmas!"

Pressure

Hey! The newspapers are full of headlines like:

POW Families Cross Fingers
U.S. Ready for the Return of POWs
Family of POW Given New Hope

But, nothing's happened.

Nixon won, we knew he would. But even after Kissinger's promise, he hasn't brought our POWs home yet.

The Air Force is practically driving us crazy. Just before Thanksgiving, we got a letter telling us that if we were going to be away for the holiday we should let them know where we could be contacted.

Wow! That blew our minds. We're waiting and thinking they've got something up their sleeve, wound up so tight . . .

Man, one of these days somebody is going to snap. The 'Peace is at Hand' sparkle is gone. I don't believe anybody any more. When they say 'Peace is at Hand,' and then it doesn't happen, you just wonder if they are going to blow it all to hell.

Mom looks so grey. They're stringing us along and it's sheer torture.

Dad took some beautiful affirmative action this month when the rest of us were stalemated. He had pre-Christmas cards printed up for the whole family. We'll each mail ours out around the first of December. He used the 'Agony of Hope' picture on the front with this message inside:

Where is the peace that President Nixon pledged? Our prisoners are still in prison camps! Our missing are still unaccounted for!
HOPE IS NOT ENOUGH

In honor of Captain John H. Nasmyth, Jr., captured September 4, 1966, WE URGE YOU to write or wire President Nixon today!

The Nasmyth Family
The Berger Family
The Loy Family

And, when those were sent off (somewhere around 8,000) we started sending last ditch telegrams:

Sent 12/16/72 via Western Union
1:23 AM

President Richard Nixon
The White House
Washington, D.C.

A Merry Christmas to you and your family, but only another bleak Christmas to our prisoners of war and missing in action in Southeast Asia. In our interminable search for an agreement that is just and fair to all, I wonder if we are losing sight of those young men who have been prisoners of Hanoi for one, two, six or eight years. What technicalities can now be worth another young man's death, or another day of imprisonment at the hands of the Communists?

Have you, Mr. President, lost sight of the real, the immediate, the humane situation in your efforts to solve the 'big picture'? I, and many thousands like me sincerely hope not.

Sincerely,
John H. Nasmyth, Sr.
Father of Capt. John H. Nasmyth, Jr.
Prisoner of war since September fourth, 1966

Happy Birthday Spike

November 14, 1972, my seventh birthday as a prisoner. I celebrate with rice and gut soup.

"Happy birthday, Spike."

"Thanks, Bob, this is a happy one."

"Why's that?"

"The last one in the slammer."

"Right on."

DECEMBER 18, 1972

After the breakdown of the Peace Talks, President Nixon ordered American B-52s to a massive air strike over Hanoi-Haiphong.

Bombing Hanoi

Oh my God, they're bombing Hanoi. The media says they've hit a prison camp, the Hanoi Hilton. Please, please don't let us lose Spike when the end of this is so near.

I was sitting at my desk at Concern for POWs when I heard the news. I burst into tears; I didn't have any control left at all. I didn't know what to do. I called our friends the Lees in Los Angeles, talked to Ruth, asked her to go and be with Mother in case anything happened, in case she needed somebody.

It was five o'clock by then, so I hurried, crying, to my car. I started for home, wanted to be there in case someone called or something happened. I was crying and I wanted to see Rick. Somewhere on the freeway about halfway home, I was really sobbing, and I hit a van driven by a woman. We pulled out of the fast lane into the dirt. She was wonderful; her truck was fine, she was fine, but my car was demolished. I'm pregnant, but I checked myself out, I was okay. She decided to take me home on the spot. We left my wrecked car and she drove me home, delivering me into the hands of Rick.

Rick just held me and smiled, he thanked the good samaritan, wasn't worried about my car, and said, "There, there, it's all right, Spike's not going to get killed by the U.S. bombers," all night long while I cried.

Rick faced the bombing with more objectivity than I did, at least outwardly. Through the night we talked. We endured the bombing with a great tangle of mixed emotions. Most of all, we were worried and anxious that the U.S. would come anywhere near the prison camps. Rick didn't really think Spike's life was in danger. He thought some POWs might get it, but not Spike. I wasn't so sure. We wanted them to bomb Hanoi, we wanted the whole thing over with. Maybe it's better if the U.S. does it, blows them up, rather than let them rot away in Hanoi.

For those days while the bombing was going on, I must have looked like a schizophrenic. I went to the office, directed the press to families, denounced the bombing and generally ran around all wound up. I was scared that the B-52s would hit a camp or, worse yet, the North Vietnamese would blow up a bunch of our POWs and blame it on the U.S. I couldn't think straight.

Bulletin

December 19, 1972

"What's all the racket?"

"The Gooks are having some sort of rally."

"They're really excited about something."

Later that day, Sweet Pea, an English-speaking guard, called us out of the cell block to our tiny walled courtyard, his face grim and a piece of paper in his hand.

"Listen carefully to these news from the camp authority."

"This oughta be good."

"Shhhh."

"Listen carefully. On the night of December eighteen, Nixon, the greatest criminal in history, and his White House clique ordered B-52 bombers to attack our beloved city of Hanoi. Many hundreds of innocent women and children were killed. Many hospitals and schools were destroyed. Many American POWs were killed or wounded by their own bombs. Hundreds of enemy aircraft were shot down by the heroic Vietnamese fighters and many pilots were captured. The Vietnamese people will never be forced to talk with bombs. We will fight until the aggressor is driven from our land and until we have destroyed every enemy aircraft. That is all."

"Do you believe him?"

"I don't know, but something has really got the Gooks excited."

Setback

The breakdown of the Paris Peace Talks and the bombing of Hanoi a little setback—hell, it looked like the war had started all over again. All of us in the family were beside ourselves. We didn't know whether to cheer or cry.

A week before Christmas, we finally broke down and sent out our 'Hanoi Release John Nasmyth' Christmas cards with another year added to Spike's tally of Christmases spent in Hanoi.

We sure thought for a while that he was going to be home this year.

For a couple of days we debated leaving the Christmas tree up to celebrate when Spike finally did come home. We thought, if we celebrate now, he may come home a couple of weeks after Christmas and say, "Hey, you guys, why didn't you wait?"

We did have presents under the tree for him, though.

Dreamin'

Christmas number seven passed, and according to the Gooks the B-52s were still bombing Hanoi. But also, according to the Gook count, more B-52s had been shot down than had ever been built.

"Happy New Year, Spike."
"Same to you, Bob, this is the last one here, I can feel it."
"You know Warner and his loony poems?"
"Yeah."
"Today he sent me two."
"HOME FREE IN SEVENTY-THREE."
"What else?"
"Well, you know this sexy picture I got of my little sister about a year ago?"
"Sure."
"When Warner and I were together in cell six he used to make up rotten little poems about Virginia. He'd look at her picture, get that crazy look in his eyes, then recite poems to her. Then he said he started having wet dreams, poor Virginia his victim."
"What was today's?"
"Let me think."

> "I burned my little finger
> Now it has a blister
> The only way to fix it
> Is stick it in your sister"

Spike brought home this photo I had sent him—worn out by being passed around to his buddies.

January 15, 1973: A big camp shuffle at 'Dogpatch.' All fourteen cell blocks had a complete lineup change. The reason for the shuffle was obvious. The Gooks were grouping us by order of capture. Everyone in my cell had been shot down just before or just after me. Why?

Obvious again. We always assumed that when we were released it would be sick and wounded first, then the rest of us in order of capture.

I couldn't sleep, couldn't do anything except daydream.

January 20, 1973: "Trucks, I hear trucks, this is it! Back to Hanoi, then home."

"I hear them too."

"Hot damn!"

Eighteen trucks pulled up. We piled in, no handcuffs, no blindfolds. The ride back to Hanoi was a breeze.

Mom

He did it again. It was a letter home that rallied us, had us so high this morning you'd think we had him instead of just his letters. What an incredible boost to our spirits. Sounds like he's going through the same things we are:

"I thought there for a while that this was going to be the year, but now I guess not. Oh well, maybe next year."

I can't get over Mother's ability to bounce back, she's euphoric, and she cracks me up. She was talking to an Associated Press reporter this morning amid our celebrating and ranting and raving. Excited, almost giddy, she was quoting from Spike's letter:

"You all look fine from recent photo. Keep smiling and stay young. There isn't anything worth worrying about."

"If he only knew," Mom said, wrung out from six and a half years of worrying. "Dumb kid."

25 Nov. 1972

Dear Mom, Dad and Family. Merry Christmas and Happy New Year to all of you. I thought there for awhile that this was going to be the year but now I guess not, oh well, mabey next year. I'm in good health as usual. I got a letter the other day from you Mom, and one picture of Pete and his boys. Put four pictures in each letter and put more in the pictures, like one of you sitting in a new sports car, how about some of Virginia and a few of her female pals in new styles, from bathing suits to mini skirts. Thanks for the financial news Mom, I should be able to make that last a few days. So Rick is going to be a lawyer, good, I may need one sometime, with a doctor and a lawyer for brothers in law I should be able to stay out of trouble. My future package request is now, one pound of freeze dried coffee, a large bottle of sweets, one pound of tobacco, half pound bag of Sail mix and half pound bag of Boskin-riff cherry brandy, and the rest the usual stuff. Send Mildred and Juan a Christmasgram for me. Tell them I plan to spend several months in their part of the world one day. My future plans are about the same, lot of travel and damn little work. Still working hard on French and Spanish. You all look fine from my recent photos, keep smiling and stay young, there isn't anything worth worrying about. As usual Pete, its up to you again this New Years, how about a blond with big jugs. I love you too Virginia.

Love Spike

Loudspeakers

January 22, 1973. Back at the 'Hilton.'

I'm put in cell number seven with the 'Old Guys.' There are about 550 prisoners. I was the 119th captured, I'm in the top one-quarter as far as longevity.

"When? Where?"

The stories about the B-52 raids are spectacular, most of us feel that the Gooks would still be bullshitting in Paris if the raids hadn't been ordered. Shit, we're getting excited.

"Hey wait, we're going home, we're going home."

We start getting so much shit on the radio. "The People's Republic of North Vietnam will never succumb . . . to force . . . blah blah blah . . ." The loudspeakers are going five, six hours a day. We can hear other speakers from the city in Vietnamese going eight, ten hours a day. We can't understand them, but they're jacking their people up to accept something.

There's not a rumble. It's so goddam quiet, there's not a sound of bombing.

In the cell we're making bets on the hour we're getting out. Except Leo:

"Oh fuck, they're gonna shoot us at dawn."

"Holy shit, how are we getting out, what time are they gonna release us?"

The 'Heavies' send down an order:

"When released say nothing bad about our treatment until every man is out of North Vietnam. We don't want the V to blackmail us with a few of our men."

Time is crawling by.

JANUARY 27, 1973

In Paris the U.S., North Vietnam, South Vietnam and the Viet Cong signed the Peace Agreement.

Going Home

The Gooks tell us all to form in the courtyard for 'important' news. We do.

The 'Agreement' signed in Paris is read to us. The Camp Commander reads the whole fucking thing in Vietnamese. Then his interpreter reads the whole thing in English. It sounds so official, so un-Gook that we know it must be real. There's just no way a Gook could have made up what that thing said.

My heart is pounding.

We are to be released in four equal groups over a two-month period. Sick and wounded first, then by order of capture.

It's pretty outrageous . . . hyped up . . . living in 'go-home' groups. I'm bunking next to Ed Davis. Ed's a great guy, with the biggest heart you've ever seen.

The Gooks eat dogs. Most of the dogs they have are the kind with black tongues, not chows but some relation to them. These cute little fur balls run around the camp. Then when a puppy gets to be three or four months old they poke them to death with sticks and cook them. The reason they poke them is to tenderize the meat.

One day, while we're waiting to go home, this tiny dog belonging to one of the guards scoots in through one of the drainage holes in the bottom of the cell. This little dog seemed to sense he was in danger. He scoots in and Ed Davis grabs him. Ed has a heart a big as a bear. He's been here since '65. He's watched a lot of guards kill these puppies.

"I'm gonna rescue this little dog, take him home with me."

We all agree. We're willing to fight to the death with these fucking guards to keep the little dog.

So Ed names him Macao. Macao sleeps between Ed and me. Ed plays with him, grooms him, uses my toothbrush to get at his fleas, which bite me anyway.

Two days before the first group is released, six of us are cut out. A few more of the recently captured men are badly wounded, so they take our place in group one.

The day before group one goes there is a giant flap. The Gooks demand that they wear new clothes. Some of the guys want to go home in their old beat-up POW stuff, to show the world what we really looked like.

The 'Heavies' say: "Wear your new duds!"

I'm ready to go nude if necessary.

The first one-quarter of the POWs leave wearing the new clothes, and Ed Davis is among them, with Macao hidden under his jacket.

A few days later the Gooks call one of us up and give him a special list of the next twenty men. They say we are going to go home early. They move us from the main part of the cell block, all twenty of us. We're sitting in this goddam place, we're all as crazy as hell, we're just within an inch of getting out of this joint and all of a sudden they isolate twenty of us, tell us some shit about a special release of a group of twenty. They are thanking Kissinger for something.

"God, what's going on?"

"This has got to be a violation of the Paris Agreement."

So we said: "Fuck it! We won't go." It was unanimous. We thought they were screwing around with us. We know the right order and two men don't belong in this group of twenty. Looks like they are trying to screw around with the order and break the agreement, or get us to go along with their breach of the agreement. By this time we're really loony.

For a whole week we said we wouldn't go. Shit, what a decision. They moved us back to the main group. Then they moved us from the big group to a cell by ourselves, fitted us up with the fancy go-home uniforms and again moved us back to the main group. We weren't cooperating. We wouldn't go.

Finally they called Colonel Gaddis, one of the high-rankers. They brought four representatives to the prison camp to meet with him, an American, an observer from Poland, a Canadian and a Vietnamese.

"Hey, man, this ain't no shit. We really want you twenty turkeys to go and you better get your fucking asses out of here today or you're gonna cause an international incident!"

We were all sitting there, waiting, not really sure we'd be going. We've become callous over the years, after so many ups and downs.

"What do you think?"

"Do you think this is really it?"

"Yeah, looks good."

Things were going so slowly. Thoughts, movements, I wished it would hurry up and happen.

Colonel Gaddis walked in. He didn't hesitate a minute. He ordered us: "Pack up and split."

We put on our go-home clothes, kind of quiet, shaking, beginning to believe. Walked out of the cell and stood around the courtyard of the 'Hilton' for a little while. Pretty soon a bus showed up.

We filed towards the gate of the 'Hanoi Hilton.' We boarded the bus. (This is it, this is really it!)

Thousands of people lined the streets, like a parade. Most gawked at us, but some shook their fists.

(Faster man, faster, move this damn bus.)

The bus left Hanoi and started across the Red River toward Gia Lam airport. Our bus had to use a temporary pontoon bridge: the real one looked like so much spaghetti. The B-52's did good work.

Approaching the airport, out of the corner of my eye, off to the right, just in time I caught the most wonderful sight of my life. It was white and silver. It had a big red cross on its belly. An American C-141 was coming in, real low, with a powerful roar she came in, right over our bus. On the side printed in big letters, "U.S. Air Force.'

(Don't crash, you beautiful doll.)

The excitement built in the bus.

The bus circled the end of the airfield, then came to a stop. Ahead of us, about fifty yards away, sat our ticket to home, the beautiful C-141. A swarm of Vietnamese and their officials were standing around. Then, for the first time, we saw some real Americans standing there. Dressed up sharp in their Class A uniforms, they were all big men, they towered over the Vietnamese.

A Gook calls our names out in the order he wants us to get off the bus. "Nahshit."

My name is called first, because I've been there longer than anyone else on the bus. We're directed to line up beside the bus in two columns.

It takes a hundred years for all twenty of us to walk down the steps of the bus and line up. All of a sudden it's quiet. A Vietnamese says something over the loudspeaker.

"Captain John Nasmyth, captured September fourth, 1966."

I can't believe it's happening.

I walk toward the tall American. Stop and salute.

"Welcome home."

Spike leaves the hands of the North Vietnamese, saluting as he passes into the custody of the United States.

Pretty choked up now, maybe I said something.

(God, I'm going home.)

As I was shaking Colonel Dennets' hand, another American grabbed my arm.

"Let's get out of here."

As my escort walked me up the rear ramp of the plane, the entire crew plus three or four flight nurses started clapping and cheering. I could hardly walk, tears streaming down my face.

The members of the crew shook my hand, I got kisses from the nurses, everybody was talking.

"Hold on a few minutes, as soon as we're all on board we'll get the hell out of here."

(Don't wake up, God, don't wake up, please don't let this be another dream.)

One after another the other nineteen were led onto the airplane. The crew knew how anxious we were. As soon as the last man got on the plane they sealed up the door. They didn't mess around a second. The pilot was already starting the engines. As we cleared the ground a spontaneous cheer went up in the plane, and a few minutes later, when the pilot announced we had crossed the coastline, it was pure bedlam.

Jim Pirie sat down next to me.

"Jesus, Jim, is this for real?"

"It's for real, Spike, it's for real."

"Let's have a toast to freedom."

"You have any booze?"

"Hey, Sarge, we need a bottle."

"Oh, Jesus, I don't have anything, besides I'd be hung if they found out."

"Bullshit, I've never known a sergeant who didn't have a bottle stashed somewhere. We haven't had a drink in seven years."

"Okay, but promise not to tell."

"Cross my heart."

The sergeant came back in a minute with a bottle of Johnny Walker Black Label Scotch, poured us each a slug in a glass.

"Here's to freedom."

"To freedom."

"To women."

"To women."

"Thanks, Sarge."

"My pleasure, mum's the word."

"No sweat."

Waiting

We've been waiting all day, the phone's been ringing constantly. The day took forever to pass. After a late dinner, sitting around the kitchen table, I'd wait for what had to have been half an hour, look up at the clock and only two or three minutes had ticked by. By evening, time started to fly by until 10 p.m. when on TV they announced there was a delay in the prisoner release. We waited out the delay. Dad, Mom, Gebo, Pete, Rick, Sue, Larry and I lay around on the living room floor talking until after midnight. It was early in the morning when KNX radio announced that the prisoners had been released, they were on the plane winging home.

I thought we'd cheer but we didn't. We just hugged each other. It was all like slow motion, subdued. We wanted to make sure he was really out of there. I have to admit we all looked pretty happy. As the minutes passed, we started asking each other:

"What do you think they're doing on the plane?"

"I'll bet Spike's up there bugging the pilot to fly it."

"Wouldn't you love to be there! It must seem unreal."

We set up two beer cans, one was Hanoi, the other, a blue can, was the Philippines. I put twenty pieces of popcorn in an empty cigarette pack, the prisoners, and scooted them away from Hanoi towards the Philippines. Dad kept moving the pack too far too soon; I'd put it back over the ocean.

About twenty minutes after the radio announced the plane had taken off, when we were sure Spike was over the ocean, really away from that stinking country, we started to feel really good.

At 1:15 a.m. the radio announced that of the twenty prisoners expected to be released, only nineteen made it. One prisoner gave up his seat for Bill Bailey, a POW who had a sick family member. Horrors! "Oh my God." All those dozing off immediately startled. "Oh, shit, sounds like something that SOB Spike would volunteer to do." Now everybody looked awful. It felt so good having him out, he just had to be on that plane. For twenty minutes we had a heated discussion as to whether or not Spike would have volunteered to stay behind. We decided that he would have.

As the time passed, it occurred to us that all twenty families of the men expected to be on the flight must be going through the same torment. Surely the Air Force would have called the family whose man stayed behind. Of course, knowing the Air Force, they'd probably screw it up. Nah, not something this important. It had been twenty minutes, the Air Force hadn't called. Surely Spike was on that plane.

1:35 a.m. "Was that the telephone?"

"Oh, God, oh no." It rang three more times. We looked at each other. I grabbed Gebo's hand and started to cry. No one wanted to get the bad news. Finally Dad answered the phone. He very quietly stood there, listening. When he said, "Please repeat that," we all sprang up from the living room floor and ran into the kitchen to the phone to listen closer. After a long pause, Dad said, "He's on the flight!" Now we started to cheer and jump around, clap our hands and hug each other.

Dad popped the cork on a little champagne for the occasion.

All teary-eyed, very sleepy and laughing, we returned to our blankets on the living room floor and continued listening to the radio.

We had the TV turned on to CBS just in case they had live coverage of Spike getting off the plane in the Philippines. I remember telling Rick, "Just think, the other nineteen families are watching this western, too."

The CBS radio broadcaster described how in the Philippines the plane could be seen at a distance, that it was circling in for a landing, that it was a beautiful sight. When the plane touched down we felt a terrific surge. What really gave us a tremendous, overwhelming, emotional feeling was hearing the cheers of the crowd when the freedom plane taxied up and opened up her doors. You could hardly hear the radio broadcaster in the Philippines for the wild cheering of the huge crowd there to meet Spike and his buddies.

All crying, holding each other, "What do you think Spike thinks of this, isn't it wonderful! Listen to the crowd cheer, there must be thousands of them."

"What are they gonna do when they see all those people.?"

"I'll bet Spike cries."

"Nah!"

"Yeah, I'll bet he cries."

Joyously, we called Western Union and sent two telegrams in the middle of the night: WE LOVE YOU, HENRY KISSINGER and WE LOVE YOU, PRESIDENT NIXON.

Re-Entry

After my first taste of American booze in damn near seven years, I calmed down a little bit, got better control of myself.

Heading toward the Philippines the islands peeked up over the horizon just as the sun was going down. Beautiful.

Touching down on friendly soil, again terribly emotional. As we approached the parking area, emotions running wild through all of us, we saw something we weren't prepared for. A giant crowd of people was standing out there to meet us: kids, men and women, cheering, waving signs, all smiling. The moment the plane landed they rolled out a red carpet.

A red carpet and cheering crowds for our first step on friendly soil; I had a hard time maintaining my composure. Everybody was all choked up. Tears running down my face again, I stepped off to be met by the Ambassador to the Philippines and an admiral.

Then, all along the highway from the flight line to the hospital, several miles, the streets were lined with cheering people, applauding and cheering, 'Welcome Home.'

They were treating us like kings. I walked into the hospital room, a nurse right behind me. She asked which bed I wanted."

"What difference does it make?"

She said, "There are going to be two people in this room."

"Over my dead body! Honey, I am never, never gonna spend another night in a room with a man." That was that.

On top of my bed was a pile of hospital clothes, a robe, pajamas and a pair of terry cloth sandals. I hollered out into the hall to get a nurse down here. A little girl came in, asked me what I wanted.

"I want to take a bath."

She informed me: "We don't have bathtubs available, there is only a shower."

"I want to take a bath. There must be a bathtub somewhere in the hospital."

She says, "There is one, but it is only authorized for staff."

"Just tell me where it is, sweetheart."

I found the staff room; it had a big tub. I locked the door, turned on the hot water and climbed in. I kept the water running hot. It filled up, ran over the side, slopped on the floor. I lay there, wallowing in it, washed off the stink. My first bath lasted about an hour, the first of half a dozen baths I took that night.

Back at my room, my escort officer was waiting for me. He had a list of things to accomplish tonight. First we went a couple of doors down. There were a bunch of Filipino tailors waiting. They measured me in about twenty different directions and said they would have my uniform ready in the morning. That through, I looked at my escort officer and said, "I'm hungry."

Down at the cafeteria the kitchen was in full swing. To begin with I had a thick steak, cooked medium rare, half a chicken, corn on the cob, green salad and shrimp salad. My first three eggs were fried hard like I always used to have 'em. After the fried eggs I had a couple hard-boiled.

I sat down for a while between courses, and a young Chinese-American girl, Cindy Chung, joined me. We talked while I had some more fried eggs and a cheese omelet. Bud Flesher joined us. We had several cups of coffee, some tomato juice, orange juice, then I topped it off with a big hot fudge sundae.

Around midnight I took another bath, visited the tailors and got to talking with a nurse.

"Boy, it would sure be nice to have a back rub."

This sweet young nurse came in and gave me a back rub for an hour and a half. Sheer ecstasy.

The rest of the night I milled around enjoying the clean things, baths in a bathtub, the toilet, hot water, a clean soft bed and a back rub, clean clothes that didn't smell like Gooks, none of that filthy crap lying around, rats and bugs on everything. Talked to the nurses about what young people are doing nowadays, what they are wearing, what movies are like, all about entertainment. Talked about everything under the sun.

Early in the morning they put us through a rush physical. They took a bunch of blood, X-rays, took every kind of sample you can think of to make sure we didn't have any wild exotic diseases. I got my feet checked, head checked, eyes, legs, stomach and arms checked. The physical lasted all day long. Then I picked up my uniform.

Back at my room getting dressed, I got a phone call from the Officers Club. It was a stewardess named Becky. She had a letter for me from Pete Lapin, a friend of mine in California. We were about to leave for the BX for a private shopping spree, so I suggested she meet me there.

We arrived at the BX in a bus. I stepped out to meet Becky and there was a crowd of people cheering, throwing kisses, shaking hands. Becky was there, she gave me a big kiss and delivered the letter.

Becky grabbed my hand, "Come on, let's go, we're having a party."

"Hell, I can't leave." Then I took a second look at her and decided it would be a pretty good idea to leave if I could. I told her I would go back to the hospital, figure out a way to get out and meet her at the Officers Club.

Back at the hospital, I had to come up with some way to get out. The Air Force helped me on this one. A sergeant gave each of us a slip of paper which we could present to the elevator operator to be taken down to the safe by the main entrance. Using my slip of paper I presented it to the guard at the elevator, said, "Look, I've got to check my valuables." He said "Okay." On the first floor I started walking toward the front door. There were three or four sergeants standing guard at the door. One of them stepped forward like he was going to ask me for my pass. I just turned around to an imaginary person: "Okay, Colonel, I'll be right back with it." It did the trick.

Out the door I took off, hailed a cab and met Becky at the Officers Club. She walked up with a double gin on the rocks. We jumped in her car and headed for the party. It was great, we talked, played all the new music, danced and talked some more. Terry, whose apartment we were at, opened up his closet and said, "Look Spike, put on some civilian duds, just take anything you want, no sweat." So I did. I picked out a pair of new mod pants and a red shirt, slipped them on, everything fit just right.

The party-goers left around 2 a.m.—left to give me and Becky some privacy, which we enjoyed all night long.

Terry drove me back to the hospital the next morning around noon, a bit to the chagrin of a few of the brass. The hospital commander was a little upset that I had taken off. But, what the hell!

Things were a little hectic now; in less than two hours we took off for Hawaii. The plane ride to Hawaii was pretty long, ten hours. I hadn't been to sleep since we left Hanoi. I was getting tired so I thought I'd lie down, try and take a nap. I tried to sleep but I couldn't. I still had this crazy feeling that if I went to sleep I'd wake up and find it was all a dream.

We refueled at Hickam Air Force Base in Hawaii, then blasted off for Travis Air Force Base in California. As we came over California, the FAA gave our plane permission to make a low pass over the Golden Gate

Bridge. We were all up, out of our seats, looking out the windows. We circled around three or four times.

At Travis I grabbed a Coors beer, walked outside, talked to the crowd, kissed a bunch of girls, talked to the press. There was a woman there waving a 'Welcome Home Spike' sign. I walked over to her, it was Barbara Murphy, a family friend from way back.

There were several planes at Travis waiting for us. They split us up, the twenty POWs. I got on the plane headed for March Air Force Base in Southern California. It's about an hour flight to March. I knew the family would be there. In the air, March AFB radioed up and said my whole family was waiting.

As we taxied up the runway at March, I looked out the window and I saw everybody standing there, the wind blowing like mad. I hadn't had any problem landing at Hickam and Travis, as far as emotions, getting all choked up and all. Then I saw everybody out there: Mom, Dad, Pete, Virginia, Gebo and everybody, and I got pretty choked up.

As Spike stepped off the plane, holding his cap with his hand, the twelve of us just started jumping up and down, waving, screaming out, "Spike, Spike, Spike . . ."

I saluted a general. He said, "Forget about the red carpet." He pointed, "There's somebody here waiting to see you."

And I ran over there. Mom was running towards me.

She practically knocked him over running into him, her arms open wide, "Oh, Spike!" Dad was right behind her, "Son, you're home!" They were squeezing him, I ran up, reached for Spike and kissed him, and kissed him, and held him. He held me, held us, speechless, tears in his eyes. Gebo, Pete ran up, the kids and brothers-in-law crushed in, his hat was knocked off. I buried my face in his shoulder, and my big brother said, "Baby, you're beautiful."

"I love you, Spike."

"I love you too, Baby."

Dad, Spike and me, right off the plane and into the hospital.

Epilogue

George Putnam was there when Spike got off the plane. He mailed me a copy of this special broadcast he delivered in honor of Spike's homecoming:

When the plane came to rest at March Air Force Base and rolled up to the waiting relatives, press, radio and TV journalists, we all surged forward to welcome the POWs. My own special concern was for Captain John Nasmyth. I felt I knew him, through his family and friends who had spent six years in an effort to bring him home. Why, they even erected a sign near the family home in South San Gabriel demanding that HANOI RELEASE JOHN NASMYTH.

I had interviewed John's mother, sister and brother and followed their day-to-day effort as they traveled to the far corners of the world in their determination to bring him home in one piece.

I recall the time that his mother, Virginia, brought a replica of a North Vietnamese bamboo prison cage up from San Diego to Los Angeles on a beatup pickup truck. John's brother and a friend had spent a couple of days in that cage at a San Diego shopping center to alert the public to the plight of our POWs in Vietnam, pleading with the public to get them out and bring them home.

I used that cage in a segment on my TV news report. Frankly, I felt like a damn fool climbing into that cage in POW pajamas. But it seemed the best way to dramatize the situation.

And then, a few weeks later, we gathered in Pershing Square and ate our POWs' prison fare—pumpkin soup and pig fat instead of a Thanksgiving turkey dinner.

And we prayed a lot. And we shook our fists. And we aroused a helluva segment of public opinion.

Meanwhile the Nasmyth family—big Virginia, little Virginia, brother Pete and Rick Loy—and John, Senior—were scrambling from radio to TV to newspapers to Washington to Paris and anywhere else they could gain recognition for their dedicated efforts and their holy cause.

They never stopped. They never gave up. They were everywhere at once. I believe that it was their efforts that culminated in the release of those hundreds of war-ravaged, sick and half-starved patriots who finally came home after serving you and me and their country.

The door opened on that plane and I held my breath. As I recall, I was crouched just beneath Christine Lund's armpit (ABC) and to one side of Bill Stout (CBS) . . . I expected Nasmyth to crawl or limp from the plane . . .

No way! He came down the steps bounding with exuberance—cocksure—and looking for action. He spied his family, rushed into their arms and it seemed the wisest for those of us in the press contingent to retire and wait for another time.

Next stop, the hospital. I waited in line with all the other reporters. He stopped for a moment, said "Hi, George," and was on his way.

The minute Spike stepped off the plane we knew he was okay.

The family made its way to the hospital where we all sat around him on couches in the lounge.

He took control. One of the first things he said was, "Listen, some general named James contacted me on the plane."

"Yeah, that's Chappy James."

"You know him?"

"Uh huh."

"I have been directly ordered *not* to go with you tonight and burn down some billboard. What is this about a billboard anyway?"

So we told him about the billboard and of course, we're not going to burn it down tonight. Not his first night home!

Spike looked so young sitting there. I held his hand, very pale and bony. I figure he weighed about 125 pounds. He looked sharp in his blue Air Force uniform, he also looked about 17 years old.

The reporters were pressing against the hospital doors. Spike couldn't talk to them because three hundred of his buddies were still in Hanoi. I went out and talked to the press. I told them he was well, he was home, he was wonderful.

After an hour or so of us talking inside with Spike, he said:

"Okay, I've got things to do. You all go on home now. I've got medical tests, de-briefings, I'll see you in a few days."

Gebo, Pete, Mom and Dad got to visit with Spike. Then, a week later, it was my turn. I was taking my big brother out for my birthday. Rick was in San Diego taking a final in law school.

General 'Chappy' James called me before I drove to Riverside to the hospital to pick up Spike.

"Virginia," he said, "You can take your brother out, but no press and no crowds. Okay?"

"Yes, sir."

One of the things Spike had asked about that first night was Sonny and Cher, were they still together? Rick picked up on it and next day called the TV station that ran the Sonny and Cher show. He asked if he could get an autographed album for Spike. Both Sonny and Cher wore POW bracelets and they were thrilled that Spike wanted an album, so thrilled they invited him on their show.

So a week later, when I picked Spike up for our quiet dinner with 'no crowds,' I asked him if he'd like to be on the show, just a few hundred people in the audience but thirty million viewers.

"Yeah," he said, he'd like that.

Spike and I wait in the audience at the Sonny and Cher TV show.

When Spike walked out on the Sonny and Cher show, Sonny on his right, Cher on his left, the audience went wild. Sonny cried, Cher cried, I cried, the only dry eye in the place was Spike's. I timed it. The audience gave him a three-minute standing ovation.

Spike's welcome to the Sonny and Cher show.

The first day Spike was released from the hospital, he axed the sign. A crowd of seven or eight hundred people stood in the rain around our billboard on the corner, playing 'When Johnny Comes Marching Home Again.' It was so moving for all of us.

The rain doesn't dampen our celebration for Spike as he prepares to take down our billboard.

The press was there, TV crews and Spike, all 130 lbs. of him soaking wet, with a splendid brass-plated axe made just for the occasion.

March 3, 1973: Spike chops down our 'Hanoi Release John Nasmyth' billboard.

He chopped on the four-by-fours of that billboard till it started to teeter. The crowd burst into cheers, he stepped back, and we watched it topple.

Then the crowd swept him back down the street to our house, axe held high, band triumphantly playing, people cheering . . .

Thank God it's over!

Six weeks after Spike's release, Dorothy Townsend, that wonderful lady from the L.A. *Times,* was trying to reach Spike.

The family was out at a giant Lion's Club 'Welcome Home' for Spike and three other guys. A TV crew from Channel 4, NBC, was there. They asked Spike for an interview about what really went on in Hanoi.

Spike said: "No. I can't tell you anything about that. Some of the guys aren't out yet."

The reporters just politely dropped the matter.

After the luncheon, back home, the Air Force was on the phone.

"Captain Nasmyth, they're all home now, they're okay."

Spike just said, "Thanks."

The next phone call was from Dorothy Townsend.

Now that all the men are out, she wanted the story. What was it really like in Hanoi?

Spike stood on the side of the kitchen counter where the dishwasher is and started telling her. Spike was talking about how it had been. Mom stayed over on the other side of the kitchen and just watched.

He just stood there and the sweat started streaming down his face and arms. The sweat was pouring off his body the whole time he talked to Dorothy about Hanoi. He was telling her the truth about torture, solitary, buddies who didn't make it and the go-home dreams.

When he was through talking his clothes were soaked, there was sweat on the floor where he had been standing.

For the next twelve months Spike accepted all the speaking engagements, parades, talk shows and appearances he could handle.

Sometimes it was two or three a day; thousands of people wanted to see him, meet him.

I stayed at Mom's house the first few weeks just to handle the phone and arrange his calendar. Rick commuted back and forth from San Diego.

People flocked to our house from all over bringing presents, their 'John Nasmyth' bracelets, asking for pictures . . . the mail was incredible. He had hundreds of letters to answer each week. And he answered them all, every one.

He was busy, too, getting re-checked out in jets and small aircraft, visiting friends all over the country and raising hell.

Over the years since Spike's return, our family has returned to normal (whatever that is).

Pete turned himself into a number-one real estate salesman. Then, in 1974, he became a broker and started running his own shop. His sons,

Pete and Jeff, are college students now. They think a lot of their Dad. In the winter, the three of them ski every chance they get. Of course, they are all terrific.

Gebo and Marty Berger built a lovely new home in Litchfield Park, Arizona. In 1974, they had a son, Jesse. So between them they have six children.

In 1975 Dad retired and later spent a great deal of time lumberjacking with Spike at Dad's childhood vacation home in Sooke, British Columbia. Dad passed away of a sudden illness in 1980. From his own plane, Spike spread Dad's ashes over the Sooke River, which Dad had loved.

Mom held down the family homestead for several years. We had our first Christmas there at home, all of us, happily including Spike, in 1974—Spike's first Christmas home since 1965. The TV crews were there. It was a heavenly Christmas.

In 1976 Mom moved out of the family home to a delightful ranch on top of a ridge in Hacienda Heights. She didn't sell our house, though; it's rented out. In fact, in 1978, we had a 'Welcome Home, Spike' five-year reunion in the old home. A thousand people trekked through.

Rick and I finished law school since Spike's return. He practices law now and I take care of our four children. Jenny was born right after Spike's release, then Mary in 1975, little Spike in 1980, and then came Bodie in 1982.

About five years ago Spike bought part of a remote island, northeast of Vancouver Island, British Columbia. He's been living up there cutting his own firewood, driving his fishing boat to pick up the mail and flying a bush plane. To top it off, he married lovely Audrey Fisher last summer.

We are all still just a little thrilled to hear Spike's voice on the phone, or to see him when he comes for a visit.

Memorial Page

Let us remember and honor these brave men. Our family became very close to their families during 'the campaign.' They formed part of the core group of active MIA and POW families in Southern California.

Alphonso R. Castro, Jr.

Alphonso, the son of Mr. and Mrs. Alphonso R. Castro, Sr., was a U.S. Army helicopter pilot. His remains were returned after the war.

Stephen Hanson

Major Steve Hanson, USMC, husband of Carol Hanson, was shot down on June 3, 1967. His status remained MIA until October 1974, when it was changed to Presumptive Finding of Death.

After the prisoners of war were released, Carol met and later married Captain James M. Hickerson, a former POW.

John Kay Hardy, Jr.

Captain Jack Hardy, USAF, was shot down over North Vietnam on October 12, 1967. His status remained MIA until August 1974, when, for lack of information, it was changed to Presumptive Finding of Death.

Jack's wife, Patricia, chose to have a marker placed in Arlington National Cemetery in memory of her beloved husband. The medals awarded Captain Hardy were presented to Pat, their children Megan and Mary Pat, and his parents at a private ceremony following his final status change.

Donavan Lyon

LTC Donavan Lyon, husband of Janice, was shot down over North Vietnam on March 22, 1968. His status was missing in action; he never returned home.

Arthur S. Mearns

The remains of Major Art Mearns, USAF, husband of Pat, were returned in October, 1977. Pat chose to have a memorial service for Major Mearns at Arlington National Cemetery on Veterans Day, November 11, 1977.

David Munoz

SSGT David Munoz, the son of Mr. and Mrs. Benjamin Munoz, was a paratrooper in the 82nd Airborne Division. He did not return home.

Darrel E. Pyle

Major Darrel Pyle, husband of Elaine, was released from Hanoi in February 1972. Darrel was killed in a private airplane crash at Elmendorf AFB, Anchorage, Alaska in 1974.

Dick Ratzlaff

After his release from North Vietnam, Dick met and married Barbara McKillip in a ceremony on May 24, 1975. Dick, a dear friend of Spike's and mine, succumbed to lymphatic cancer on February 28, 1981.

Larry James Stevens

Lieutenant Commander Larry Stevens, husband of Charlene, did not return home. His status was changed to Killed in Action after the war.

Mother and I attended the memorial service Larry's folks, Jack and Gladys Fleckenstein, held for him. I will never forget the pride and sorrow I felt as the American flag was presented to Larry's mother.

Samuel Edwin Waters, Jr.

Major Sam Waters, USAF, husband of Mary Ann, was shot down on December 13, 1966. His remains were returned to the United States in March 1977.